STATE LEGISLATURES

STATE LEGISLATURES

A Bibliography

Robert U. Goehlert

Frederick W. Musto

ABC–Clio Information Services
Santa Barbara, California
Denver, Colorado
Oxford, England

©1985 by Robert U. Goehlert and Frederick W. Musto

All rights reserved. No part of this publication may be reproduced, stored in a retrieval system, or transmitted, in any form or by any means, electronic, mechanical, photocopying, recording, or otherwise, except for the inclusion of brief quotations in a review, without prior permission in writing from the publishers.

This book is printed on acid-free paper to meet library standards.

Cover and book design by Tanya Cullen

Library of Congress Cataloging in Publication Data

Goehlert, Robert, 1948–
    State legislatures.

    Includes indexes.
    1. Legislative bodies—United States—States—Bibliography. I. Musto, Frederick W. II. Title.
Z7164.R4G574 1984   [JK2488]   016.328'3'0973   84-24404
ISBN 0-87436-422-1 (alk. paper)

10 9 8 7 6 5 4 3 2 1

ABC-Clio Information Services
2040 Alameda Padre Serra
Santa Barbara, California 93103

Clio Press Ltd.
55 St. Thomas Street
Oxford OX1 1JG, England

Manufactured in the United States of America

Contents

Introduction, ix

Part I: Theoretical and Empirical Studies, 1

General Studies	3
Constitutional Aspects	9
Structures of Legislatures	12
Reapportionment and Redistricting	15
Elections and Formation of Legislatures	21
Legislator-Constituency Relations	23
Legislative Recruitment and Careers	26
Political Parties and Groups in Legislatures	30
Legislative Committees	33
Legislative Councils	35
Organization of Legislative Business	36
Legislative Behavior	39
Legislative Power	43
Leadership in Legislatures	45
Decision Making	47
Legislative Voting Behavior	49
Economic and Fiscal Powers	51
Legislative Oversight	54
Legislative-Executive Relations	57
Judicial Powers and Relations	59
Interest Groups and Legislatures	60
Legislatures and Public Opinion	62
Reform	64
Legislative Staffing and Information	68
Policy Outputs	74

Part II: Studies on Individual Legislatures, 81

Alabama	83
Alaska	85
Arizona	85
Arkansas	86
California	87
Colorado	99
Connecticut	101
Delaware	104
Florida	104
Georgia	108
Hawaii	110
Idaho	111
Illinois	111
Indiana	117
Iowa	120
Kansas	122
Kentucky	125
Louisiana	128
Maine	130
Maryland	130
Massachusetts	133
Michigan	134
Minnesota	139
Mississippi	142
Missouri	144
Montana	146
Nebraska	146
Nevada	149
New Hampshire	150
New Jersey	151
New Mexico	153
New York	154
North Carolina	159
North Dakota	161
Ohio	162
Oklahoma	165
Oregon	167
Pennsylvania	169
Rhode Island	171

Contents

South Carolina 172
South Dakota 173
Tennessee 174
Texas 177
Utah 181
Vermont 182
Virginia 183
Washington 185
West Virginia 187
Wisconsin 189
Wyoming 192

Author Index, 195
Subject Index, 217

Introduction

During the past twenty-five years, research on U.S. state legislatures has changed significantly. Theoretical and comparative works have supplanted descriptive, single-state studies. American state legislatures have changed dramatically as well. In short, they have become more professional, with better staffs, full-time legislators, and complex committee systems. These changes in the literature and the legislatures themselves warrant a bibliography that brings together all of the research.

This bibliography is designed to assist librarians, researchers, and government personnel in researching state legislatures. The bibliography includes works drawn from a variety of fields, including political science, law, history, public administration, and the social sciences. The scope and arrangement of the bibliography make it unique: it is the first bibliography to focus exclusively on state legislative research.

Scope

This volume is intended to be comprehensive; it treats all major aspects of state legislatures, including their history, functions, organization, structure, and procedures. The bibliography includes books, articles, dissertations, essays, research reports, and selected documents. As a wealth of state documents deal with legislative studies, they are omitted here. The researcher can identify state documents by using a number of indexes, including *Legislative Research Checklist*, *Monthly Checklist of State Publications*, and *Index to Current State Documents*.

All citations are to English-language works. In general, coverage extends from 1945 to the first half of 1984. While most works cited were published within the last twenty years, earlier works have been included if they provide coverage for areas that have not been extensively researched. Much of the earliest research produced single-legislature studies. A number of these studies are included in Part II, which is arranged by state, because they provide a historical record of the development of state legislative research.

All materials included are analytical, not merely descriptive, and scholarly. Hence, emphasis is on research monographs, articles from major journals, and dissertations. From the abundant descriptive material, we selected only works covering areas in which little scholarly research has been done. We tended toward materials that were available in larger academic libraries. However, since much early research on state legislatures rendered processed materials and pamphlet-like publications, we included such publications when they were judged still of value. To have excluded these works completely would have been to overlook a vast amount of material that constitutes a major area of research.

Arrangement

The bibliography is divided into two major parts. Part I is subdivided into twenty-five topical categories, covering all aspects of legislative studies. Part II includes materials that focus on particular states. The materials here are arranged alphabetically by state. A subject index identifies more specific subjects and indexes all state-arranged entries according to the topics used in the first part. An author index provides further access.

Compilation

In compiling this bibliography, we checked a variety of sources, including numerous older bibliographies on state government and politics. Primarily, we searched seven indexes: *Index to Legal Periodicals, United States Political Science Documents, Social Sciences Index, Humanities Index, Public Affairs Information Service Bulletin, ABC POL SCI,* and *Writings on American History*. For dissertations, we made an exhaustive key word search of *Comprehensive Dissertation Index*. For books and research reports, we checked all relevant bibliographies on state politics, bibliographies on state legislatures contained in books, *Books in Print, Public Affairs Information Service Bulletin,* and the holdings of the Indiana University Libraries.

The seven indexes were chosen for their coverage of a variety of disciplines, including history, political science, and law, and they seem to provide the best coverage of state government and politics in general. We hope that this most comprehensive bibliography on state legislatures will not only prove beneficial to researchers and students, but also, by surveying what has been done and pointing out areas of neglected research, generate further interest in state legislative research.

PART I
Theoretical and Empirical Studies

General Studies

1. Adrian, Charles R. *State and Local Governments*. New York: McGraw-Hill, 1967.

2. American Assembly. *State Legislatures in American Politics*. Englewood Cliffs, NJ: Prentice-Hall, 1966.

3. American Political Science Association. Committee on American Legislatures. *American State Legislatures*. New York: Crowell, 1954.

4. "American State Legislatures in Mid-Twentieth Century." *State Government* 34 (Fall 1961): 245–252.

5. Anderson, William, and Edward Weilder. *State and Local Government in America*. New York: Henry Holt, 1951.

6. Black, Merle. "Legislative Politics in the Deep South, 1939–1967." Ph.D. dissertation, University of Chicago, 1972.

7. Bradley, Phillips. "American State Legislatures: Some Comparisons and Contrasts." *India Quarterly* 14 (Jan. 1958): 442–448.

8. Buechner, John C. *State Government in the Twentieth Century*. Boston: Houghton Mifflin, 1967.

9. Buell, Erwin C., and William E. Brigman. *The Grass Roots: Readings in State and Local Government*. Glenview, IL: Scott, Foresman, 1968.

10. Campbell, Ballard. *Representative Democracy: Public Policy and Midwestern Legislatures in the Late Nineteenth Century*. Cambridge: Harvard University Press, 1980.

11. Citizens Conference on State Legislatures. *The Sometimes Governments: A Critical Study of the 50 American Legislatures*. 2d ed. Kansas City: Citizens Conference on State Legislatures, 1973.

12. Clarke, Mary Patterson. *Parliamentary Privilege in the American Colonies*. New Haven: Yale University Press, 1943.

13. Crane, Edgar G., et al. *State Government Productivity: The Environment Improvement*. New York: Praeger, 1976.

14. Council of State Governments. Western Office. *Lawmaking in the West. Vol. 1: Summary and Analysis of Procedures*. San Francisco: Council of State Governments, 1967.

15. Council of State Governments. Western Office. *Lawmaking in the West. Vol. 2: State-by-State Digests of Procedures*. San Francisco: Council of State Governments, 1967.

16. Council of State Governments. National Legislative Conference. *American State Legislatures in Mid-Twentieth Century.* Chicago: Council of State Governments, National Legislative Conference, 1961.

17. Crew, Robert E. *State Politics.* Belmont, CA: Wadsworth, 1968.

18. Day, William L. "British Parliament and State Legislatures." *State Government* 48 (Summer 1975): 160–163.

19. Dishman, Robert B., and George Goodwin. *State Legislatures in New England Politics. Final Report of the New England Assembly on State Legislatures.* Durham: New England Center for Continuing Education, 1968.

20. Dye, Thomas R. *Politics in States and Communities.* Englewood Cliffs, NJ: Prentice-Hall, 1969.

21. Dye, Thomas R. "State Legislative Politics." In *Politics in the American States,* edited by Herbert Jacob and Kenneth Vines. Boston: Little, Brown, 1965, pp. 151–206.

22. Fellman, David, Lane W. Lancaster, and A. Breckenridge. *Readings in American National and State Government.* New York: Rinehart, 1950.

23. Fesler, James W. *The 50 States and Their Local Governments.* New York: Knopf, 1967.

24. Fordham, Jefferson B. "Challenge Legislatures." *National Municipal Review* 47 (Dec. 1958): 551–555.

25. Francis, Wayne L. *Legislative Issues in the Fifty States: A Comparative Analysis.* Chicago: Rand-McNally, 1967.

26. Frost, Richard T., ed. *Cases in State and Local Governments.* Englewood Cliffs, NJ: Prentice-Hall, 1961.

27. Garland, Michael. "Politics, Legislation, and Natural Death." *Hastings Center Report* 6 (Oct. 1976): 5–6.

28. Gosnell, Cullen B., and Lynwood Holland. *State and Local Government in America.* New York: Prentice-Hall, 1951.

29. Grant, Daniel R., and H. C. Nixon. *State and Local Government in America.* 3d ed. Boston: Allyn and Bacon, 1975.

30. Graves, W. Brooke. *American State Government.* Boston: D. C. Heath, 1954.

General Studies

31. Harrold, Frances. "The Upper House in Jeffersonian Political Theory." *Virginia Magazine of History and Biography* 78 (July 1970): 281–294.

32. Heard, Alexander. *State Legislatures in American Politics.* Englewood Cliffs, NJ: Prentice-Hall, 1966.

33. Hofferbert, Richard I. "Classification of American State Party Systems." *Journal of Politics* 26 (Aug. 1964): 550–567.

34. Holloway, William V. *State and Local Government in the United States.* New York: McGraw-Hill, 1951.

35. Howorth, L. S. "Place of State Legislatures." *Federal Bar Association Journal* 3 (Apr. 1937): 45–47.

36. Hurst, James W. *The Growth of American Laws: The Law Makers.* Boston: Little, Brown, 1950.

37. Hyneman, Charles S. "Who Makes Our Laws." *Political Science Quarterly* 55 (Dec. 1940): 550–581.

38. Ingram, Denny L. "The Legislature." *Natural Resources Journal* 8 (Jan. 1968): 148–168.

39. Jacob, Herbert, and Kenneth N. Vines. *Politics in American States: A Comparative Analysis.* 3d ed. Boston: Little, Brown, 1976.

40. Jennings, M. Kent, and Harmon Zeigler. "The Salience of American State Politics." *American Political Science Review* 64 (June 1970): 523–535.

41. Jewell, Malcolm E. *The State Legislature: Politics and Practice.* 2d ed. New York: Random House, 1969.

42. Jewell, Malcolm E. "State Legislatures in Southern Politics." *Journal of Politics* 26 (Feb. 1964): 177–197.

43. Jewell, Malcolm E., and Samuel C. Patterson. *The Legislative Process in the United States.* 3d ed. New York: Random House, 1977.

44. Joffee, J. M. "An Unusual Occurrence in the State Legislature." *Journal of the Missouri Bar* 5 (Oct. 1934): 150–160.

45. Johnson, Claudius O. *American State and Local Government.* 2d ed. New York: Crowell, 1956.

46. Keith, Gary A. "Comparing Legislative Studies Groups in Three States." *Legislative Studies Quarterly* 6 (Feb. 1981): 69–86.

47. Kendell, Willmoore. "The Two Majorities." *Midwest Journal of Political Science* 4 (Nov. 1960): 317–345.

48. Kerle, Donald F. "An Analysis of the Representational Role-Perceptions of State Legislatures." Ph.D. dissertation, University of Kansas, 1972.

49. Key, V. O. *American State Politics.* New York: Knopf, 1965.

50. Key, V. O. *Southern Politics in State and Nation.* New York: Knopf, 1949.

51. Kurfess, Charles F. "State Legislatures: A Record of Accomplishment." *State Government* 47 (Autumn 1974): 247–251.

52. Kurtz, Karl T., et al. "The State of U.S. State Legislative Research: A Comment." *Legislative Studies Quarterly* 6 (Feb. 1981): 27–34.

53. Lancaster, Lane W., and A. Breckenridge. *Readings in American State Government.* New York: Rinehart, 1950.

54. Ledbetter, Cal L. "State Legislators and the Electing of Presidents." *State Government* 49 (Summer 1975): 138–140.

55. Lepawsky, Albert. "The Statehouse as a School for State Craft." *State Government* 24 (Oct. 1951): 246–248.

56. Lockard, Duane. *Governing the States and Localities.* New York: Macmillan, 1969.

57. Lockard, Duane. *New England State Politics.* Princeton: Princeton University Press, 1959.

58. Lockard, Duane. *The Politics of State and Local Government.* 2d ed. New York: Macmillan, 1969.

59. Lowi, Theodore J. *Legislative Politics, U.S.A.* 3d ed. Boston: Little, Brown, 1973.

60. Luttbeg, N. R. "Structure of Public Beliefs on State Policies: A Comparison with Local and National Findings." *Public Opinion Quarterly* 35 (Spring 1971): 114–116.

61. McCurdy, Kathleen B. "More Stately Mansions for the Governors." *Historic Preservation* 17 (Nov.-Dec. 1965): 218–229.

62. MacDonald, Austin F. *American State Government and Administration.* New York: Crowell, 1960.

63. MacDonald, Austin F. *State and Local Government in the United States.* New York: Crowell, 1955.

General Studies

64. Main, Jackson T. "Government by the People: The American Revolution and the Democratization of the Legislatures." *William and Mary Quarterly* 23 (July 1966): 391–407.

65. Main, Jackson T. *The Upper House in Revolutionary America, 1763–1788.* Madison: University of Wisconsin Press, 1967.

66. Mead, Lawrence M. "Institutional Analysis for State and Local Government." *Public Administration Review* 39 (Jan.-Feb. 1979): 26–30.

67. Mid-America Assembly on State Legislatures in American Politics. *Midwest Legislative Politics, Participants' Edition.* Iowa City: University of Iowa, 1966.

68. Mitau, G. T. *State and Local Government: Politics and Processes.* New York: Scribner, 1966.

69. Murray, Keith. "The Legislative Scene." *Liberal Democrat* (Aug. 1963): 7–8.

70. National Legislative Conference. Committee on Legislative Processes and Procedures. *American State Legislatures in Mid-Twentieth Century: Final Report.* Chicago: Council of State Governments, 1961.

71. Neuberger, Richard L. "Government by the People." *Survey* 86 (Nov. 1950): 53–57.

72. Nixon, H. Clarence. "The Southern Legislature and Legislation." *Journal of Politics* 10 (May 1948): 410–417.

73. Norris, George W. "The One-House Legislature." *National Municipal Review* 24 (Feb. 1935): 87–89.

74. Norris, George W. "Only One House." *State Government* 7 (Oct. 1934): 209–210.

75. Patterson, Samuel C. *Midwest Legislative Politics.* Iowa City: University of Iowa, Institute of Public Affairs, 1967.

76. Perkins, John A. "The Legislatures and the Future of the States." *State Government* 19 (Oct. 1946): 254–257.

77. Paschman, Gene S. "The Images of Organization, Pluralism, and Community in American Social Science Literature on the Legislature." Ph.D. dissertation, University of California, Berkeley, 1970.

78. Prendergast, William B. "State Legislatures and Communism: The Current Scene." *American Political Science Review* 44 (Sept. 1950): 556–574.

79. Ringold, May S. *The Role of the State Legislatures in the Confederacy.* Athens: University of Georgia Press, 1966.

80. Rosenthal, Alan. "Separate Roads: The Legislator as an Individual and the Legislature as an Institution." *State Legislatures* 5 (Mar. 1979): 21–23.

81. Rosenthal, Alan, and R. Forth. "There Ought to Be a Law." *State Government* 51 (Spring 1978): 81–87.

82. Rossell, Beatrice S. *Working with a Legislature.* Chicago: American Library Association, 1948.

83. Saffell, David C. *State and Local Government: Politics and Public Policies.* Reading, MA: Addison-Wesley, 1978.

84. Sanford, Terry. *Storm over the States.* New York: McGraw-Hill, 1967.

85. Schmidt, Karl M. *American Government in Action.* Belmont, CA: Dickenson, 1967.

86. Smith, Thomas V. "In Praise of the Legislative Way." *Antioch Review* 9 (Mar. 1949): 46–59.

87. Smith, Thomas V. *The Legislative Way of Life.* Chicago: University of Chicago Press, 1940.

88. Snider, Clyde F. *American State and Local Government.* New York: Appleton-Century-Crofts, 1950.

89. Southern Assembly. *Our State Legislatures: Prospects and Problems.* New Orleans: Tulane University, 1967.

90. Stever, James A. *Diversity and Order in State and Local Politics.* Columbia: University of South Carolina Press, 1980.

90A. Steinbach, Carol. "Calling on Congress: What Some State Legislatures are Doing to Improve Relations with Federal Lawmakers." *State Legislatures* 10 (Feb. 1984): 17–20.

91. Stoiber, Susanne A. *Legislative Politics in the Rocky Mountain West: Colorado, New Mexico, Utah, and Wyoming.* Boulder: University of Colorado, Bureau of Governmental Research and Service, 1967.

92. Texas Pre-Session Legislative Conference. Lyndon B. Johnson School of Public Affairs. *Legislative Issues of the 'Seventies: Proceedings.* Austin: University of Texas, Lyndon B. Johnson School of Public Affairs, 1971.

93. Toepel, M. G. "Putting a Price Tag on Legislation." 31 *State Government* (May 1958): 502–505.

94. Toll, Henry W. "Today's Legislatures." *Annals of the American Academy of Political and Social Sciences* 195 (Jan. 1958): 1–10.

95. Trippett, Frank. *The States: United They Fell.* Cleveland: World, 1967.

96. Unruh, Jesse M. "Taking the Initiative." *National Civic Review* 57 (Sept. 1968): 407–410.

97. Wahlke, John C., Heinz Eulau, William Buchanan, and LeRoy C. Ferguson. *The Legislative System.* New York: Wiley, 1962.

98. Walker, Harvey. *The Legislative Process: Lawmaking in the United States.* New York: Ronald, 1952.

99. Walker, Harvey. "Role of the Legislature in Government." *State Government* 33 (Spring 1960): 96–102.

100. Weeks, O. Douglas. *Research in the American State Legislative Process: Need, Scope, Methods, Suggested Problems.* Ann Arbor, MI: J. W. Edwards, 1947.

101. Wheare, K. C. *Legislatures.* New York: Oxford University Press, 1963.

102. Willis, Simeon S. *The Process of Government: Lectures by Simeon S. Willis and Others.* Lexington: University of Kentucky, Bureau of Government Research, 1949.

103. Wolfinger, Raymond. *The Politics of Progress.* Englewood Cliffs, NJ: Prentice-Hall, 1974.

104. Zeller, Belle. *American State Legislatures.* New York: Crowell-Collier, 1954.

Constitutional Aspects

105. Citizens Conference on State Legislatures. *State Constitutional Provisions Affecting Legislatures.* Kansas City: Citizens Conference on State Legislatures, 1967.

106. "Constitutional Law—Legislative Bodies—Freedom of Religion—Tennessee Constitutional Provision Barring Ministers and Priests from Serving in the State Legislature Offends Neither the Free

Exercise Clause Nor the Establishment Clause of the First Amendment." *University of Cincinnati Law Review* 46 (1977): 893–904.

107. Dodd, Walter F. "State Constitutional Conventions and State Legislative Power." *Vanderbilt Law Review* 2 (Dec. 1948): 27–34.

108. English, A., and Carroll, J. J. "Teaching Constitutional Conventions in Legislative Process and State and Local Government Courses." *Teaching Political Science* 7 (Apr. 1980): 337–343.

109. Fordham, Jefferson B. "An Effective Legislature: Freed from Constitutional and Structural Limits, State Lawmaking Bodies Could Fill Rightful Role." *National Civic Review* (Mar. 1966): 135–140.

110. Friedman, Robert S., and S. L. Stokes. "The Role of Constitution-Maker as Representative." *Midwest Journal of Political Science* 9 (May 1965): 148–166.

111. Goodman, Jay S., Robert Arseneau, Elmer E. Cornwell, and Wayne R. Swanson. "Public Responses to State Constitutional Revision." *American Journal of Political Science* 17 (Aug. 1973): 571–596.

112. Grant, Edward D. "State Constitutional Revision and the Forces that Shape It." *State and Local Government Review* 9 (May 1977): 60–64.

113. Graves, W. Brooke. *Major Problems in State Constitutional Revision.* Chicago: Public Administration Service, 1960.

114. Haines, Charles G. *The Revival of Natural Law Concepts: A Study of the Establishment and of the Interpretation of Limits on Legislatures with Special Reference to the Development of Certain Phases of American Constitutional Law.* Cambridge: Harvard University Press, 1930.

115. Jung, Peter M. "Validity of a State's Rescision of Its Ratification of a Federal Constitutional Amendment." *Harvard Journal of Law and Public Policy* 2 (Summer 1979): 233–278.

116. Kirby, James C. "Limitations on the Power of State Legislatures over Presidential Elections." *Law and Contemporary Problems* 27 (Summer 1962): 495–509.

117. "Legislative Sessions: Constitutional Provisions, Principal State Officers, 1945." *State Government* 18 (Jan. 1945): 16–17.

118. Lutz, Donald S. "The Theory of Consent in Early State Constitutions." *Publius* 9 (Spring 1979): 11–42.

119. Marcantonio, Edward J. "Constitutional Requirements as to the Title of a Bill." *Temple Law Quarterly* 25 (July 1951): 63–67.

120. National Municipal League. "Proposals for a Model State Constitution." *National Municipal Review* 9 (Nov. 1920): 711–715.

121. National Municipal League. *Salient Issues of Constitutional Revision.* New York: National Municipal League, 1961.

122. National Municipal League. Committee on State Government. *Model State Constitution, with Explanatory Articles.* New York: National Municipal League, Committee on State Government, 1948.

123. Nortrup, Jack. "Yates, the Prorogued Legislature, and the Constitutional Convention." *Journal of the Illinois State Historical Society* 62 (Spring 1969): 5–34.

123A. Proffer, Lanny. "Legislative Veto Alternatives." *State Legislatures* 10 (Jan. 1984): 23–25.

124. Roll, Charles W. "We, Some of the People: Apportionment in the Thirteen State Conventions Ratifying the Constitution." *Journal of American History* 56 (June 1969): 21–40.

125. Schnader, William A. "The Constitution and the Legislature." *Annals of the American Academy of Political and Social Science* 181 (Sept. 1935): 39–49.

126. Sturm, Albert L. *Methods of State Constitutional Reform.* Ann Arbor: University of Michigan Press, 1954.

127. Sturm, Albert L. "The 1971 Revised Virginia Constitution and Recent Constitution-Making." *State Government* 44 (Summer 1971): 166–176.

128. Thompson, William N. "An Analysis of the Legislative Ambitions of State Constitutional Convention Delegates." *Western Political Quarterly* 29 (Sept. 1976): 425–439.

129. Tobin, Richard J. "Some Observations on the Use of State Constitutions to Protect the Environment." *Environmental Affairs* 3 (1974): 473–493.

130. Weinstein, Jack B. *A New York Constitution Meeting Today's Needs and Tomorrow's Challenges.* New York: National Municipal League, 1967.

131. Zenor, Dean. *State Constitutional Conventions: The Legislature's Role Preparing for a Convention.* Iowa City: University of Iowa, Institute of Public Affairs, 1960.

Structures of Legislatures

132. Aly, Bower. *Unicameral Legislatures.* Columbia, MO: Lucas Brothers, 1950.

133. Blair, George S. *American Legislatures: Structure and Process.* New York: Harper and Row, 1967.

134. Blank, Robert H. "State Electoral Structure." *Journal of Politics* 35 (Nov. 1973): 988–994.

135. Brademas, John. "Federal Reorganization and Its Likely Impacts on State and Local Government." *Publius* 8 (Spring 1978): 25–38.

136. Bryan, Frank M. "The Metamorphosis of a Rural Legislature." *Polity* 1 (Winter 1968): 191–212.

137. Buehler, Ezra C., ed. *Unicameral Legislatures.* New York: Noble and Noble, 1937.

138. Chaffey, Douglas C. "The Institutionalization of State Legislatures: A Comparative Study." *Western Political Quarterly* 23 (Mar. 1970): 180–196.

139. Citizens Conference on State Legislatures. *State Legislatures: An Evaluation of Their Effectiveness.* New York: Praeger, 1971.

140. Clayton, Dorothy H. "A Comparative Analysis of American State Legislatures: A Study of Institutionalization." Ph.D. dissertation, University of California, Berkeley, 1976.

141. Council of State Governments. *American Legislatures, Structure and Procedures: Summary and Tabulations of a 1953 Survey.* Chicago: Council of State Governments, 1954.

142. Council of State Governments. *American State Legislatures: Their Structures and Procedures.* Rev. ed. Lexington, KY: Council of State Governments, 1977.

143. Council of State Governments. *Unicameral Legislation.* Chicago: Council of State Governments, 1937.

144. Crane, Wilder, and Meredith W. Watts. *State Legislative Systems.* Englewood Cliffs, NJ: Prentice-Hall, 1968.

145. Culver, Dorothy C., comp. *Unicameral Legislatures—A Digest of Materials.* Berkeley: University of California, Bureau of Public Administration, 1934.

146. DeClercq, Eugene R. "A Comparative Study of the Economic and Political Influences on State Legislative Structures." Ph.D. dissertation, Florida State University, 1974.

147. DeClercq, Eugene R. "Inter-House Differences in American State Legislatures." *Journal of Politics* 39 (Aug. 1977): 774–785.

148. "The Facts Condemn the Unicameral System of Legislation...." *Texas Tax Journal* (Apr.-May 1938): 3–5, 6–9.

149. Fordham, Jefferson B. *The State Legislative Institution.* Philadelphia: University of Pennsylvania Press, 1959.

150. Greene, Jack P. "Political Mimesis: A Consideration of the Historical and Cultural Roots of Legislative Behavior in the British Colonies in the Eighteenth Century." *American Historical Review* 75 (Dec. 1969): 337–367.

151. Grumm, John G. "The Consequences of Structural Change for the Performance of State Legislatures: A Quasi-Experiment." In *Legislative Reform and Public Policy*, edited by Susan Welch and John G. Peters. New York: Praeger, 1977, pp. 201–213.

152. Grumm, John G. "The Effects of Legislative Structure on Legislature Performance." In *State and Urban Politics*, edited by Richard I. Hofferbert and Ira Sharkansky. Boston: Little, Brown, 1971, pp. 298–322.

153. Grumm, John G. *A Paradigm for the Comparative Analysis of Legislative Systems.* Beverly Hills, CA: Sage, 1973.

154. Grumm, John G. *Structure and Policy in the Legislature.* Kansas City: Citizens Conference on State Legislatures, 1966.

155. Herzberg, Donald G., and Jesse Unruh. *Essays on the State Legislative Process.* New York: Holt, Rinehart and Winston, 1970.

156. Johnson, Alvin W. *The Unicameral Legislature.* Minneapolis: University of Minnesota Press, 1938.

157. Johnson, Alvin W. "Unicameralism Marks Time." *State Government* 12 (June 1939): 101–103.

158. Keefe, William J., and Morris S. Ogul. *The American Legislative Process: Congress and the States.* 5th ed. Englewood Cliffs, NJ: Prentice-Hall, 1981.

159. McHenry, Dean E. *The Third House.* Stanford: Stanford University Press, 1963.

160. Mather, W. W. "Geographic Basis for a Unicameral Legislature." *Annals of the American Academy of Political and Social Science* 248 (Nov. 1946): 236–238.

161. Moran, T. F. *The Rise and Development of the Bicameral System in America.* New York: AMS Press, 1973.

162. Moschos, Demitrios M., and David Katsky. "Unicameralism and Bicameralism: History and Tradition." *Boston University Law Review* 45 (Spring 1965): 250–270.

163. National Legislative Conference. Committee on Legislative Rules. *Key Points in Legislative Procedure: Twenty Ways to Expedite the Legislative Process.* Lexington, KY: Council of State Governments, 1970.

164. Olson, David M. *The Legislative Process: A Comparative Approach.* New York: Harper and Row, 1980.

165. Perkins, John A. "State Legislative Reorganization." *American Political Science Review* 40 (June 1946): 510–521.

166. Putney, Bryant. "Unicameral Legislatures." *Editorial Research Reports* (Feb. 9, 1935): 101–119.

167. Senning, John P. *The One House Legislature.* New York: McGraw-Hill, 1937.

168. Senning, John P. "Unicameralism Passes Test." *National Municipal Review* 33 (Feb. 1944): 60–65.

169. Shull, Charles W. *American Experience with Unicameral Legislatures.* Detroit: Bureau of Governmental Research, 1937.

170. Shull, Charles W. *The Unicameral Legislature.* Detroit: Citizens' Research Council of Michigan, 1960.

171. Spencer, Richard C. "Highest Score Sheet: Unicameral System Lacks Old Abuses of Railroading, Last Minute Peak Load, Buck Passing, Trickery, Patronage." *National Municipal Review* 46 (Nov. 1957): 502–505.

172. Spicer, Erik J. "State Senates: Are They Really Necessary?" *State Government* 48 (Summer 1975): 156–159.

173. Stigler, G. J. "Sizes of Legislatures." *Journal of Legal Studies* 5 (Jan. 1976): 17–34.

174. Summers, Harrison B., comp. *Unicameral Legislatures.* New York: H. W. Wilson, 1936.

175. Tubbesing, Carl D. "Does Changing the Rules Change the Players?" *State Government* 48 (Spring 1975): 79–84.

176. University of Kentucky. Bureau of Government Research. *Unicameral Legislation in the States.* Lexington: University of Kentucky, Bureau of Government Research, 1938.

177. Wahlke, John C. "Organization and Procedure." In *State Legislatures in Politics.* Englewood Cliffs, NJ: Prentice-Hall, 1966, pp. 126–153.

178. Weeks, O. Douglas. "Recent Developments in the State Legislative Process: Structural, Organizational, and Procedural Developments Appraised." *State Government* 16 (July 1943): 162–166.

179. Willoughby, William F. *Principles of Legislative Organization and Administration.* Washington, D.C.: Brookings Institution, 1934.

Reapportionment and Redistricting

180. Adams, Bruce. "Model State Reapportionment Process: The Continuing Quest For 'Fair and Effective Representation.'" *Harvard Journal on Legislation* 14 (June 1977): 825–904.

181. *Apportionment Acts of the Legislature.* Norman: University of Oklahoma, Bureau of Government Research, 1961.

182. Baker, Gordon E. "America's Rotten Boroughs: Urban Under-Representation in State Legislatures." Ph.D. dissertation, Princeton University, 1952.

183. Baker, Gordon E. *State Constitutions: Reapportionment.* New York: National Municipal League, 1960.

184. Belsky, M. H. "Reapportionment in the 1970's—A Pennsylvania Illustration." *Temple Law Quarterly* 47 (Fall 1973): 3–37.

185. Bickerstaff, S. "Reapportionment by State Legislatures: A Guide for the 1980's." *Southwestern Law Journal* 34 (June 1980): 607–687.

186. Boyd, W. J. D. *Apportionment in the Nineteen Sixties: State Legislatures, Congressional Districts.* New York: National Municipal League, 1967.

187. Brady, D. W., and D. Edmonds. *The Effects of Malapportionment on Policy Outputs in the American States.* Iowa City: University of Iowa, Department of Political Science, 1966.

188. Broach, Glen T. "Party, Apportionment, and Conflict in State Legislatures: A Comparative Roll Call Analysis." Ph.D. dissertation, University of Alabama, 1971.

189. Bureau of Municipal Research. *Redistribution of State Legislative Representation in Philadelphia*. Philadelphia: Bureau of Municipal Research, 1951.

190. Bushman, Donald O., and William R. Stanley. "State Senate Reapportionment in the Southeast." *Annals of the Association of American Geographers* 61 (Dec. 1971): 654–670.

191. Bushnell, E. *Impact of Reapportionment on Thirteen Western States*. Salt Lake City: University of Utah Press, 1970.

192. Cho, Y. H., and H. G. Frederickson. *Measuring the Effects of Reapportionment in the American States*. New York: National Municipal League, 1976.

193. Clem, Alan L., and W. Faber. "Manipulated Democracy: The Multi-Member District." *National Civic Review* 68 (May 1979): 235–243.

194. Clem, Alan L. "Measuring Legislative Malapportionment: In Search of a Better Yardstick." *American Journal of Political Science* 7 (May 1963): 125–144.

195. "Constitutional Law—Elections—Representative Government—In Apportioning Its Legislative Districts, a State May Deviate from One Man, One Vote If It Can Show a Rational State Policy and Maintain Substantial Equality." *University of Cincinnati Law Review* 42 (Fall 1973): 788–794.

196. "Constitutional Law: State Apportionment—A Still-Emerging Standard for Equal Protection." *University of Florida Law Review* 25 (Summer 1973): 829–837.

197. Council of State Governments. *Legislative Reapportionment in the States*. Chicago: Council of State Governments, 1964.

198. Derfner, Armand. "Pro Affirmative Action in Districting." *Policy Studies Journal* 8 (1980–1981): 851–862.

199. Dines, A. "A Reapportioned State." *National Civic Review* 55 (1966): 70–76.

200. Dixon, Robert G. "Local Representation: Constitutional Mandates and Apportionment Options." *George Washington Law Review* 36 (May 1968): 693–712.

201. Dye, Thomas R. "Malapportionment and Public Policy in the States." *Journal of Politics* 27 (Aug. 1965): 586–601.

202. "Elections—Reapportionment—Section 5 of the Voting Rights Act of 1965, which Requires Prior Approval by Federal Officials of Changes in State Voting Laws, Held Applicable to Reapportionment Plans of State Legislatures." *Indiana Law Review* 7 (Jan. 1974): 579–591.

203. Erikson, Robert S. "The Partisan Impact of State Legislative Reapportionment." *American Journal of Political Science* 15 (Feb. 1971): 57–71.

204. Eulau, Heinz, et al. "The Role of the Representative: Some Empirical Observations on the Theory of Edmund Burke." *American Political Science Review* 53 (Sept. 1959): 742–756.

205. Fairlie, John A. "The Nature of Political Representation, II." *American Political Science Review* 34 (June 1940): 456–466.

206. Firestine, R. E. "Some Effects of Reapportionment on State Government Fiscal Activity." Ph.D. dissertation, Syracuse University, 1971.

207. "Flexible Standard for State Reapportionment Cases." *Fordham Law Review* 42 (Mar. 1974): 641–652.

208. Frederickson, H. George, and Yong Hyo Cho. "Legislative Apportionment and Fiscal Policy in the American States." *Western Political Quarterly* 27 (Mar. 1974): 5–37.

209. Hamm, Keith, et al. "Ethnic and Partisan Minorities in Two Southern State Legislatures." *Legislative Studies Quarterly* 8 (May 1983): 177–190.

210. Hanson, Roger A., and Robert E. Crew. "The Policy Impact of Reapportionment." *Law and Society Review* 8 (Fall 1973): 69–94.

211. Hardin, Charles M. "Issues in Legislative Reapportionment." *Review of Politics* 27 (Apr. 1965): 147–172.

212. Hastings, Fred W. "Voters Initiate Reapportionment." *State Government* 4 (Feb. 1931): 7.

213. Hill, A. Spencer. "The Reapportionment Decisions: A Return to Dogma?" *Journal of Politics* 31 (Feb. 1969): 186–213.

214. Kaiser, Henry F. "A Measure of the Population Quality of Legislative Apportionment." *American Political Science Review* 62 (Mar. 1968): 208–215.

215. Kaiser, Henry F. "An Objective Method for Establishing Legislative Districts." *American Journal of Political Science* 10 (May 1966): 200–213.

216. Kenton, Carolyn L., and S. W. Wanat. *Reapportionment in the States*. Lexington, KY: National Legislative Conference and Council of State Governments, 1972.

217. Key, V. O. "Procedures in State Legislative Apportionment." *American Political Science Review* 26 (Dec. 1932): 1050–1058.

218. Knight, Barbara B. "The States and Reapportionment: One Man, One Vote Reevaluated." *State Government* 49 (Summer 1976): 155–160.

219. "Legislatures Continue to Be Unrepresentative: 1950 Census Evokes New Apportionment Studies." *National Municipal Review* 41 (Nov. 1952): 523–525.

220. Leonard, James M. *Redistricting Detroit for Representation in the State Legislature*. Detroit: Bureau of Governmental Research, 1941.

221. "Limits to State Reapportionment through Multimember Districting." *De Paul Law Review* 23 (Spring 1974): 821–837.

222. Lyons, William E. "Legislative Redistricting by Independent Commissions." *Polity* 1 (Summer 1969): 428–458.

223. McClain, Robert H. "Compulsory Reapportionment." *National Municipal Review* 40 (June 1951): 305–307.

224. McKay, Robert B. "Reapportionment and Local Government." *George Washington Law Review* 36 (May 1968): 713–740.

225. McNickle, R. K. "Legislative Apportionment." *Editorial Research Reports* (Jan. 3, 1950): 1–19.

226. Montague, R. L. "Role of Federal Courts in the Reapportionment of State Legislatures." *Washington and Lee Law Review* 24 (Fall 1967): 227–240.

227. Morrill, Richard L. "Ideal and Reality in Reapportionment." *Annals of the Association of American Geographers* 63 (Dec. 1973): 463–477.

228. Murray, Richard W., and Donald S. Lutz. "Redistricting Decisions in the American States: A Test of the Minimal Winning Coalition Hypothesis." *American Journal of Political Science* 18 (May 1974): 233–255.

229. Neuberger, Richard L. "Why Social Progress Lags at the State Line! Our Rotten Borough Legislatures." *Survey* 86 (Nov. 1950): 53–57.

230. Newell, C. *County Representation and Legislative Reapportionment.* Austin: University of Texas, Institute of Public Affairs, 1965.

231. O'Rourke, Timothy G. "A Comparative Analysis of the Impact of Reapportionment on Six State Legislatures." Ph.D. dissertation, Duke University, 1977.

232. O'Rourke, Timothy G. *The Impact of Reapportionment.* New Brunswick, NJ: Transaction Books, 1980.

233. Peel, Roy V. "Political Implications of the 1950 Census of Population." *Western Political Quarterly* 3 (Dec. 1950): 615–619.

234. Pilcher, Dan. "Reapportionment: The New Ingredients." *State Legislatures* 6 (Apr. 1980): 6–11.

235. Pilcher, Dan. "Reapportionment: What's the Law?" *State Legislatures* 6 (Apr. 1980): 12–17.

236. Pulsipher, Allan G., and James L. Weatherby. "Malapportionment, Party Competition, and the Functional Distribution of Governmental Expenditures." *American Political Science Review* 62 (Dec. 1968): 1207–1219.

237. Reock, Ernest C. "Procedures and Standards for the Apportionment of State Legislatures." Ph.D. dissertation, Rutgers University, 1960.

238. Rossotti, J. E. "Measuring Some Effects of Apportionment on State Policy Outcomes, 1957–1969." Ph.D. dissertation, Syracuse University, 1972.

239. Saffell, David C. "Reapportionment and Public Policy: State Legislators' Perspectives." *Policy Studies Journal* 9 (1980–1981): 916–937.

240. Sanders, J. L. *Data on North Carolina Congressional Districts, State Senatorial Districts, and Apportionment of the State House of Representatives.* Chapel Hill: University of North Carolina, Institute of Government, 1961.

241. Shull, Charles W. "Legislative Apportionment and the Law." *Temple Law Quarterly* 18 (June 1944): 388–403.

242. Shull, Charles W. "Reapportionment: A Chronic Problem. . . ." *National Municipal Review* 30 (Feb. 1941): 73–79.

243. Shull, Charles W. "Revitalizing Representation." *Social Science* 25 (Oct. 1950): 234–238.

244. Silva, Ruth C. "Relation of Representation and the Party System to the Number of Seats Apportioned to a Legislative District." *Western Political Quarterly* 17 (Dec. 1964): 742–769.

245. Simons, Janet. "Reapportionment: Here It Comes Again." *State Legislatures* 4 (Nov.-Dec. 1978): 14–17.

246. Smith, George B. "The Failure of Reapportionment: The Effect of Reapportionment on the Election of Blacks to Legislative Bodies." *Howard Law Journal* 18 (1975): 639–684.

247. Smith, George B. "Reapportionment and Black America: A Study of the Effect of Reapportionment on the Election of Blacks to American Legislatures." Ph.D. dissertation, New York University, 1974.

248. Stanley, W. R. "State Senate Reapportionment in the Southeast." *Annals of the American Association of Geographers* 61 (1971): 654–670.

249. "State Legislative Reapportionment: A New Era." *Albany Law Review* 38 (1974): 798–825.

249A. Tucker, Harvey J. "Toward Consistent Legal Standards of State Legislative Apportionment." *National Civic Review* 73 (Feb. 1984): 64–69.

250. University of Chicago Law School. *Methods of Reapportionment*. Chicago: University of Chicago Law School, 1952.

251. Vickrey, William. "On the Prevention of Gerrymandering." *Political Science Quarterly* 76 (Mar. 1961): 105–110.

252. Walter, David O. "Legislative Reapportionment and Redistricting." Ph.D. dissertation, Harvard University, 1937.

253. Walter, David O. "Reapportionment and Urban Representation." *Annals of the American Academy of Political and Social Science* 195 (Jan. 1938): 11–20.

254. Walter, David O. "Reapportionment of State Legislative Districts." *Illinois Law Review* 37 (May 1942): 20–42.

255. Wells, Thomas L. "A Pattern Emerges: Two Sessions of Reapportioned Virginia Legislature Break Tradition in Volume and Number of Enactments." *National Civic Review* 57 (Oct. 1968): 453–457.

256. Wheeler, John P., and John Bebout. "After Reapportionment: New Appraisals, Thinking, Understanding Called For." *National Civic Review* 51 (May 1962): 246–250.

257. White, John P., and Norman C. Thomas. "Urban and Rural Representation and State Legislative Apportionment." *Western Political Quarterly* 17 (Dec. 1964): 724–741.

Elections and Formation of Legislatures

258. Bibby, John F. "Political Parties and Federalism: The Republican National Committee Involvement in Gubernatorial and Legislative Elections." *Publius* 9 (Winter 1979): 229–236.

259. Broh, C. Anthony. "Whether Bellwethers or Weather-Jars Indicate Election Outcomes." *Western Political Quarterly* 33 (Dec. 1980): 564–570.

260. Caldeira, Gregory A., and Samuel C. Patterson. "Contexual Influences on Participation in U.S. State Legislative Elections." *Legislative Studies Quarterly* 7 (Aug. 1982): 359–382.

260A. Cohen, Jeffrey E. "Perceptions of Electoral Insecurity Among Members Holding Safe Seats in a U.S. State Legislature." *Legislative Studies Quarterly* 9 (Mar. 1984): 365–370.

261. "Comparison of Legislative Campaign Costs." *Comparative State Politics Newsletter* 1 (1980): 16–20.

262. Cosman, Bernard. "Republicans in the South: Goldwater's Impact upon Voting Alignments in Congressional, Gubernatorial, and Senatorial Races." *Social Science Quarterly* 48 (June 1967): 13–23.

263. Cowart, Andrew T. "Electoral Choice in the American States: Incumbency Effects, Partisan Forces, and Divergent Partisan Majorities." *American Political Science Review* 67 (Sept. 1973): 835–853.

264. Dubeck, Paula J. "Women and Access to Political Office: A Comparison of Female and Male State Legislators." *Sociological Quarterly* 17 (Winter 1976): 42–52.

265. Frost, Richard T. "On Derge's Metropolitan and Outstate Legislative Delegations." *American Political Science Review* 53 (Sept. 1959): 792–795.

266. Grau, Craig H. "Competition in State Legislative Primaries." *Legislative Studies Quarterly* 6 (Feb. 1981): 35–54.

267. Hall, William K. "The 'Divisive' Primary in State Legislative Elections." Ph.D. dissertation, University of Kansas, 1969.

268. Jewell, Malcolm E. "Electoral Research and the Analysis of State Politics." *Louisiana Studies* 7 (Spring 1968): 31–46.

269. Jewell, Malcolm E. "Voter Turnout in State Gubernatorial Primaries." *Western Political Quarterly* 30 (June 1977): 236–254.

270. Jones, Charles O. "From the Suffrage of the People: An Essay of Support and Worry for Legislatures." *State Government* 47 (Summer 1974): 137–141.

271. Key, V. O. "The Direct Primary and Party Structure: A Study of State Legislative Nominations." *American Political Science Review* 48 (Mar. 1954): 1–26.

272. Kuklinski, James H. "Representativeness and Elections: A Policy Analysis." *American Political Science Review* 72 (Mar. 1978): 165–177.

273. Lijphart, Arend. "Comparative Perspectives on Fair Representation: The Plurality-Majority Rule, Geographical Districting, and Alternate Electoral Arrangements." *Policy Studies Journal* 9 (1980–1981): 899–915.

274. McNitt, Andrew D. "The Impact of State Legislation on Political Campaigns." *State Government* 53 (Summer 1980): 135–139.

275. Mervin, David. "Personality and Ticket Splitting in U.S. Federal and Gubernatorial Elections." *Political Studies* 21 (Sept. 1973): 306–310.

276. Neuberger, Richard L. "Toward Winning States' Rights." *National Municipal Review* 42 (Feb. 1953): 68–72.

277. Olson, David M. "The Structure of Electoral Politics." *Journal of Politics* 29 (May 1967): 352–361.

278. Penning, James M., and Corwin E. Smidt. "Public Funding of Gubernatorial Elections: The Views of State Legislators." *American Politics Quarterly* 10 (July 1982): 315–332.

279. Ray, David H., and John Harick. "A Longitudinal Analysis of Party Competition in State Legislative Elections." *American Journal of Political Science* 25 (Feb. 1981): 119–128.

280. Shull, Charles W. "Filling Legislative Vacancies." *County Officer* 17 (Nov. 1952): 334–336.

281. Tedin, Kent L., and Richard W. Murray. "Dynamics of Candidate Choice in a State Election." *Journal of Politics* 43 (May 1981): 435–455.

282. Tobin, Richard J. "The Influence of Nominating Systems on the Political Experiences of State Legislators." *Western Political Quarterly* 28 (Sept. 1975): 553–566.

283. Weber, Ronald E. "Gubernatorial Coattails: A Vanishing Phenomenon?" *State Government* 53 (Summer 1980): 153–156.

284. Weber, Ronald E., Anne H. Hopkins, Michael Mezey, and Frank J. Munger. "Computer Simulation of State Electorates." *Public Opinion Quarterly* 36 (Winter 1972): 549–565.

285. Webster, Donald H. "Voters Take the Law in Hand." *National Municipal Review* 35 (May 1946): 240–245.

286. Wiltz, John E. "The 1895 Election—A Watershed in Kentucky Politics." *Filson Club Historical Quarterly* 37 (Apr. 1963): 117–136.

Legislator-Constituency Relations

287. Abney, Glenn, and Thomas Henderson. "Representation of Local Officials by U.S. State Legislators." *Legislative Studies Quarterly* 4 (Feb. 1979): 63–78.

288. Adams, William C., and Paul H. Ferber. "Measuring Legislator-Constituency Congruence: Liquor, Legislators and Linkage." *Journal of Politics* 42 (Feb. 1980): 202–208.

289. Baker, Earl M. "Community and Party: Perceptions of the Political Party Among Local Legislators." Ph.D. dissertation, American University, 1971.

290. Baker, Gordon E. "Cities Resent Stepchild Lot." *National Municipal Review* 42 (Sept. 1953): 387–392.

291. Boynton, G. R., Samuel C. Patterson, and Ronald D. Hedlund. "The Missing Links in Legislative Politics: Attentive Constituents." *Journal of Politics* 31 (Aug. 1969): 700–721.

292. Bruner, Charles H. "Representation by Surrogate: The Politics of Aging in a State Legislative Setting." Ph.D. dissertation, Stanford University, 1978.

293. Buchanan, William, et al. "The Legislator as Specialist." *Western Political Quarterly* 13 (Sept. 1960): 636–661.

294. Clausen, Aage. "The Accuracy of Leader Perceptions of Constituency Views." *Legislative Studies Quarterly* 2 (Nov. 1977): 361–384.

295. Council of State Governments. *Single-Member and Multi-Member Districts in State Legislatures as of December, 1966; and Use of Numbered Positions in Multi-Member Districts.* Chicago: Council of State Governments, 1967.

296. Crane, Wilder. "Do Representatives Represent?" *Journal of Politics* 22 (May 1960): 295–299.

297. David, Paul T., and Ralph Eisenberg. *Devaluation of the Urban and Suburban Vote: A Statistical Investigation of Long-Term Trends in State Legislative Representation.* 2 vols. Charlottesville: University of Virginia, Bureau of Public Administration, 1961–1962.

298. Dixon, Robert. "Fair Criteria and Procedures for Establishing Legislative Districts." *Policy Studies Journal* 9 (1980–1981): 839–850.

299. Driscoll, Jean C. "The Legislator-District Relationship: A Case Study in Representation." Ph.D. dissertation, Northwestern University, 1953.

300. Dye, Thomas R. "A Comparison of Constituency Influences in the Upper and Lower Chambers of a State Legislature." *Western Political Quarterly* 14 (June 1961): 473–481.

301. Edsall, Preston W. "State Legislatures and Legislative Representation." *Journal of Politics* 30 (May 1968): 277–290.

302. Engle, R. H. "Weighting Legislators' Votes to Equalize Representation." *Western Political Quarterly* 12 (June 1959): 442–448.

303. Erikson, Robert S., Norman R. Luttbeg, and William V. Holloway. "Knowing One's District: How Legislators Predict Referendum Voting." *American Journal of Political Science* 19 (May 1975): 231–246.

304. Fenton, John H., and Daniel W. Chamberlayne. "The Literature Dealing with the Relationships between Political Processes, Socio-Economic Conditions and Public Policies in the American States: A Bibliographical Essay." *Polity* 1 (Spring 1969): 388–404.

305. Hain, Paul L. "Constituency Characteristics, Political Ambition and Advancement." *American Politics Quarterly* 4 (Jan. 1976): 47–62.

306. Hamilton, H. D. "Legislative Constituencies: Single-Member Districts, Multi-Member Districts, and Floterial Districts." *Western Political Quarterly* 20 (June 1967): 321–340.

307. Harvey, Lashley G. "Some Problems of Representation in State Legislatures." *Western Political Quarterly* 2 (June 1949): 265–271.

308. Hedlund, Ronald D., and H. Paul Friesema. "Representatives' Perceptions of Constituency Opinion." *Journal of Politics* 34 (Aug. 1972): 730–752.

309. Ingram, Helen M. "The Impact of Constituency on the Process of Legislating." *Western Political Quarterly* 22 (June 1969): 265–279.

310. Ingram, Helen M., Nancy K. Laney, and John R. McCain. *A Policy Approach to Representation: Lessons from the Four Corners States*. Baltimore: Johns Hopkins University Press, 1980.

311. Jewell, Malcolm E. "Legislative Casework: Serving Constituents, One at a Time." *State Legislatures* 5 (Nov. 1979): 14–18.

312. Jewell, Malcolm E. *Legislative Representation in the Contemporary South*. Durham, NC: Duke University Press, 1967.

313. Jewell, Malcolm E. *Representation in State Legislatures*. Lexington: University Press of Kentucky, 1982.

314. Klain, Maurice. "A New Look at the Constituencies: The Need for a Recount and Reappraisal." *American Political Science Review* 49 (Dec. 1955): 1105–1119.

315. Kuklinski, James H., and Richard Elling. "Representational Role, Constituency Opinion, and Legislative Roll-Call Behavior." *American Journal of Political Science* 21 (Feb. 1977): 135–148.

316. McCrone, Donald J., and James Kuklinski. "The Delegate Theory of Representation." *American Journal of Political Science* 23 (May 1979): 278–300.

317. MacNeil, Douglas H. "Urban Representation in State Legislatures." *State Government* 18 (Apr. 1945): 59–61.

318. Martin, John B. "Backstage at the State House: What Those Politicians Do to You." *Saturday Evening Post* (Dec. 1953): 30–31.

319. Neuman, Dale A. "Operative Conceptions of Political Representation in the United States: Some Preliminary Findings." *Journal of Politics* 33 (Aug. 1971): 831–839.

320. O'Loughlin, John. "Black Representation Growth and the Seat-Vote Relationship." *Social Science Quarterly* 60 (June 1979): 72–86.

321. Pierce, John C., and Nicholas P. Lovrich. "Belief Systems Concerning the Environment: The General Public, Attentive Publics, and State Legislators." *Political Behavior* 2 (1980): 259–286.

322. Prewitt, Kenneth, and Heinz Eulau. "Political Matrix and Political Representation: Prolegomenon to a New Departure from an Old Problem." *American Political Science Review* 63 (June 1969): 427–444.

323. Rehfuss, John A. "Multipurpose District Legislation for California: 1958–1963." D.P.A. dissertation, University of Southern California, 1966.

324. Robeck, Bruce W. "Legislative Partisanship, Constituency and Malapportionment." *American Political Science Review* 66 (Dec. 1972): 1246–1255.

325. Schneider, Mark. "Migration, Ethnicity, and Politics: A Comparative State Analysis." *Journal of Politics* 38 (Nov. 1976): 938–962.

326. Schulman, Mark A. "Legislators, Bureaucrats and Judges: A Comparative Analysis of Some Predispositions of Democratic Accountability." Ph.D. dissertation, Rutgers University, 1980.

327. Uslaner, Eric M., and Ronald E. Weber. "U.S. State Legislators' Opinions and Perceptions of Constituency Attitudes." *Legislative Studies Quarterly* 4 (Nov. 1979): 563–596.

328. Yarwood, Dean L., and Dan P. Nimmo. "Subjective Environment of Bureaucracy: Accuracies and Inaccuracies in Roll-Taking Among Administrators, Legislators, and Citizens." *Western Political Quarterly* 29 (Sept. 1976): 337–352.

329. Zeller, Belle. "Lawmaker—Legislator or Lobbyist?" *National Municipal Review* 29 (Aug. 1940): 523–531.

330. Ziegler, Martha J. "Legislators Work Between Sessions." *State Government* 10 (Nov. 1937): 236–237.

Legislative Recruitment and Careers

331. Barber, James D. *The Lawmakers: Recruitment and Adaption to Legislative Life*. New Haven: Yale University Press, 1965.

332. Calvert, Jerry. "Revolving Doors: Volunteerism in State Legislatures." *State Government* 52 (Summer 1979): 174–181.

333. Clark, Calvin W. *Compensation for Legislators in the Fifty States*. Kansas City: Citizens Conference on State Legislatures, 1968.

334. Clark, Calvin W., and Walter Nunn. *Recent and Proposed Changes in Compensation for Legislators in the Fifty States.* Kansas City: Citizens Conference on State Legislatures, 1967.

335. Clarke, Harold D., and Allan Kornberg. "Moving Up the Political Escalator: Women Party Officials in the United States and Canada." *Journal of Politics* 41 (May 1979): 442–477.

336. Council of State Governments. *Retirement Plans for State Legislators.* Chicago: Council of State Governments, 1967.

337. Diamond, Irene. *Sex Roles in the State House.* New Haven: Yale University Press, 1977.

338. Diamond, Irene. "Women and State Legislatures: A Macro and Micro Analysis." Ph.D. dissertation, Princeton University, 1975.

339. Eulau, Heinz. "Career Perspectives of American State Legislators." In *Political Decision Makers*, edited by Dwaine Marvick. Glencoe, IL: Free Press, 1960, pp. 218–263.

340. Eulau, Heinz, and John Sprague. *Lawyers in Politics: A Study in Professional Convergence.* Indianapolis: Bobbs-Merrill, 1964.

341. Eulau, Heinz, and David Kaff. "Occupational Mobility and Political Career." *Western Political Quarterly* 15 (Sept. 1962): 507–521.

342. Githens, Marianne, and Jewel Prestage. "Women State Legislators: Styles and Priorities." *Policy Studies Journal* 7 (Winter 1978): 264–270.

343. Gold, David. "Lawyers in Politics: An Empirical Exploration of Biographical Data on State Legislators." *Pacific Sociological Review* 4 (Fall 1961): 84–86.

344. Goodman, Jay S., Wayne R. Swanson, and Elmer E. Cornwell. "Political Recruitment in Four Selection Systems." *Western Political Quarterly* 23 (Mar. 1970): 92–103.

345. Graves, W. Brooke, ed. "Our State Legislators." *Annals of the American Academy of Political and Social Science* 195 (Jan. 1938): 1–252.

346. Grumm, John G., and Calvin W. Clark. *Compensation for Legislators in the Fifty States.* Kansas City: Citizens Conference on State Legislatures, 1966.

347. Hain, Paul L. "American State Legislators' Ambitions and Careers: The Effects of Age and District Characteristics." Ph.D. dissertation, Michigan State University, 1971.

348. Hightower, Nikki R. Van. "The Recruitment of Women for Public Office." *American Political Quarterly* 5 (July 1977): 301–314.

349. Jacob, Herbert. "Initial Recruitment of Elected Officials in the U.S.: A Model." *Journal of Politics* 24 (Nov. 1962): 703–716.

350. Keynes, Edward, Richard Tobin, and Robert Danziger. "Institutional Effects on Elite Recruitment: The Case of State Nominating Systems." *American Politics Quarterly* 7 (July 1979): 283–302.

351. "The Legislators of 1949 Face Their Jobs." *State Government* 22 (Feb. 1949): 28–31.

352. Lockard, Duane. "Tribulations of a State Senator." *Reporter* (May 1956): 24–28.

353. Main, Jackson T. "Social Origins of a Political Elite: The Upper House in the Revolutionary Era." *Huntington Library Quarterly* 27 (Feb. 1964): 147–158.

354. Marvick, Dwaine. *Political Decision-Makers.* Glencoe, IL: Free Press, 1961.

355. Mason, John B. "State Legislatures: The Proving Grounds of American Statesmanship." *State Government* 11 (Dec. 1938): 230–232.

356. Matthews, Donald C. *The Social Background of Political Decision-Makers.* Garden City, NY: Doubleday, 1954.

357. Patterson, Samuel C., and G. R. Boynton. "Legislative Recruitment in a Civic Culture." *Social Science Quarterly* 50 (Sept. 1969): 243–263.

358. Pindur, Wolfgang. "Comparative Recruitment Styles of Urban Legislators." *Michigan Academician* 5 (Summer 1972): 29–40.

359. Ray, David H. "Membership Stability in Nine State Legislatures: 1891–1970." Ph.D. dissertation, Stanford University, 1979.

360. Ray, David H. "Voluntary Retirement and Electoral Defeat in Eight State Legislatures." *Journal of Politics* 38 (May 1976): 426–433.

360A. Rosenthal, Alan. "Where Do You Sit?: Where a Lawmaker Sits in a Legislative Chamber Affects His or Her Standing on the Floor." *State Legislatures* 10 (Mar. 1984): 22–24.

361. Ruchelman, Leonard I. *Political Careers: Recruitment Through the Legislature.* Rutherford, NJ: Fairleigh Dickinson University Press, 1970.

362. Rule, Wilma. "Why Women Don't Run: The Critical Contextual Factors in Women's Legislative Recruitment." *Western Political Quarterly* 34 (Mar. 1981): 60–77.

363. Schapiro, Beth S. "The Recruitment of Southern State Legislators: A Comparison of Men and Women." Ph.D. dissertation, Emory University, 1979.

364. Schumaker, Waldo. "What Price Law-Makers?" *State Government* 4 (Feb. 1931): 10.

365. Seligman, Lester G. "Elite Recruitment and Political Development." *Journal of Politics* 26 (Aug. 1964): 612–626.

366. Staub, Stephen A. "Antecedents and Consequences of Political Ambition: A Study of Legislators in Four States." Ph.D. dissertation, Indiana University, 1974.

367. Strange, M. L. "Case for the Citizen Legislator." *State Government* 47 (Summer 1974): 130–131.

368. Thurber, James A. "The Impact of Party Recruitment Activity upon Legislative Role Orientations: A Path Analysis." *Legislative Studies Quarterly* 1 (Nov. 1976): 533–550.

369. Tobin, Richard J. "A Comparative Analysis of the Impact of Nominating Systems on State Legislative Recruitment and Behavior." Ph.D. dissertation, Northwestern University, 1973.

370. Tobin, Richard J., and Edward Keynes. "Institutional Differences in the Recruitment Process: A Four-State Study." *American Journal of Political Science* 19 (Nov. 1979): 667–682.

371. Toll, Henry W. "Should We Pay Law-Makers?" *State Government* 4 (Feb. 1931): 11–13.

372. Tucker, W. P. "Characteristics of State Legislators." *Social Science* 29 (Apr. 1955): 94–98.

373. "Turnover in State Legislatures." *American Journal of Political Science* 18 (Aug. 1974): 609–616.

374. "Two in One." *State Government* 8 (Dec. 1935): 245–247.

375. Van der Vries, Bernice T. "Women in Government." *State Government* 21 (July 1948): 127–128.

376. Weinberg, A. A. "Retirement Planning for Public Employees." *State Government* 20 (Jan. 1947): 10–19.

377. Welch, Susan. "Recruitment of Women to Public Office: A Discriminant Analysis." *Western Political Quarterly* 31 (Sept. 1978): 372–380.

378. Werner, Emmy E. "Women in the State Legislatures." *Western Political Quarterly* 21 (Mar. 1968): 40–50.

379. "Women in State Legislatures." *State Government* 10 (Oct. 1937): 214–215.

Political Parties and Groups in Legislatures

380. Broussard, James H. "Party and Partisanship in American Legislatures: The South Atlantic States, 1800–1812." *Journal of Southern History* 43 (Feb. 1977): 39–58.

381. Carmines, Edward G. "Mediating Influence of State Legislatures on the Linkage Between Interparty Competition and Welfare Policies." *American Political Science Review* 68 (Sept. 1974): 1118–1124.

382. Clark, Robert B., and Charles Wiggins. "The Persistence of Divided Party Control of State Governments: A Post-Reapportionment Note." *Polity* 8 (Spring 1976): 490–495.

383. Dreyer, Edward C. "Change and Stability in Party Identifications." *Journal of Politics* 35 (Aug. 1973): 712–722.

384. Elling, Richard C. "State Party Platforms and State Legislative Performance: A Comparative Analysis." *American Journal of Political Science* 23 (May 1979): 383–405.

385. Erikson, Robert S. "The Relationship Between Party Control and Civil Rights Legislation in the American States." *Western Political Quarterly* 24 (Mar. 1971): 178–182.

386. Flinn, Thomas A. "Party Responsibility in the States: Some Causal Factors." *American Political Science Review* 58 (Mar. 1964): 60–71.

387. Francis, Wayne L. "Coalitions in American State Legislatures." In *The Study of Coalitions Behavior*, edited by Sven Groennings, E. W. Kelley, and Michael Leiserson. New York: Holt, Rinehart and Winston, 1970, pp. 409–423.

388. Garcia, Thomas V. "Inter-Party Competition, Direct Legislation, and Electoral Participation in the American States, 1950–1960." Ph.D. dissertation, University of Massachusetts, 1967.

389. Gatlin, Douglas S. "The Development of a Responsible Party System in the Florida Legislature." In *State Legislative Innovation: Case Studies of Washington, Ohio, Florida, Illinois, Wisconsin, and California*, edited by James A. Robinson. New York: Praeger, 1973, pp. 1–45.

390. Hanson, Russell. "Political Culture, Interparty Competition and Political Efficacy in the American States." *Publius* 10 (Spring 1980): 17–36.

391. Ippolito, Dennis S. "Motivational Reorientation and Change Among Party Activists." *Journal of Politics* 31 (Nov. 1969): 1098–1101.

392. "Is the Party Over? Political Parties in State Legislatures." *State Legislatures* 7 (Nov.-Dec. 1981): 23–27.

393. Jacob, Herbert. "Dimensions of State Politics." In *State Legislatures in American Politics*, edited by Alexander Heard. Englewood Cliffs, NJ: Prentice-Hall, 1966, pp. 377–412.

394. Jennings, M. Kent, and Norman Thomas. "Men and Women in Party Elites: Social Roles and Political Resources." *American Journal of Political Science* 12 (Nov. 1968): 469–472.

395. Jewell, Malcolm E., and David Olson. *American State Political Parties and Elections*. Homewood, IL: Dorsey Press, 1982.

396. Jones, Bryan D. "Competitiveness, Role Orientations, and Legislative Responsiveness." *Journal of Politics* 35 (Nov. 1973): 924–947.

397. Keefe, William J. "Comparative Study of the Role of Political Parties in State Legislatures." *Western Political Quarterly* 9 (Sept. 1956): 726–742.

398. Klein, Bernard W. "Political Partisanship in Four State Legislatures." Ph.D. dissertation, Michigan State University, 1966.

399. Kornberg, Allan, Joel Smith, and Harold Clarke. "Attributes of Ascribed Influence in Local Party Organizations in Canada and the United States." *Canadian Journal of Political Science* 5 (June 1972): 206–233.

400. Meltz, David B. "Legislative Party Cohesion: A Model of the Bargaining Process in State Legislatures." *Journal of Politics* 35 (Aug. 1973): 649–681.

401. Monsma, Stephen V. "Integration and Goal Attainment as Functions of Formal Legislative Groups." *Western Political Quarterly* 22 (Mar. 1969): 19–28.

402. Morehouse, Sarah M. "The State Political Party and the Policy-Making Process." *American Political Science Review* 67 (Mar. 1973): 55–72.

403. Morehouse, Sarah M. *State Politics, Parties, and Policy.* New York: Holt, Rinehart and Winston, 1981.

404. Myers, Thomas R. "Legislative Factionalism in a One-Party System." Ph.D. dissertation, University of Kentucky, 1977.

405. "Party Control Shifts in Many Legislatures." *National Civic Review* 53 (Dec. 1964): 600–601.

406. Patterson, Samuel C. "Party Oppositions in the Legislature." *Polity* 4 (Spring 1972): 344–365.

406A. Pilcher, Dan. "Legislators as Party Leaders: Why Wear Two Hats?" *State Legislatures* 10 (Jan. 1984): 15–18.

407. Riley, Dennis D. "Party Competition and State Policy Making: The Need for a Reexamination." *Western Political Quarterly* 24 (Sept. 1971): 510–513.

408. Shaffer, William R. "Partisan Loyalty and the Perceptions of Party, Candidates and Issues." *Western Political Quarterly* 25 (Sept. 1972): 424–433.

408A. Sherman, Sharon. "Powersplit: When Legislatures and Governors are of Opposing Parties." *State Legislatures* 10 (May-June 1984): 9–12.

409. Sprague, John. "One-Party Dominance in Legislatures." *Legislative Studies Quarterly* 6 (May 1981): 259–286.

410. Tucker, Harvey J. "Interparty Competition in the American States: One More Time." *American Politics Quarterly* 10 (Jan. 1982): 93–116.

411. Walker, Dennis L. "A Comparative Analysis of the Factors Influencing Party Voting Cohesion in Democratic Legislatures." Ph.D. dissertation, Washington State University, 1971.

412. Wiggins, Charles W., and William L. Turk. "State Party Chairman: A Profile." *Western Political Quarterly* 23 (June 1970): 321–332.

413. Wolf, T. Philip. "Party Loyalty Among Party Workers." *Rocky Mountain Social Science Journal* 2 (Oct. 1965): 134–144.

Legislative Committees

414. "Ad Interim: Committees and Commissions Left on the Beach by the Legislative Tide of 1931." *State Government* 5 (Feb. 1932): 12–19.

415. Council of State Governments. *Handbook for Legislative Committees*. Rev. ed. Lexington, KY: Council of State Governments, 1969.

416. Council of State Governments. *Professional Assistance for Legislative Standing and Interim Committees and Legislative Leaders*. Chicago: Council of State Governments, 1961.

417. Council of State Governments. Midwest Regional Conference. *Handbook on Standing and Interim Committees in Midwestern States*. Springfield: State of Illinois Commission on Intergovernmental Cooperation, 1966.

418. Ethridge, Marcus E. "Legislative-Administrative Interaction as 'Intrusive Access': An Empirical Analysis." *Journal of Politics* 43 (May 1981): 473–492.

419. Fairlie, John A. "Legislative Committees and Commissions in the United States." *Michigan Law Review* 31 (Nov. 1932): 25–39.

420. Fountain, M. R. "Validity of Functioning of Interim Committees After Legislature Has Adjourned." *Temple Law Quarterly* 23 (Apr. 1950): 411–416.

421. Gallup, Christopher M. "Our Invisible Government: The Committee System in Our Legislative Bodies and How It Works." *National Municipal Review* 28 (Nov. 1939): 795–796.

422. Hamm, Keith E. "U.S. State Legislative Committee Decisions: Similar Results in Different Settings." *Legislative Studies Quarterly* 5 (Feb. 1980): 31–54.

423. Hamm, Keith E., and Gary Moncrief. "Effects of Structural Change in Legislative Committee Systems on Their Performance in U.S. States." *Legislative Studies Quarterly* 7 (Aug. 1982): 383–400.

424. Huwa, Randy, and Alan Rosenthal. *Politicians and Professionals: Interactions Between Committee and Staff in State Legislatures*. New Brunswick, NJ: Rutgers University, Eagleton Institute of Politics, Center for State Legislative Research and Service, 1977.

425. Irwin, Frank. "Interim Committees: State Legislators Study Many Problems." *Tax Digest* 31 (Nov. 1953): 365–367.

426. Lees, John D., and Malcolm Shaw, eds. *Committees in Legislatures: A Comparative Analysis.* Durham, NC: Duke University Press, 1979.

427. National Legislative Conference. Committee on Legislative Rules. *Handbook for Legislative Committees.* Lexington, KY: Council of State Governments, 1969.

428. Oxendale, James R. "Membership Stability on Standing Committees in Legislative Lower Chambers." *State Government* 54 (Autumn 1981): 126–129.

429. Ray, Robert F. *Appointment of State Legislative Committees.* Iowa City: University of Iowa, Institute of Public Affairs, 1955.

430. Rhode, William E. *Committee Clearance of Administrative Decisions.* East Lansing: Michigan State University, College of Business and Public Service, Bureau of Social and Political Research, 1959.

431. Rosenthal, Alan. "Legislative Committee Systems: An Exploratory Analysis." *Western Political Quarterly* 26 (June 1973): 252–262.

432. Rosenthal, Alan. *Legislative Performance in the States: Explorations of Committee Behavior.* New York: Free Press, 1974.

433. Shapley, T. S., and Martin Shubik. "A Method for Analysis in the Distribution of Power in a Committee System." *American Political Science Review* 48 (Sept. 1954): 787–792.

434. Wellman, Charles. "Effect of *Sine Die* Adjournment upon Legislative Committees." *Southern California Law Review* 13 (Mar. 1940): 363–365.

435. Wilkenfield, H. C. "Power of Legislative Committee to Function After Adjournment of Legislature." *Georgetown Law Journal* 28 (Jan. 1940): 560–562.

436. Winslow, Clinton I. "Committees in State Legislatures." Ph.D. dissertation, Harvard University, 1931.

437. Winslow, Clinton I. "Standing Committees in 48 Senates and 48 Houses." *State Government* 4 (Aug. 1931): 4.

438. Winslow, Clinton I. *State Legislative Committees: A Study in Procedure.* Baltimore: Johns Hopkins University Press, 1931.

439. Winslow, Clinton I. "Who Appoints the Standing Committees in the 48 Legislatures?" *State Government* 4 (Mar. 1931): 10–12.

Legislative Councils

440. Asch, S. H. "The Legislative Council Movement in the United States." *St. John's Law Review* 31 (Dec. 1956): 49–64.

441. Corrick, Franklin. "Previews: The New Legislative Council." *State Government* 7 (Nov. 1934): 250–252.

442. Council of State Governments. *Legislative Councils: Organization, Staff, and Appropriations.* Chicago: Council of State Governments, 1959.

443. Davey, Harold W. "The Legislative Council Movement, 1933–1953." *American Political Science Review* 47 (Sept. 1953): 785–797.

444. Evans, Alvin E. "Municipal Councils Compared with State Legislatures." *Missouri Law Review* 17 (Apr. 1952): 139–158.

445. Gallagher, Hubert R. "Legislative Councils." *National Municipal Review* 24 (Mar. 1935): 147–151.

446. Guild, Frederic H. "The Development of the Legislative Council Idea." *Annals of the American Academy of Political and Social Science* 195 (Jan. 1938): 144–150.

447. Guild, Frederic H. *Legislative Councils After Thirty Years.* Carbondale: Southern Illinois University, Public Affairs Research Bureau, 1964.

448. Guild, Frederic H. "Legislative Councils: An Article and Bibliography." *Law Library Journal* 36 (Nov. 1943): 169–190.

449. Guild, Frederic H. "Legislative Councils: Objectives and Accomplishments." *State Government* 22 (Sept. 1949): 217–219.

450. Johnson, Roy H. "A Review of Legislative Councils." *University of Kansas City Law Review* 8 (Feb. 1940): 65–72.

451. "The Legislative Councils in Action: Round-Up of State Legislative Councils—Their Financing, Operation, and Results." *State Government* 16 (Feb. 1943): 34–36.

452. Lindsay, Jim T. "Legislative Councils." *Texas Bar Journal* 13 (Dec. 1950): 621–625.

453. Putney, Bryant. "Legislative Councils." *Editorial Research Reports* (Aug. 12, 1937): 111–126.

454. Rhodes, Jack A. "The Legislative Council: A Program for Planning and Research." *Oklahoma Bar Association Journal* 17 (July 1946): 1205–1209.

455. Rhodes, Jack A. "Light for State Legislatures: Three New Legislative Councils." *National Municipal Review* 35 (Sept. 1946): 393–399.

456. Siffin, William J. *The Legislative Council in the American States.* Bloomington: Indiana University Press, 1959.

457. Smith, David W. "The Legislative Council Movement in the United States." Ph.D. dissertation, University of Utah, 1955.

458. "Three More Legislative Councils Established." *Public Administration Review* 10 (Winter 1950): 62.

459. "Tools for the Legislative Council." *National Municipal Review* 28 (Oct. 1939): 684–686.

460. Walker, Harvey. "Legislative Councils—An Appraisal." *National Municipal Review* 28 (Dec. 1939): 839–842.

Organization of Legislative Business

461. "Availability of the Testimonial Privilege for State Legislators: The Seventh Circuit's Current Position." *Chicago-Kent Law Review* 53 (1976): 541–561.

462. Barker, Twiley W. "A Long, Long Ballot." *National Civic Review* 53 (Apr. 1964): 170–175.

463. Bartley, David M. "The Legislative Organization from a Speaker's Perspective." *Public Administration Review* 35 (Sept.-Oct. 1975): 494–496.

464. Butler, F., and R. Craft. "Toward a More Efficient Use of Legislative Time." *State Government* 50 (Spring 1977): 110–115.

465. Chamberlain, Joseph P. *Legislative Processes: National and State.* New York: Appleton-Century, 1936.

466. Christensen, Asher N. "Days and Days." *State Government* 4 (July 1931): 7–9.

467. Clark, Calvin W., and Walter Nunn. *Charts Showing Recent and Proposed Changes in Legislative Sessions in the Fifty States.* Kansas City: Citizens Conference on State Legislatures, 1967.

468. Council of State Governments. *Our State Legislatures: Report of the Committee on Legislative Processes and Procedures.* Rev. ed. Chicago: Council of State Governments, 1948.

Organization of Legislative Business

469. Council of State Governments. *Parliamentary Authorities Used by State Legislative Bodies.* Chicago: Council of State Governments, 1961.

470. Council of State Governments. National Legislative Conference. *Debate and Decorum in State Legislatures.* Chicago: Council of State Governments, 1965.

471. Crain, W. M., and R. D. Tollison. "Sizes of Majorities." *Economic Journal* 46 (Jan. 1980): 726–734.

472. Dickerson, Reed. "Three Aspects of Legislative Drafting." *State Legislatures* 3 (Sept.-Oct. 1977): 12.

473. Dodds, Harold W. "Procedure in State Legislatures." Ph.D. dissertation, University of Pennsylvania, 1917.

474. Grant, J. A. C. "The Introduction of Bills." *Annals of the American Academy of Political and Social Science* 195 (Jan. 1938): 116–122.

475. Gupton, Kevin. "State Legislative Security: A New Perspective." *State Legislatures* 2 (May-June 1976): 17–19.

476. Harlow, Ralph Volney. *The History of Legislative Methods in the Period Before 1825.* New Haven: Yale University Press, 1917.

477. Hart, James. "Limits of Legislative Delegation." *Annals of the American Academy of Political and Social Science* 221 (May 1942): 87–100.

478. Lester, J. P. "Partisanship and Environmental Policy: The Mediating Influence of State Organizational Structures." *Environment and Behavior* 12 (Mar. 1980): 101–131.

479. "Limitations on Even-Year Legislative Sessions." *Maryland Law Review* 12 (Spring 1951): 124–144.

480. Luce, Robert. *Legislative Assemblies: Their Framework, Make-Up, Character, Characteristics, Habits, and Manners.* Boston: Houghton Mifflin, 1924.

481. McGeary, M. Nelson. "Changes in Legislative Sessions." *Temple Law Quarterly* 25 (Apr. 1952): 449–459.

482. McKenna, William J. "The Legislative Special Session as an American Political Institution." Ph.D. dissertation, University of Pennsylvania, 1951.

483. Mason, Paul. "Procedure in State Legislatures." *State Government* 36 (Spring 1963): 101–107.

484. Mazur, Gilbert G. "Senatorial Confirmation Procedure in American State Governments." M.A. thesis, University of California, 1951.

485. Moffat, Abbot L. "The Legislative Process." *Cornell Law Quarterly* 24 (Feb. 1939): 223–233.

486. Moflitt, H. L. "Lawyer's Role as a Legislator." *Florida Bar Journal* 51 (Mar. 1977): 134–135.

487. National Legislative Conference. *A Guide to the Objectives, Organization, and Operations of a Legislative Reference Service in State Government.* Chicago: Council of State Governments, 1957.

488. National Legislative Conference. Committee on Organization of Legislative Services. *Mr. President... Mr. Speaker... Report.* Chicago: Council of State Governments, 1963.

489. Rosenthal, Alan. *Legislative Life: People, Process, and Performance in the States.* New York: Harper and Row, 1981.

490. Rosenthal, Alan. "Legislative Life: The Rules of the Game." *State Legislatures* 7 (Oct. 1981): 15–19.

491. Rosenthal, Alan, and Rod Forth. "The Assembly Line: Law Production in the American States." *Legislative Studies Quarterly* 3 (May 1978): 265–291.

492. Sands, C. Dallas. "Developments in the Field of Legislation." *Rutgers Law Review* 10 (Fall 1955): 2–26.

493. Senning, John P. "One House, Two Sessions." *National Municipal Review* 28 (Dec. 1939): 843–847.

494. Sheldon, Addison E., and Myrtle Keegan. *Legislative Procedure in the Forty-Eight States.* Lincoln, NE: State Journal, 1914.

495. Silverman, Corinne. "The Legislators' View of the Legislative Process." *Public Opinion Quarterly* 18 (Summer 1954): 180–190.

496. Smith, Morgan. "The Legislative Maze." *Colorado Quarterly* 23 (Winter 1975): 373–387.

497. Solomon, Samuel R. "Master of the House." *National Civic Review* 57 (Feb. 1968): 68–74.

498. "Ten States Now Have Annual Legislative Sessions." *National Municipal Review* 40 (June 1951): 312.

499. University of North Carolina. Institute of Government. "Institute of Government Legislative Service—1951: Organization and Objectives." *Popular Government* 17 (Apr. 1951): 1–6.

500. Wilkes, James C. "Better Legislation Through Co-operation—The Work of the Drafting Committee of the Council of State Governments." *State Government* 22 (Jan. 1949): 16–18.

501. Williams, W. "Longest Legislative Session." *Christian Century* 78 (May 1961): 660–662.

502. Worthley, John A., and Edgar C. Crane. "Organizational Dimensions of State Legislatures." *Midwest Review of Public Administration* 10 (Mar. 1976): 14–30.

Legislative Behavior

503. Asher, Herbert B. "The Learning of Legislative Norms." *American Political Science Review* 67 (June 1973): 499–513.

504. Barber, James D. "The Legislator's First Session." Ph.D. dissertation, Yale University, 1960.

505. Basehart, Hubert H. "The Effect of Membership Stability on Continuity and Experience in U.S. State Legislative Committees." *Legislative Studies Quarterly* 5 (Feb. 1980): 55–68.

506. Belknap, George M. "A Method for Analyzing Legislative Behavior." *Midwest Journal of Political Science* 2 (Nov. 1958): 377–402.

507. Blair, Diane K., and Ann R. Henry. "The Family Factor in State Legislative Turnover." *Legislative Studies Quarterly* 6 (Feb. 1981): 55–68.

508. Conklin, Patrick J. "A Hard Look at the Training Ground Thesis: A Study of County and Township Experience in the Backgrounds of Legislators, Selected Executive Officers, and Supreme Court Justices in Five States." Ph.D. dissertation, University of Michigan, 1959.

509. Elling, Richard C. "State Legislative Casework and State Administrative Performance." *Administration and Society* 12 (Nov. 1980): 327–356.

510. Entman, Robert M. "The Psychology of Legislative Behavior: Ideology, Personality, Power, and Policy." Ph.D. dissertation, Yale University, 1977.

511. Ershkowitz, Herbert, and William G. Shade. "Consensus or Conflict? Political Behavior in the State Legislatures During the Jacksonian Era." *Journal of American History* 58 (Dec. 1971): 591–621.

512. Eulau, Heinz, et al. "The Political Socialization of the American State Legislature." *Midwest Journal of Political Science* 3 (May 1959): 188–206.

513. Fletcher, Mona. "Wanted: Experienced Legislators." *National Municipal Review* 30 (May 1941): 268–274.

514. Francis, Wayne L. "The Role Concept in Legislatures: A Probability Model and a Note on Cognitive Structure." *Journal of Politics* 27 (Aug. 1965): 567–587.

515. Grumm, John G. "Factor Analysis of Legislative Behavior." *Midwest Journal of Political Science* 7 (Nov. 1963): 336–356.

516. Havard, William C. "Lawmakers Take Initiative." *National Municipal Review* 43 (Mar. 1954): 130–133.

517. Hebert, F. Ted, and Lelan McLemore. "Character and Structure of Legislative Norms." *American Journal of Political Science* 17 (Aug. 1973): 506–527.

518. Hedlund, Ronald D., and Keith E. Hamm. "Conflict and Perceived Group Benefits from Legislative Rules Changes." *Legislative Studies Quarterly* 1 (May 1976): 181–199.

519. Hill, David B. "Political Culture and Female Political Representation." *Journal of Politics* 43 (Feb. 1981): 159–168.

520. Howe, C. B. "Case for the Professional Legislator." *State Government* 47 (Summer 1974): 130–134.

521. Hyneman, Charles S. "Tenure and Turnover of Legislative Personnel." *Annals of the American Academy of Political and Social Science* 195 (Jan. 1938): 21–31.

522. Janda, Kenneth F. "Democratic Theory and Legislative Behavior: A Study of Legislator-Constituency Relationships." Ph.D. dissertation, Indiana University, 1961.

523. Kane, Thomas J. "Legislative Role Orientations: An Interlevel Inquiry." Ph.D. dissertation, Indiana University, 1978.

524. Kirkpatrick, Samuel A., and Lelan McLemore. "Perceptual and Affective Components of Legislative Norms: A Social-Psychological Analysis of Congruity." *Journal of Politics* 39 (Aug. 1977): 685–711.

525. Kornberg, Allan. "Perception and Constituency Influence on Legislative Behavior." *Western Political Quarterly* 19 (June 1966): 285–292.

526. Lowrie, S. G. "The Makers of Our Laws." *University of Cincinnati Law Review* 17 (Mar. 1948): 144–158.

527. McCormick, Robert E., and Robert Tollison. "Legislatures as Unions." *Journal of Political Economy* 86 (Feb. 1978): 63–78.

528. McLemore, Lelan E. "The Structuring of Legislative Behavior: Norm Patterns in a State Legislature." Ph.D. dissertation, University of Oklahoma, 1973.

529. Meller, Norman. "Legislative Behavior Research." *Western Political Quarterly* 13 (Mar. 1960): 131–153.

530. Meller, Norman. "Legislative Behavior Research Revisited: A Review of Five Years' Publications." *Western Political Quarterly* 18 (Dec. 1965): 776–793.

531. Michael, Jerry B., and Ronald C. Dillehay. "Reference Behavior Theory and the Elected Representative." *Western Political Quarterly* 22 (Dec. 1969): 759–773.

532. Neuberger, Maurine. "Footnotes on Politics by a Lady Legislator." *New York Times Magazine* (May 27, 1951): 18.

533. Oxendale, James R. "Compensation and Turnover in State Legislative Lower Chambers." *State and Local Government Review* 11 (May 1979): 60–63.

534. Patterson, Samuel C., ed. *American Legislative Behavior: A Reader.* Princeton, NJ: Van Nostrand, 1968.

535. Patterson, Samuel C. "Comparative Legislative Behavior: A Review Essay." *Midwest Journal of Political Science* 12 (Nov. 1968): 599–616.

536. Patterson, Samuel C. "The Political Cultures of the American States." *Journal of Politics* 30 (Feb. 1968): 187–209.

537. Patterson, Samuel C. *Toward a Theory of Legislative Behavior.* Stillwater: Oklahoma State University, 1963.

538. Prewitt, Kenneth, and William Nowlin. "Political Ambitions and the Behavior of Incumbent Politicians." *Western Political Quarterly* 22 (June 1969): 298–308.

539. Prewitt, Kenneth, Heinz Eulau, and Betty H. Zisk. "Political Socialization and Political Roles." *Public Opinion Quarterly* 30 (Winter 1966–1967): 569–582.

540. "Protection of State Legislative Activity from Federal Prosecution: Common-Law and Constitutional Immunity." *Boston University Law Review* 58 (May 1978): 469–491.

541. Ray, David H. "Membership Stability in Three State Legislatures: 1893–1969." *American Political Science Review* 68 (Mar. 1974): 106–112.

542. Rosen, Corey M. "Programmatic and Non-Programmatic Orientations in State Legislatures." Ph.D. dissertation, Cornell University, 1973.

543. Rosenthal, Alan. "Legislative Turnover in the States." *State Government* 47 (Summer 1974): 148–152.

544. Rosenthal, Alan. "Turnovers in State Legislatures." *American Journal of Political Science* 18 (Aug. 1974): 609–616.

545. Schlesinger, Joseph A. "Lawyers and American Politics." *Midwest Journal of Political Science* 1 (May 1957): 26–39.

546. Schramm, Sarah S. "Women and Representation: Self Government and Role Change." *Western Political Quarterly* 34 (Mar. 1981): 46–59.

547. Shin, Kwang, and John Jackson. "Membership Turnover in U.S. State Legislatures 1931–1976." *Legislative Studies Quarterly* 4 (Feb. 1979): 95–104.

548. Stevens, Arthur R. "State Boundaries and Political Cultures: An Exploration in the Tri-State Area of Michigan, Indiana, and Ohio." *Publius* 4 (Winter 1974): 111–125.

549. Swanson, Wayne R., Sean A. Kelleher, and Arthur English. "Socialization of Constitution-Makers: Political Experience, Role Conflict, and Attitude Change." *Journal of Politics* 34 (Feb. 1972): 183–198.

550. Thomas, Norman C., and Allan Kornberg. "The Purposive Roles of Canadian and American Legislators: Some Comparisons." *Political Science* 17 (Sept. 1965): 36–50.

551. Toll, Henry W. "What 6,620 Legislators Are Thinking About." *National Municipal Review* 24 (Jan. 1935): 7–10.

552. Uslaner, Eric M., and Ronald Weber. "Partisan Cues and Decision Loci in U.S. State Legislatures." *Legislative Studies Quarterly* 2 (Nov. 1977): 423–444.

553. Wahlke, John C., et al. "The Annals of Research: A Case of Collaboration in Comparative Study of Legislative Behavior." *American Behavioral Scientist* 4 (May 1961): 3–9.

554. Wahlke, John C., and Heinz Eulau. *Legislative Behavior: A Reader in Theory and Research.* Glencoe, IL: Free Press, 1959.

555. Wahlke, John C., et al. "The Legislator as a Specialist." *Western Political Quarterly* 13 (Sept. 1960): 636–651.

556. Wahlke, John C., et al. "The Political Socialization of American State Legislators." *Midwest Journal of Political Science* 3 (May 1959): 188–206.

557. Welch, Susan, and John Peters. "Attitudes of U.S. State Legislators Toward Political Corruption: Some Preliminary Findings." *Legislative Studies Quarterly* 2 (Nov. 1977): 445–463.

558. Welch, Susan, and John G. Peters. "Elite Attitudes on Economic Welfare and Social Issues." *Polity* 14 (Fall 1981): 160–177.

559. Welch, Susan, and John G. Peters. "State Political Culture and the Attitudes of State Senators Toward Social, Economic Welfare, and Corruption Issues." *Publius* 10 (Spring 1980): 59–67.

560. Wiggins, Charles W., and Lee Bernick. "Legislative Turnover Reconsidered." *Policy Studies Journal* 5 (Summer 1977): 419–424.

561. Zemsky, Robert M. "American Legislative Behavior." *American Behavioral Scientist* 16 (May-June 1973): 675–694.

Legislative Power

562. Bachrach, Peter, and Morton S. Baratz. "The Two Faces of Power." *American Political Science Review* 57 (Dec. 1962): 947–952.

563. Bernick, E. Lee. "Gubernatorial Tools: Formal vs. Informal." *Journal of Politics* 41 (May 1979): 656–664.

564. Beyle, Thad. "The Governor as Chief Legislator." *State Government* 51 (Winter 1978): 2–10.

565. Beyle, Thad L., and Robert Dalton. "Appointment Power: Does It Belong to the Government?" *State Government* 54 (Winter 1981): 2–13.

566. Beyle, Thad, and J. O. Williams. *The American Governor in Behavioral Perspective.* New York: Harper and Row, 1972.

567. Dometrius, Nelson C. "Measuring Gubernatorial Power." *Journal of Politics* 41 (May 1979): 589–610.

568. Dye, Thomas R. "Executive Power and Public Policy in the States." *Western Political Quarterly* 22 (Dec. 1969): 926–939.

569. Eulau, Heinz. "Bases of Authority in Legislative Bodies." *Administrative Science Quarterly* 7 (Dec. 1962): 309–321.

570. Farber, Stephen B., et al. "Politics and the American Governors." *State Government* 53 (Summer 1980): 114–165.

571. Francis, Wayne L. "Influence and Interaction in a State Legislative Body." *American Political Science Review* 56 (Dec. 1962): 953–960.

572. Gallagher, Hubert R. "Crisis Management Legislation: An Overview of the Problems Facing State Governments." *State Government* 47 (Summer 1974): 189–192.

573. Gross, Bertram M. *The Legislative Struggle: A Study in Social Combat.* New York: McGraw-Hill, 1953.

574. Grumm, John G. "The Means of Measuring Conflict and Cohesion in the Legislature." *Social Science Quarterly* 44 (Mar. 1964): 377–388.

575. Jacob, Herbert, and Michael Lipsky. "Outputs, Structure, and Power: An Assessment of Changes in the Study of State and Local Politics." *Journal of Politics* 30 (May 1968): 510–538.

576. Jones, Lloyd P. "Controlling the Agenda in an American State Legislature." Ph.D. dissertation, Northern Illinois University, 1981.

577. LeLoup, Lance T. "Reassessing the Mediating Impact of Legislative Capability." *American Political Science Review* 72 (June 1978): 616–621.

578. Lyons, William V., and Russell L. Smith. "The Impact of State Legislative Reform on Legislative Efficiency and Turnover: A Reply." *State and Local Government Review* 11 (May 1979): 76–81.

579. Michaelson, Ronald D. "An Analysis of the Chief Executive: How the Governor Uses His Time." *State Government* 45 (Summer 1972): 153–160.

580. Miller, Edward J. "The Governor and Legislation." *State Government* 47 (Spring 1974): 93–95.

581. Olsen, Raymond T. "The American Governor: Executive Management for System Change." *State Government* 44 (Winter 1971): 26–30.

582. Prescott, Frank W. "The Executive Veto in American States." *Western Political Quarterly* 3 (Mar. 1950): 98–112.

583. Prescott, Frank W. "The Executive Veto in the Southern States." *Journal of Politics* 10 (Nov. 1948): 659–675.

584. Ransone, Coleman B. "The Governor, the Legislature, and Public Policy." *State Government* 52 (Summer 1979): 117–120.

585. Roper, Donald M. "The Governorship in History." *Proceedings of the Academy of Political Science* 31 (May 1974): 16–30.

586. Rosen, Corey M. "Legislative Influence and Policy Orientation in American State Legislatures." *American Journal of Political Science* 18 (Nov. 1974): 681–691.

587. Schen, Seymour. "Conditions for Legislative Control." *Journal of Politics* 25 (Aug. 1963): 526–551.

588. Uslaner, Eric M., and Ronald E. Weber. "Changes in Legislator Attitudes Toward Gubernatorial Power." *State and Local Government Review* 9 (May 1977): 40–43.

589. Wiggins, Charles W. "Executive Vetoes and Legislative Overrides in the American States." *Journal of Politics* 42 (Nov. 1980): 1110–1117.

Leadership in Legislatures

590. Barber, James D. "Leadership Strategies for Legislative Party Cohesion." *Journal of Politics* 28 (May 1966): 347–367.

591. Beardsley, Janet. "Legislative Leadership: Is Everybody Leaving." *State Legislatures* 7 (May 1981): 16–21.

592. Beardsley, Janet. "Legislative Leadership Today." *State Legislatures* 5 (1979): 4–7.

593. Chaffey, Douglas C., and Malcolm E. Jewell. "Selection and Tenure of State Legislative Party Leaders: A Comparative Analysis." *Journal of Politics* 34 (Nov. 1972): 1278–1286.

594. Cleary, Robert E. "Gubernatorial Leadership and State Policy on Desegregation in Public Higher Education." *Phylon* 27 (Summer 1966): 165–170.

595. Cleary, Robert E. "The Role of Gubernatorial Leadership in Desegregation in Public Higher Education." *Journal of Negro Education* 35 (Fall 1966): 439–444.

596. Council of State Governments. *State Legislative Leaders: 1976.* Lexington, KY: Council of State Governments, 1976.

597. Crain, W. M., and R. D. Tollison. "Influence of Representation on Public Policy." *Journal of Legal Studies* 6 (June 1977): 355–361.

598. Evans, Alvin E. "Personal Responsibility of Members of Municipal Legislative Bodies." *Washington University Law Quarterly* 1951 (Apr. 1951): 205–213.

599. Hofferbert, Richard I. "Elite Influence in State Policy Formation: A Model for Comparative Inquiry." *Polity* 2 (Spring 1970): 316–343.

600. Keefe, William J. "Legislative Leadership: A Time to Rebuild." *State Legislatures* 7 (May 1981): 22–27.

601. Kennedy, Patrick J., and Tom W. Rice. "Popularity and the Vote: The Gubernatorial Case." *American Politics Quarterly* 11 (Apr. 1983): 237–242.

602. McCally, Sarah P. "The Governor and His Legislative Party." *American Political Science Review* 60 (Dec. 1966): 923–942.

603. Muchmore, Lynn, and Thad L. Beyle "The Governor as Party Leader." *State Government* 53 (Summer 1980): 121–124.

604. Patterson, Samuel C. "Characteristics of Party Leaders." *Western Political Quarterly* 16 (June 1963): 332–352.

605. Patterson, Samuel C. "Legislative Leadership and Political Behavior." *Public Opinion Quarterly* 27 (Fall 1963): 399–410.

606. Prewitt, Kenneth, and Heinz Eulau. "Social Bias in Leadership Selection, Political Recruitment, and Electoral Contact." *Journal of Politics* 33 (May 1971): 293–315.

607. Ragsdale, Lyn. "Responsiveness and Legislative Elections: Toward a Comparative Study." *Legislative Studies Quarterly* 8 (Aug. 1983): 339–378.

608. Ransone, Coleman B. "Political Leadership in the Governor's Office." *Journal of Politics* 26 (Feb. 1964): 197–220.

609. Rosenthal, Alan, and Susan Fuhrman. "Higher Education Leadership in State Legislatures." *Policy Studies Journal* 10 (Autumn 1981): 47–58.

610. Routt, Garland C. "Interpersonal Relationships and the Legislative Process." *Annals of the American Academy of Political and Social Science* 195 (Jan. 1938): 129–136.

611. Salamon, Lester M. "Leadership and Modernization: The Emerging Black Political Elite in the American South." *Journal of Politics* 35 (Aug. 1973): 615–646.

612. Scott, Robert W. "Governor's Records: Public Records." *American Archivist* 33 (Jan. 1970): 5–10.

613. Solomon, Samuel R. "The Governor as Legislator." *National Municipal Review* 40 (Nov. 1951): 515–520.

614. "Survey on Selection of State Legislative Leaders." *Comparative State Politics Newsletter* 1 (1980): 7–21.

615. Swanson, Wayne R., Jay S. Goodman, and Elmer E. Cornwell. "Leadership Perception and Voting Behavior in the Nonpartisan Legislature." *Polity* 5 (Fall 1972): 129–135.

616. Turett, J. Stephen. "The Vulnerability of American Governors, 1900–1969." *American Journal of Political Science* 15 (Feb. 1971): 108–132.

Decision Making

617. Bosworth, Carl A. *Lawmaking in State Government—The Forty-Eight States: Their Task as Policy Makers and Administrators.* New York: Columbia University Press, 1955.

618. Council of State Governments. National Conference on Comparative Statistics. *Information Needs for Decision Making by State and Local Governments.* Chicago: Council of State Governments, 1966.

619. Derge, David R. "The Lawyer as a Decision-Maker in the American State Legislature." *Journal of Politics* 21 (Aug. 1959): 408–433.

620. Hedlund, Ronald D. "Perceptions of Decisional Referents in Legislative Decision Making." *American Journal of Political Science* 19 (Aug. 1975): 527–542.

621. Hedlund, Ronald D., and Patricia K. Freeman. "A Stategy for Measuring the Performance of Legislatures in Processing Decisions." *Legislative Studies Quarterly* 6 (Feb. 1981): 87–114.

622. Huckshorn, Robert J. "Decision-Making Stimuli in the State Legislative Process." *Western Political Quarterly* 18 (Mar. 1965): 164–185.

623. Kampelman, Max M. "The Legislative Bureaucracy: Its Response to Political Change, 1953." *Journal of Politics* 16 (Aug. 1954): 539–550.

624. Klay, William E. "Planners' Strategies and Population Growth Attitudes of Local Officials." *State and Local Government Review* 9 (Jan. 1977): 13–17.

625. Luce, Robert. *Legislative Problems: Development, Status, and Trend of the Treatment and Exercise of Law-Making Powers.* Boston: Houghton, 1935.

626. Michel, J. B. *Legislative Decision-Making: A Case Study of Reference Behavior.* Austin: University of Texas, 1964.

627. Morehouse, S. M. "State Political Party and the Policy-Making Process." *American Political Science Review* 67 (Mar. 1973): 55–72.

628. Patterson, Samuel C. "American State Legislatures and Public Policy." In *Politics in the American States: A Comparative Analysis,* edited by Herbert Jacob and Kenneth N. Vines. 3d ed. Boston: Little, Brown, 1976, pp. 139–195.

629. Patterson, Samuel C. "Conclusions: On the Study of Legislative Reform." In *Legislative Reform and Public Policy,* edited by Susan Welch and J. G. Peters. New York: Praeger, 1977, 214–222.

630. Rakoff, Stuart H., Ralph L. Nickell, and Ronald Sarner. *Policy Making Models in State Legislatures: A Preliminary Analysis.* Binghamton, NY: State University at Binghamton, Center for Comparative Political Research, 1971.

631. Rowell, David T. "The Legislators' Decision Process: The Politics of the 1977 Extension of the Massachusetts Police and Firefighter Binding Arbitration Statute." Ph.D. dissertation, State University of New York at Albany, 1980.

632. Thompson, Fred. "American Legislative Decision Making and the Size Principle." *American Political Science Review* 73 (Dec. 1979): 1100–1108.

633. Unruh, Jesse M. "Scientific Inputs to Legislative Decision Making." *Western Political Quarterly* 17 (Sept. 1964): 53–60.

634. Uslaner, Eric M., and Ronald E. Weber. *Patterns of Decision Making in State Legislatures.* New York: Praeger, 1977.

Legislative Voting Behavior

635. Abrams, Burton A. "Legislative Profits and the Economic Theory of Representative Voting: An Empirical Investigation." *Public Choice* 31 (Fall 1977): 111–119.

636. Anderson, Lee F., Meredith Watts, and Allen Wilcox. *Legislative Roll Call Analysis.* Evanston: Northwestern University Press, 1966.

637. Bernick, E. Lee. "The Impact of U.S. Governors on Party Voting in One-Party Dominated Legislatures." *Legislative Studies Quarterly* 3 (Aug. 1978): 431–444.

638. Broach, Glen T. "A Comparative Dimensional Analysis of Partisan and Urban-Rural Voting in State Legislatures." *Journal of Politics* 34 (Aug. 1972): 905–921.

639. Crain, W. M., and R. D. Tollison. "Legislative Size and Voting Rules." *Journal of Legal Studies* 6 (Jan. 1977): 235–240.

640. Crane, Wilder. "A Caveat on Roll-Call Studies of Party Voting." *Midwest Journal of Political Science* 4 (Aug. 1960): 237–249.

641. Dyer, J. A. "Do Lawyers Vote Differently? A Study of Voting on No-Fault Insurance." *Journal of Politics* 38 (May 1976): 452–456.

642. "Electric Roll Call Systems in State Legislatures." *Kansas Government Journal* 35 (Feb. 1949): 34–35.

643. Ferguson, L. C., and B. Klein. "An Attempt to Correlate the Voting Records of Legislators with Their Attitudes Toward Party." *Public Opinion Quarterly* 31 (Fall 1967): 422–426.

644. Greenfield, Arnold L. "Two Theories of Legislative Voting Behavior: A Theoretical and Empirical Assessment." Ph.D. dissertation, Michigan State University, 1980.

645. Greenstein, Fred I., and Alton Jackson. "A Second Look at the Validity of Roll Call Analysis." *Midwest Journal of Political Science* 7 (May 1963): 156–166.

646. Hahn, Harlan. "Leadership Perceptions and Voting Behavior in a One-Party Legislative Body." *Journal of Politics* 32 (Feb. 1970): 140–155.

647. Hedlund, Ronald D., and Keith E. Hamm. "Institutional Innovation and Performance Effectiveness in Public Policy Making." In *Legislative Reform: The Policy Impact*, edited by Leroy N. Rieselbach. Lexington, MA: Lexington Books, 1978, pp. 117–132.

648. Jewell, Malcolm E. "Party Voting in American State Legislatures." *American Political Science Review* 49 (Sept. 1955): 773–791.

649. Le Blanc, Hugh L. "Voting in State Senates: Party and Constituency Influences." *Midwest Journal of Political Science* 13 (Feb. 1969): 33–57.

650. LeLoup, Lance T. "Policy, Party, and Voting in U.S. State Legislatures: A Test of the Content-Process Linkage." *Legislative Studies Quarterly* 1 (May 1976): 213–230.

651. Lutz, Donald S., and James R. Williams. *Minimum Coalitions in Legislatures: A Review of the Evidence*. Beverly Hills, CA: Sage, 1976.

652. McMurray, Carl D. "A Factor Method for Roll Call Vote Studies." *Prod* 6 (Apr. 1963): 26–27.

653. MacRae, Duncan. "A Method for Identifying Issues and Factions from Legislative Votes." *American Political Science Review* 59 (Dec. 1965): 909–926.

654. MacRae, Duncan. "Roll Call Votes and Leadership." *Public Opinion Quarterly* 20 (Fall 1956): 543–558.

655. MacRae, Duncan. "Some Underlying Variables in Legislative Roll Call Votes." *Public Opinion Quarterly* 18 (Summer 1954): 191–196.

656. MacRae, Duncan, and E. MacRae. "Legislators' Social Status and Their Votes." *American Journal of Sociology* 66 (May 1951): 599–603.

657. Patterson, Samuel C. "Dimensions of Voting Behavior in a One Party State Legislature." *Public Opinion Quarterly* 26 (Summer 1962): 185–201.

658. Patterson, Samuel C. "Inter-Generational Occupational Mobility and Legislative Voting Behavior." *Social Forces* 43 (Oct. 1964): 90–92.

659. Rakoff, Stuart H., and Ronald Sarner. "Bill History Analysis: A Probability Model of the State Legislative Process." *Polity* 7 (Spring 1975): 402–414.

660. Riker, William H., and Lloyd S. Shapley. *Weighted Voting: A Mathematical Analysis for Instrumental Judgments.* Santa Monica, CA: Rand Corporation, 1966.

661. Silbey, Joel H. "Congressional and State Legislative Roll-Call Studies by U.S. Historians." *Legislative Studies Quarterly* 6 (Nov. 1981): 597–607.

662. Swanson, Wayne R., Jay S. Goodman, and Elmer E. Cornwell. "Voting Behavior in a Nonpartisan Legislative Setting." *Western Political Quarterly* 25 (Mar. 1972): 39–50.

663. Welch, Susan, and Eric H. Carlson. "The Impact of Party on Voting Behavior in a Nonpartisan Legislature." *American Political Science Review* 67 (Sept. 1973): 854–867.

664. Wohlenberg, E. H. "Correlates of Equal Rights Amendment Ratification." *Social Science Quarterly* 60 (Mar. 1980): 676–684.

Economic and Fiscal Powers

665. Austermann, Winnie. "Can Legislatures Control Federal Funds?" *State Legislatures* 4 (Jan.-Feb. 1978): 12–14.

666. Balutis, Alan P., and Daron Butler. *The Political Pursestrings: The Role of the Legislature in the Budgetary Process.* New York: Wiley, 1975.

667. Beardsley, Janet. "State Legislative Control of Federal Funds." *State Legislatures* 6 (Mar. 1980): 6–13.

668. Blankenbeckler, George M. "Cash Management by State and Local Governments." *State and Local Government Review* 10 (Sept. 1978): 106–109.

699. Blankenbeckler, George M. "Excess Cash Management at the State and Local Levels." *State and Local Government Review* 10 (Jan. 1978): 2–7.

670. Campbell, Alan K. "National-State-Local Systems of Government and Intergovernmental Aid." *Annals of the American Academy of Political and Social Science* 359 (May 1965): 94–106.

671. Case, Karl E., and V. Rogers. "Financing State and Local Governments: Crisis of the 1970's." *Current History* 69 (Nov. 1975): 183–188.

672. Council of State Governments. *Fiscal Service for State Legislatures.* Chicago: Council of State Governments, 1961.

673. Council of State Governments. *State Legislative Appropriations Process.* Lexington, KY: Council of State Governments, 1975.

674. Deleon, Richard E. "Politics, Economic Surplus and Redistribution in the American States: A Test of a Theory." *American Journal of Political Science* 17 (Nov. 1973): 781–796.

675. Dye, Thomas R. "Taxing, Spending, and Economic Growth in the American States." *Journal of Politics* 42 (Nov. 1980): 1085–1107.

676. Farber, W. O. "State Governments and Pump Priming." *State Government* 48 (Autumn 1975): 206–209.

677. Feig, D. G. "Expenditures in the American States: The Impact of Court Ordered Legislative Reapportionment." *American Politics Quarterly* 6 (July 1978): 309–324.

678. Gray, Virginia. "Expenditures and 'Progressivism': A Note on the American States." *American Journal of Political Science* 18 (Nov. 1974): 693–699.

679. "Growth and the States." *State Government* 47 (Spring 1974): 75–92.

680. Guhde, Robert, and Husain Mustafa. "Partisan Politics and Legislative-Gubernatorial Competition in Budgeting." *State and Local Government Review* 13 (Jan. 1981): 124–127.

681. Hatry, Harry P. "Status of PPBS in Local and State Governments in the United States." *Policy Sciences* 2 (June 1971): 177–190.

682. Hrebenar, R. J. "Utility of Role in Budgetary Decision-Making." *Western Political Quarterly* 29 (Dec. 1976): 575–588.

683. Kelly, F. "Computerization of Budgetary Processes in the States." *Public Administration Review* 38 (July 1978): 381–386.

684. Lawton, Frederick J. "Legislative-Executive Relationships in Budgeting as Viewed by the Executive." *Public Administration Review* 13 (Summer 1953): 169–176.

Economic and Fiscal Powers

685. Lee, Robert D., and Raymond Staffeldt. "Executive and Legislative Use of Policy Analysis in the State Budgetary Process: Survey Results." *Policy Analysis* 3 (Summer 1977): 395–405.

686. LeMay, Michael. "Expenditure and Nonexpenditure Measures of State Urban Policy Output: A Research Note." *American Politics Quarterly* 1 (Oct. 1973): 511–528.

687. Logan, John W., and John A. Donaho. "The Performance Budget and Legislative Review." *State Government* 26 (July 1953): 185–187.

688. Long, Russell B. "Revenue-Sharing: A Legislative Landmark." *State Government* 46 (Winter 1973): 9–11.

689. McGee, Vernon A. "A Legislative Approach to State Budgeting." *State Government* 26 (Aug. 1953): 200–204.

690. Mason, R. P. "The Interactions of Policy and Urban Growth: A Simulation Model." *State and Local Government Review* 9 (May 1977): 65–68.

691. Mikesell, J. L. "Local Legislative Behavior in Tax Substitution." *Quarterly Review of Economics and Business* 14 (Winter 1974): 83–91.

692. Moncrief, Gary F., and Joel A. Thompson. "Partisanship and Purse-Strings: A Research Note on Sharkansky." *Western Political Quarterly* 33 (Sept. 1980): 336–340.

693. Muchmore, Lynn. "Planning and Budgeting Offices: On Their Relevance to Gubernatorial Decisions." *State Government* 52 (Summer 1979): 126–130.

694. Portney, Kent E. "State Tax Preference Orderings and Partisan Control of Government." *Policy Studies Journal* 9 (Autumn 1980): 87–95.

695. Ratchford, William R. "The Legislature's Role in Revenue Sharing." *State Government* 46 (Winter 1973): 19–21.

696. Rosebaugh, D. L. "State Planning as a Policy-Coordinative Process." *Journal of the American Institute of Planners* 42 (Jan. 1976): 52–63.

697. Ross, John P., and S. Calkins. "Economic Stimulus Package at Mid-Stream: The Role of State and Local Governments." *Publius* 9 (Winter 1979): 45–65.

698. Sharkansky, Ira. "Agency Requests, Gubernatorial Support and Budget Success in State Legislatures." *American Political Science Review* 62 (Dec. 1968): 1220–1231.

699. Sharkansky, Ira. "Economic Development, Representative Mechanisms, Administrative Professionalism and Public Policies: A Comparative Analysis of Within-State Distributions of Economic and Political Traits." *Journal of Politics* 33 (Feb. 1971): 112–132.

700. Sharkansky, Ira. "Governmental Expenditures and Public Services in the American States." *American Political Science Review* 61 (Dec. 1967): 1066–1077.

701. Sharkansky, Ira. "Regional Patterns in the Expenditures of American States." *Western Political Quarterly* 20 (Dec. 1967): 955–971.

702. Sharkansky, Ira. *Spending in the American States.* Chicago: Rand-McNally, 1968.

703. Simmons, Robert H. "American State Executive Systems: An Heuristic Model." *Western Political Quarterly* 18 (Mar. 1965): 19–26.

704. Welch, William P. "The Effectiveness of Expenditures in State Legislative Races." *American Politics Quarterly* 4 (July 1976): 333–356.

705. Wright, Deil S., and A. Light. "The Indeterminants of State Revenue Sharing Expenditure: Reactions to the Havick Research Note." *Journal of Politics* 39 (May 1977): 457–463.

Legislative Oversight

706. Adams, Bruce, and Betsy Sherman. "Sunset Implementation: A Positive Partnership to Make Government Work." *Public Administration Review* 38 (Jan.-Feb. 1978): 78–82.

707. Brown, Richard E., ed. *The Effectiveness of Legislative Program Review.* New Brunswick, NJ: Aldine-Atherton, 1979.

708. Brown, Richard E. "Legislative Performance Auditing: Its Goals and Pitfalls." *State Government* 52 (Winter 1979): 31–34.

709. Brown, Richard E., and Ralph Craft. "Auditing and Public Administration: The Unrealized Partnership." *Public Administration Review* 40 (May-June 1980): 259–265.

710. Brown, R. E., and R. D. Pethtel. "Matter of Facts: State Legislative Performance Auditing." *Public Administration Review* 34 (July 1974): 318–327.

711. Chadwin, Mark L., ed. *Legislative Program Evaluation in the United States.* New Brunswick, NJ: Rutgers University, Eagleton Institute of Politics, 1974.

712. Council of State Governments. *Legislative Investigations: A Survey and Recommendations.* Chicago: Council of State Governments, 1968.

713. Council of State Governments. National Legislative Conference. Committee on Legislative Rules. *Legislative Investigations.* Chicago: Council of State Governments, National Legislative Conference, Committee on Legislative Rules, 1964.

714. Craft, Ralph. *Legislative Follow-Through: Profile of Oversight in Five States.* New Brunswick, NJ: Rutgers University, Eagleton Institute of Politics, 1977.

715. Craft, Ralph. "Successful Legislative Oversight: Lessons from State Legislatures." *Policy Studies Journal* 10 (Autumn 1981): 161–171.

716. Crane, Edgar G. *Legislative Review of Government Programs: Tools for Accountability.* New York: Praeger, 1977.

717. Crane, Stephen C. "The Legislative Marketplace: A Model of Political Exchange to Explain State Health Regulatory Policy." Ph.D. dissertation, University of Michigan, 1981.

718. Dittenhofer, Mortimer A. "Is Auditing a Fourth Power in State Government?" *State Government* 43 (Summer 1970): 179–183.

719. Elling, Richard C. "The Utility of State Legislative Casework as a Means of Oversight." *Legislative Studies Quarterly* 4 (Aug. 1979): 353–380.

719A. Ethridge, Marcus E. "Consequences of Legislative Review of Agency Regulations in Three U.S. States." *Legislative Studies Quarterly* 9 (Feb. 1984): 161–178.

720. Fogarty, Andrew B., and Augustus B. Turnbull. "Legislative Oversight Through a Rotating Zero-Base Budget." *State and Local Government Review* 9 (Jan. 1977): 18–22.

721. Hamm, Keith E., and Roby D. Robertson. "Factors Influencing the Adoption of New Methods of Legislative Oversight in the U.S. States." *Legislative Studies Quarterly* 6 (Feb. 1981): 133–150.

722. Hedlund, Ronald D., and Keith E. Hamm. "Reconceptualizing Legislative Accountability." In *Accountability in Urban Society: Public Agencies Under Fire,* edited by Scott Greer, Ronald D. Hedlund, and James L. Gibson. Beverly Hills, CA: Sage, 1978, pp. 63–86.

723. Herwitz, Oren C., and William G. Mulligan. "The Legislative Investigating Committee: A Survey and Critique." *Columbia Law Review* 33 (Jan. 1933): 1–27.

724. Hodes, Richard S. "Legislative Evaluation of Human Resources Programs." *State Government* 47 (Summer 1974): 175–179.

725. Jackson, Edwin L., and Alan J. Howard. *Legislative Oversight.* Athens: University of Georgia, Institute of Government, 1976.

726. Kopel, Gerald H. "Sunset in the West." *State Government* 49 (Summer 1976): 135–138.

727. Lewis, C. "State Regulation of Local Government Labor Relations." *Public Management* 57 (Feb. 1975): 7–9.

727A. Lyons, William V., and Patricia K. Freeman. "Sunset Legislation and the Legislative Process in Tennessee." *Legislative Studies Quarterly* 9 (Feb. 1984): 151–160.

728. Lyons, William V., and Larry W. Thomas. *Legislative Oversight: A Three State Study.* Knoxville: University of Tennessee, Bureau of Public Administration, 1978.

729. Lyons, William V., and Larry W. Thomas. "Oversight in State Legislatures: Structural-Attitudinal Interaction." *American Politics Quarterly* 10 (Jan. 1982): 117–133.

730. Marvel, Richard D., Robert J. Parsons, Winn Sanderson, and N. Dale Wright. "Legislative Intent and Oversight." *State Government* 49 (Winter 1976): 39–42.

731. Peters, John G., and Susan Welch. "Political Corruption in America: A Search for Definitions and a Theory, or if Political Corruption Is in the Mainstream of American Politics, Why Is It Not in the Mainstream of American Politics Research." *American Political Science Review* 72 (Sept. 1978): 974–984.

732. Peters, John G., and Susan Welch. "Politics, Corruption, and Political Culture." *American Politics Quarterly* 6 (July 1978): 345–356.

733. Pethtel, Roy D., and Richard E. Brown, eds. *Legislative Review of State Program Performance.* New Brunswick, NJ: Rutgers University, Eagleton Institute of Politics, Center for State Legislative Research and Science, 1972.

734. Rosenthal, Alan. "Legislative Behavior and Legislative Oversight." *Legislative Studies Quarterly* 6 (Feb. 1981): 115–132.

735. Weissert, Carol S. "State Legislative Oversight of Federal Funds." *State Government* 53 (Spring 1980): 77–80.

Legislative-Executive Relations

736. Abney, Glenn, and Thomas Henderson. "An Exchange Model of Intergovernmental Relations: State Legislators and Local Officials." *Social Science Quarterly* 59 (Mar. 1979): 720–731.

737. Abrams, A. J. "Legislative Administrator." *Public Administration Review* 35 (Dec. 1975): 780–785.

738. Adrian, Charles R. "State and Local Government Participation in the Design and Administration of Intergovernmental Programs." *Annals of the American Academy of Political and Social Science* 359 (May 1965): 35–43.

739. Balutis, Alan P. "Legislative-Executive Integration." *State and Local Government Review* 9 (Sept. 1977): 88–94.

740. Bernick, E. Lee, and Charles W. Wiggins. "Executive-Legislative Power Relationships: Perspectives of State Lawmakers." *Legislative Studies Quarterly* 6 (Oct. 1981): 467–478.

741. Brockbank, W. Hughes. "The Legislature's Role in Restoring Balance to Federalism." *State Government* 43 (Autumn 1970): 221–224.

742. Conolly, John H., and Robert M. Rhodes. "The Challenge of State Legislatures in Federal-State Relations." *State Government* 44 (Winter 1971): 12–16.

743. Daley, Dennis M. "Administrative Responsibility and Control of the Bureaucracy: An Examination of Administrative, Executive, and Legislative Attitudes in Five States." Ph.D. dissertation, Washington State University, 1980.

744. Edmar, F. Robert. "Federal Grants-in-Aid to State Legislatures." *State Government* 44 (Summer 1971): 154–161.

745. Elazar, Daniel J. *American Federalism: A View from the States.* New York: Crowell, 1967.

746. Engelbert, Ernest A., and Kenneth Wernimont. "Administrative Aspects of the Federal-State Legislative Relationships." *Public Administration Review* 2 (Spring 1942): 126–140.

747. Fairlie, John A. "The Legislature and the Administration." *American Political Science Review* 30 (Apr.-June 1936): 494–506.

748. Ficklin, L. R. "City Council and the State Legislature." *Public Management* 42 (Dec. 1960): 276–278.

749. Fyock, J. W., and J. J. Long. "New Federalism: A Challenge to State Legislative Responsibility." *State Government* 50 (Spring 1977): 77–82.

750. Gilbert, Charles E., and Max Kampelman. "Legislative Control of the Bureaucracy." *Annals of the American Academy of Political and Social Sciences* 292 (Mar. 1954): 76–88.

751. Goldberg, Delphis C. "Intergovernmental Relations: From the Legislative Perspective." *Annals of the American Academy of Political and Social Science* 416 (Nov. 1974): 52–66.

752. Gove, Samuel K. "State Management and Legislative-Executive Relations." *State Government* 54 (Summer 1981): 99–101.

753. Hardy, John L. "Federal Grants? To State Legislatures?" *State Legislatures* 4 (Jan.-Feb. 1978): 10–11.

754. Hardy, John L. "Federal Grants to State Legislatures." *State Government* 51 (Winter 1978): 34–40.

755. Henderson, Thomas A., and G. Abney. "The State Legislator and Intergovernmental Relations: The Job of Local Governance." *Publius* 7 (Spring 1977): 85–100.

756. Herring, Pendleton. "Executive-Legislative Responsibilities." *American Political Science Review* 38 (Dec. 1944): 1153–1165.

757. Kemp, K. A. "Nationalization of the American States: A Test of the Thesis." *American Politics Quarterly* 6 (Apr. 1978): 237–247.

758. Moore, Dan K. "The Partnership of State and Local Governments." *Popular Government* 35 (Oct. 1968): 17–19.

759. Plosila, Walter H. "State Legislative Involvement in Federal-State Relations." *State Government* 48 (Summer 1975): 170–176.

760. Pye, Lucian W. "Effects of Legislative and Administrative Accessibility on Interest Group Politics." *Prod* 1 (Jan. 1958): 11–14.

761. Simmons, Robert H. "American State Executive Studies: A Suggested New Departure." *Western Political Quarterly* 17 (Dec. 1964): 777–783.

762. Skok, James E. "Federal Funds and State Legislatures: Executive-Legislative Conflict in State Government." *Public Administration Review* 40 (Nov.-Dec. 1980): 561–567.

763. Thurber, James A. "Legislative-Administrative Relations." *Policy Studies* 5 (Autumn 1976): 56–65.

764. United States Advisory Commission on Intergovernmental Relations. *ACIR State Legislative Program.* Washington, D.C.: United States Advisory Commission on Intergovernmental Relations, 1975.

765. Wilson, S. L. "Role of State Municipal Leagues in Local/State Legislative Relations." *Public Management* 56 (Nov. 1974): 8–10.

766. Worthley, John A. *Public Administration and Legislatures: Examination and Exploration.* Chicago: Nelson-Hall, 1976.

767. Wyner, Alan J. "Gubernatorial Relations with Legislators and Administrators." *State Government* 41 (Summer 1968): 199–203.

Judicial Powers and Relations

768. Beiser, Edward N. "A Comparative Analysis of State and Federal Judicial Behavior: The Reapportionment Cases." *American Political Science Review* 62 (Sept. 1968): 788–795.

769. Frohnmayer, David. "Legislating and Judging." *State Legislatures* 7 (Nov.-Dec. 1981): 18–22.

770. Jewell, Malcolm E. "Local Systems of Representation: Political Consequences and Judicial Choices." *George Washington Law Review* 36 (May 1968): 790–807.

771. "Legislative Journals, Impeachment by Parol Evidence." *Minnesota Law Review* 25 (Mar. 1941): 528–529.

772. Lloyd, William J. "Judicial Control of Legislative Procedure." *Syracuse Law Review* 4 (Fall 1952): 6–30.

773. Proffer, Lanny. "Litigating Legislatures." *State Legislatures* 3 (Feb.-Mar. 1977): 5.

774. Rainey, Robert L. "Comparing Courts and Legislatures: Value Allocations in State Political Systems." Ph.D. dissertation, University of North Carolina, 1974.

775. Satter, Robert. "Changing Roles of Courts and Legislatures." *Connecticut Law Review* 11 (Winter 1979): 230–246.

776. Shattuck, H. L. "Discussion of Proposal that Members of the Legislature Be Prohibited from Acting as Counsel on Matters Within the Jurisdiction of State Departments, Boards, and Commissions." *Massachusetts Law Quarterly* 12 (Aug. 1927): 35–38.

777. Thomas, Robert D. "Legislator Attitudes Toward Inter-Jurisdictional Policy Responsibilities." *Publius* 9 (Summer 1979): 119–133.

778. Thompson, Joel A., and Robert T. Roper. "The Determinants of Legislators' Support for Judicial Reorganization." *American Politics Quarterly* 8 (Apr. 1980): 221–236.

779. Tyler, G. "Court Versus Legislature." *Law and Contemporary Problems* 27 (Summer 1962): 390–407.

780. Watson, George H. "The Concept of the Legislative Court." Ph.D. dissertation, University of Chicago, 1942.

781. Wood, John W. "State Judicial Selection: Realities vs. Legalities." *State Government* 31 (Jan. 1958): 17–19.

Interest Groups and Legislatures

782. Allen, Russ, and Jill Clark. "State Policy Adoption and Innovation: Lobbying and Education." *State and Local Government Review* 13 (Jan. 1980): 18–25.

783. Baer, Michael A. "Environmental Effects on State Legislators and Lobbyists." Ph.D. dissertation, University of Oregon, 1968.

784. Crane, Wilder. "A Test of the Effectiveness of Interest Group Pressures on Legislators." *Social Science Quarterly* 41 (Dec. 1960): 335–340.

785. Dunn, Charles W. "Black Caucuses and Political Machines in Legislative Bodies." *American Journal of Political Science* 17 (Feb. 1973): 148–158.

786. Elkins, F. Clark. "State Politics and the Agricultural Wheel." *Arkansas Historical Quarterly* 38 (Autumn 1979): 248–258.

787. Fiellin, Alan. "The Functions of Informal Groups in Legislative Institutions: A Case Study." *Journal of Politics* 24 (Feb. 1962): 72–91.

788. Francis, Wayne L. "A Profile of Legislator Perception of Interest Group Behavior Relating to Legislative Issues in the States." *Western Political Quarterly* 24 (Dec. 1971): 702–712.

789. Froman, Lewis A. "Some Effects of Interest Group Strength in State Politics." *American Political Science Review* 60 (Dec. 1966): 952–962.

Interest Groups and Legislatures

790. Garceau, Oliver, and Corinne Silverman. "A Pressure Group and the Pressured: A Case Report." *American Political Science Review* 48 (Sept. 1954): 672–691.

791. Gibbs, Clayton R. *State Regulation of Lobbying, Constitutional and Statutory Provisions of the State*. Chicago: Council of State Governments, 1951.

792. Greenhouse, Linda. "Press vs. Courts vs. Legislatures." *State Legislatures* 4 (Oct. 1978): 20–23.

793. Grumm, John G. "The Systematic Analysis of Blocs in the Study of Legislative Behavior." *Western Political Quarterly* 18 (June 1965): 350–362.

794. Henry, C. T. "Strategies for City Lobbying in State Legislatures." *Public Management* 56 (Nov. 1974): 11–13.

795. Hotard, Ken. "State Legislatures and Small Business." *State Legislatures* 5 (1979): 11–14.

796. "Improving the Legislative Process: Federal Regulation of Lobbying." *Yale Law Journal* 56 (Jan. 1947): 304–332.

797. Kelleher, Sean, Jay S. Goodman, and Elmer E. Cornwell. "Political Attitudes of Activists in the American States: Some Comparative Data." *Western Political Quarterly* 26 (Mar. 1973): 162–169.

798. Killpatrick, E. W. "Bay Lobbyists Toe Mark." *National Civic Review* 34 (Dec. 1945): 536–569.

799. Lane, Edgar. *Lobbying and the Law*. Berkeley: University of California Press, 1964.

800. Longley, Lawrence D. "The Effectiveness of Interest Groups in a State Legislature." *Tennessee Historical Quarterly* 26 (Fall 1967): 279–294.

801. Longley, Lawrence D. "Interest Group Interaction in a Legislative System." *Journal of Politics* 29 (Aug. 1967): 637–658.

802. Pitstick, W. J. "COGs/Strategies for Legislative Lobbying." *Public Management* 56 (Nov. 1974): 14–16.

803. "Potpourri/Legislative Lobbying Programs." *Public Management* 56 (Nov. 1974): 17–20.

804. Robey, John S., et al. "American State Policies and the Women's Movement." *State Government* 54 (Spring 1981): 58–64.

805. Schriftgiesser, Karl. *The Lobbyists: The Art and Business of Influencing Lawmakers.* Boston: Little, Brown, 1951.

806. Sigelman, Lee, and Albert Karnig. "Black Representation in the American States: A Comparison of Bureaucracies and Legislatures." *American Politics Quarterly* 4 (Apr. 1976): 237–246.

807. Smith, Peter W. *A Survey of State Lobbying Laws.* Chicago: National College Press Service, 1966.

808. Teune, Henry J. "Legislative Attitudes Toward Interest Groups." *Midwest Journal of Political Science* 11 (Nov. 1967): 489–504.

809. Wahlke, John C., et al. "American State Legislators' Role Orientations Toward Pressure Groups." *Journal of Politics* 22 (May 1960): 203–227.

810. Weeks, O. Douglas. "Politics in the Legislatures: Pressure Groups and Blocks in Most States." *National Municipal Review* 41 (Feb. 1952): 80–86.

811. Zeigler, Harmon. "The Effects of Lobbying: A Comparative Assessment." *Western Political Quarterly* 22 (Mar. 1969): 122–140.

812. Zeigler, Harmon, and Michael A. Baer. *Lobbying: Interaction and Influence in American State Legislatures.* Belmont, CA: Wadsworth, 1969.

813. Zeigler, Harmon, and Michael A. Baer. "The Recruitment of Lobbyists and Legislators." *American Journal of Political Science* 12 (Nov. 1968): 493–513.

814. Zeller, Belle. "Regulation of Pressure Groups and Lobbyists." *Annals of the American Academy of Political and Social Science* 319 (Sept. 1958): 94–104.

Legislatures and Public Opinion

815. Baker, Kendall L., and Oliver B. Walter. "The Press as a Source of Information about Activities of a State Legislature." *Journalism Quarterly* 52 (Winter 1975): 735–740.

816. Boynton, G. R., et al. "The Structure of Public Support for Legislative Institutions." *Midwest Journal of Political Science* 12 (May 1968): 163–180.

817. Cantwell, Frank V. "Public Opinion and the Legislative Process." *American Political Science Review* 40 (Oct. 1946): 924–935.

818. Citizens Conference on State Legislatures. *The National Press Report on the Legislative Evaluation Study.* Kansas City: Citizens Conference on State Legislatures, 1972.

819. Dunn, Delmer D. "Differences Among Public Officials in Their Reliance on the Press for Information." *Social Science Quarterly* 49 (Mar. 1969): 829–839.

820. Erikson, Robert S. "The Relationship Between Public Opinion and State Policy: A New Look Based on Some Forgotten Data." *American Journal of Political Science* 20 (Feb. 1976): 25–36.

821. Gormley, William T. "Coverage of State Government in the Mass Media." *State Government* 52 (Spring 1979): 46–51.

822. Gormley, William T. "Television Coverage of State Government." *Public Opinion Quarterly* 42 (Fall 1978): 354–359.

823. Grupp, Fred W., and Alan Richards. "Variations in Elite Perceptions of American States as Referents for Public Policy Making." *American Political Science Review* 69 (Sept. 1975): 850–858.

824. Hamilton, T. H. "Citizen Views the Legislature." *State Government* 37 (Winter 1964): 30–35.

825. Hartmann, George W. "Judgments of State Legislators Concerning Public Opinion." *Journal of Social Psychology* 21 (Feb. 1945): 105–114.

826. Hattery, Lowell H. "The Legislators' Source of Expert Information." *Public Opinion Quarterly* 18 (Fall 1954): 300–302.

827. Hopkins, A. H. "Opinion Publics and Support for Public Policy in the American States." *American Journal of Political Science* 18 (Feb. 1974): 167–177.

828. Key, V. O. *Public Opinion and American Democracy.* New York: Knopf, 1961.

829. McMurray, Carl D., and M. Parsons. "Public Attitudes Toward the Representational Role of Legislators and Judges." *American Journal of Political Science* 9 (May 1965): 167–185.

830. Newkirk, Glenn. "The Legislative Use (and Misuse) of Polls." *State Legislatures* 4 (Mar.-Apr. 1978): 16–19.

831. Newkirk, Glenn. "State Legislatures Through the People's Eye." *State Legislatures* 5 (Aug.-Sept. 1979): 6–11.

832. Peterson, C. Petrus. "The Legislatures and the Press." *State Government* 27 (Nov. 1954): 223–224.

833. Pilcher, Dan. "Building Trust: The Role of Public Information in State Legislatures." *State Legislatures* 7 (Apr. 1981): 11–15.

834. Porter, H. Owen. "Legislative Experts and Outsiders: The Two-Step Flow of Communication." *Journal of Politics* 36 (Aug. 1974): 703–730.

835. Porter, H. Owen. "Legislative Information Needs and Staff Resources in the American States." In *Legislative Staffing: A Comparative Perspective*, edited by James J. Heaphey and Alan Balutis. New York: Halstead, 1975, pp. 39–59.

836. Richards, Barbara. "Newsgathering in the Legislature: The Impact of Reporter-Source Exchanges." Ph.D. dissertation, University of Minnesota, 1981.

837. Schuiteman, John G. "Ideology, Cognitive Style, and Belief Systems about Crime Among City, State, and Federal Legislators." Ph.D. dissertation, Michigan State University, 1977.

838. Smylie, Robert E. "The Legislative Workshop—A Method of Improving Communication with Higher Education." *State Government* 32 (Autumn 1959): 266–271.

839. Sorenson, Robert C. "The Influence of Public Opinion Polls on the Legislator." *Sociology and Social Research* 34 (May 1950): 323–328.

840. Spadaro, R. "Role Perceptions of Politicians Vis-a-Vis Public Administrators: Parameters for Public Policy." *Western Political Quarterly* 26 (Dec. 1973): 717–725.

Reform

841. American Legislators' Association. "Two Houses—Or One?" *State Government* 7 (Oct. 1934): 207–208.

842. Baaklini, Abdo, and James J. Heaphey, eds. *Comparative Legislative Reforms and Innovations*. Albany: State University of New York at Albany, Graduate School of Public Affairs, Comparative Development Studies Center, 1977.

843. Balutis, Alan P. "Legislative Reform in the American States: A Comment." *State and Local Government Review* 11 (May 1979): 70–75.

844. Brake, Hale D. "Practical Suggestions and Prospects for Legislative Reform." *State Government* 20 (June 1947): 161–164.

845. Buck, A. E. *Modernizing our State Legislatures.* Philadelphia: American Academy of Political and Social Science, 1936.

846. Caldwell, Lynton K. "Strengthening State Legislatures." *American Political Science Review* 41 (Apr. 1947): 281–289.

847. Citizens Conference on State Legislatures. *Agenda for Reform.* Kansas City: Citizens Conference on State Legislatures, 1971.

848. Citizens Conference on State Legislatures. *Compilation of Recommendations Pertaining to Legislative Improvement in the Fifty States.* Kansas City: Citizens Conference on State Legislatures, 1969.

849. Citizens Conference on State Legislatures. *Legislatures Move to Improve Their Effectiveness: A Report on Legislative Progress from Mid-1970 through 1971.* Kansas City: Citizens Conference on State Legislatures, 1972.

850. Citizens Conference on State Legislatures. *Report on an Evaluation of the 50 State Legislatures.* Kansas City: Citizens Conference on State Legislatures, 1971.

851. Committee for Economic Development. Research and Policy Committee. *Modernizing State Government.* Washington, D.C.: Committee for Economic Development, Research and Policy Committee, 1967.

852. Council of State Governments. *Legislative Modernization. Report of the Committee on Legislative Modernization of the Council of State Governments.* Lexington, KY: Council of State Governments, 1969.

853. Crittenden, John. "Dimensions of Modernization in the American States." *American Political Science Review* 61 (Dec. 1967): 989–1001.

854. Culver, Margaret S. *Proposals for Legislative Reorganization.* Chicago: Council of State Governments, 1939.

855. D'Alemberte, Talbot, and Charles Fishburne. "Why A Second House?" *National Civic Review* 55 (Sept. 1966): 431–437.

856. Engstrom, Richard L., and Patrick F. O'Connor. "Lawyer-Legislators and Support for State Legislative Reform." *Journal of Politics* 42 (Feb. 1980): 267–276.

857. Garnett, James L. "Strategies for Governors Who Want to Reorganize." *State Government* 52 (Summer 1979): 135–143.

858. Harris, Joseph P. "Modernizing the Legislature." *National Municipal Review* 36 (Mar. 1947): 142–146.

859. Harris, Joseph R. "To Get Better Legislatures." *Tax Outlook* 2 (July 1947): 7–10.

860. Horack, Frank E. "Bicameral Legislatures Are Effective." *State Government* 14 (Apr. 1941): 79–80.

861. Humphrey, Hubert H. "Ethical Standards in American Legislative Chambers." *Annals of the American Academy of Political and Social Science* 280 (Mar. 1952): 51–59.

862. Karnig, Albert K., and Lee Sigelman. "State Legislative Reform and Public Policy: Another Look." *Western Political Quarterly* 28 (Sept. 1975): 548–552.

863. Kassel, Charles. "The Collapse of the State Legislature: A Study of the Legislative Commission." *South Atlantic Quarterly* 36 (Apr. 1937): 140–153.

864. Keefe, William J. "Reform and the American Legislature." In *Strengthening the States: Essays on Legislative Reform*, edited by Donald G. Herzberg and Alan Rosenthal. Garden City, NY: Doubleday, 1971, pp. 183–193.

865. Lederle, John W. "State Legislative Reorganization." *Marquette Law Review* 31 (Feb. 1948): 272–280.

866. "Legislative Reorganization Since World War II." *State Government* 27 (Feb. 1954): 33–36.

867. Lentz, Gilbert G. "Better State Government Through Better Legislative Services." *Western Political Quarterly* 10 (June 1957): 448–449.

868. Mackey, E. S. "State Legislature in the 1970's—How to Help Your State Legislature Help You." *Public Management* 56 (Nov. 1974): 5–7.

869. Margolis, Larry. "States on the Spot." *National Civic Review* 57 (June 1968): 303–306.

870. Michelson, S. "Reform through State Legislatures: What Is a Just System for Financing Schools? An Evaluation of Alternative Reforms." *Law and Contemporary Problems* 38 (Winter 1974): 436–458.

871. Miller, James N. "Hamstrung Legislatures." *National Civic Review* 54 (Apr. 1965): 178–187.

872. Moncrief, Gary F. "The Consequences of State Legislative Reform." Ph.D. dissertation, University of Kentucky, 1977.

873. Moncrief, Gary F., and Malcolm E. Jewell. "Legislators' Perceptions of Reform in Three States." *American Politics Quarterly* 8 (Jan. 1980): 106–127.

874. Murphy, Jerome T. "The Paradox of State Government Reform." *Public Interest* 64 (Summer 1981): 124–139.

875. National Conference of State Legislatures. *Strengthening the Legislative Process: An Agenda for Improvement: Recommendations.* Denver: National Conference of State Legislatures, 1980.

876. Northwest Regional American Assembly on State Legislatures in American Politics. *Final Report: The Northwest Regional American Assembly on State Legislatures in American Politics.* Seattle: University of Washington, 1966.

877. Ohio Regional American Assembly on State Legislatures in American Politics (Indiana-Michigan-Ohio). *Final Report and Recommendations: Regional American Assembly on State Legislatures in American Politics (Indiana-Michigan-Ohio).* Kent, OH: Kent State University, 1966.

878. Pennsylvania General Assembly's Commission for Legislative Modernization. *Toward Tomorrow's Legislature: The Report of the Commission.* Harrisburg: Commission for Legislative Modernization, 1969.

879. Peters, John G., and Susan Welch. "Legislative Reform and Public Policy: An Overview." *Policy Studies Journal* 5 (Summer 1977): 408–414.

880. Press, Charles. "Second Thoughts on Strengthening State Legislatures." *Publius* 4 (Spring 1974): 117–122.

881. Press, Charles, and Charles R. Adrian. "Why Our State Governments Are Sick." *Antioch Review* 24 (Summer 1964): 149–165.

882. Ritt, Leonard B. "State Legislative Reform: Does It Matter?" *American Politics Quarterly* 1 (Oct. 1973): 499–510.

883. Roeder, Philip W. "State Legislative Reform: Determinants and Policy Consequences." *American Politics Quarterly* 7 (Jan. 1979): 51–70.

884. Rosenthal, Alan. "The Effectiveness of Legislative Study and Interim Work." *State Government* 44 (Spring 1971): 93–101.

885. Rosenthal, Alan. "Legislative Review and Evaluation—The Task Ahead." *State Government* 45 (Winter 1972): 42–50.

886. Rosenthal, Alan, and Thomas Mann, eds. "Can the House Be a Home?" *State Legislatures* 6 (Jan. 1980): 22–27.

887. Rousse, Thomas A. *Bicameralism vs. Unicameralism.* New York: Nelson, 1937.

888. Shull, Charles W. "Legislative Reforms." *Social Science* 29 (Jan. 1954): 35–40.

889. Silliman, J. W. "Streamlined Lawmaking: More Improvements Ahead." *Tax Digest* 32 (Feb. 1954): 53–55.

890. Smith, Russell L., and Ronald E. Weber. "Legislative Reform in the American States: Some Preliminary Observations." *State and Local Governmment Review* 9 (May 1977): 35–39.

891. Spencer, Charles F. "Improvement of Procedure in State Legislatures." Ph.D. dissertation, University of Wisconsin, 1938.

892. "Strengthening of Legislatures Urged." *National Civic Review* 51 (Jan. 1962): 23–24.

893. University of California. School of Law. *Streamlining State Legislatures: Report of a Conference Held at the University of California, Berkeley, October 27–29, 1955.* Berkeley: University of California. School of Law, 1956.

894. Uhruh, Jesse M. "Unicameralism—The Wave of the Future," In *Strengthening the States: Essays on Legislative Reform*, edited by Donald G. Herzberg and Alan Rosenthal. Garden City, NY: Doubleday, 1971, pp. 87–94.

895. Walker, Harvey. "The Legislature Today: Major Overhauling, Streamlining Urged to Gain Support and Public Confidence So Sorely Needed." *National Civic Review* 49 (Nov. 1960): 530–536.

896. White, H. "Can Legislatures Learn from City Councils?" *American Political Science Review* 21 (Feb. 1927): 95–100.

897. Witt, S. K. "Modernization of the Legislature." *Proceedings of the Academy of Political Science* 31 (May 1974): 45–57.

Legislative Staffing and Information

898. American Historical Association. "The Colonial Assemblies and Their Legislative Journals." *Annual Report of the American Historical Association* (1897): 403–453.

Legislative Staffing and Information

899. Balutis, Alan P. "Legislative Staffing: A View from the States." In *Legislative Staffing: A Comparative Perspective*, edited by James J. Heaphey and Alan P. Balutis. New York: Sage, 1975, pp. 106–137.

900. Bradley, Phillips. "Legislative Recording in the United States." *American Political Science Review* 29 (Feb. 1935): 74–83.

901. Bradley, Robert B. "Motivations in Legislative Information Use." *Legislative Studies Quarterly* 5 (Aug. 1980): 393–406.

902. Caldwell, Mary Ellen. "Legislative Record Keeping in a Computer Journal." *Harvard Journal on Legislation* 5 (Nov. 1967): 1–30.

903. Clark, Calvin W. *A Survey of Legislative Services in the Fifty States.* Kansas City: Citizens Conference on State Legislatures, 1967.

904. Cohen, Julius. *Materials and Problems on Legislation.* Indianapolis: Bobbs-Merrill, 1949.

905. Coigne, Armand B. *Statute Making: A Treatise on the Means and Methods for the Enactment of Statute Law in the United States.* Chicago: Commerce Clearing House, 1948.

906. "Computers in the Legislatures." *State Legislatures* 2 (May-June 1976): 6–8.

907. Conard, Alfred F. "New Ways to Write Laws." *Yale Law Journal* 56 (Feb. 1947): 458–481.

908. Council of State Governments. *A Guide to the Objectives and Functions of the Legislative Reference Service.* Chicago: Council of State Governments, 1957.

909. Council of State Governments. *Interstate Conference on Automated Data Processing: Its Impact on Public Policy and Service.* Chicago: Council of State Governments, 1965.

910. Council of State Governments. *Legal Services for State Legislatures.* Chicago: Council of State Governments, 1960.

911. Council of State Governments. *Legislative Staff Improvement Survey.* Chicago: Council of State Governments, 1968.

912. Council of State Governments. *The Offices of Legislative Clerks and Secretaries in the States.* Chicago: Council of State Governments, 1957.

913. Council of State Governments. *Permanent Legislative Service Agencies: A Roster of Staff Heads and Services Provided.* Chicago: Council of State Governments, 1975.

914. Council of State Governments. *State Bill-Drafting Manuals.* Chicago: Council of State Governments, 1950.

915. Council of State Governments. *Suggested Basic List of Periodicals Useful for Legislative Reference and Research.* Chicago: Council of State Governments, 1967.

916. Council of State Governments and Public Administration Service. *Automated Data Processing in State Government.* Chicago: Public Administration Service, 1965.

917. Council of State Governments. National Legislative Conference. *Legislative Research Agency Relations with Universities.* Chicago: Council of State Governments, 1967.

918. Day, William L. "Legislative Broadcasting and Recording." *State Government* 25 (Oct. 1952): 225–226.

919. Duke University. Law School. Department of Legislative Research and Drafting. *The Cost of Legislation: A Report on the Actual Cost of the Legislative Department of Government in the States of the Union.* Durham, NC: Duke University, Law School, 1934.

920. Elkins, James S. *A Survey of the Use of Electronic Data Processing by State Legislatures.* Athens: University of Georgia, Institute of Government and Institute of Community and Area Development, 1974.

921. Feller, Irwin. "Providing a University-Based Science and Technology Input to State Legislatures." *State Government* 47 (Summer 1974): 142–147.

922. Feller, Irwin, et al. "Scientific and Technological Information in State Legislatures." *American Behavioral Scientist* 22 (Jan. 1979): 417–436.

923. Fisher, Mary L., ed. *Guide to State Legislative Materials.* Littleton, CO: American Association of Law Libraries, 1979.

924. Fletcher, Mona. "The Use of Mechanical Equipment in Legislative Research." *Annals of the American Academy of Political and Social Science* 195 (Jan. 1938): 168–175.

925. Guild, Frederic H. "Streamlining Legislative Journals." *State Government* 16 (June 1943): 135–138.

926. Guzzo, Peter P. "Confidentiality of Legislative Research Papers." *State Government* 51 (Autumn 1978): 220–224.

Legislative Staffing and Information

927. Hall, Kristin, comp. *A Bibliography of Current Publications on Access to Legislative Information and Activities*. Kansas City: Citizens Conference on State Legislatures, 1974.

928. Harris, Joseph P. *Aids for Lawmakers: A Legislative Council and a Legislative Reference Service*. Chicago: American Legislators' Association, 1933.

929. Heaphey, James J., ed. *Legislative Security*. Albany: State University of New York at Albany, Graduate School of Public Affairs, Research Center, 1972.

930. Heaphey, James J., and Alan Balutis. *Legislative Staffing: A Comparative Perspective*. New York: Halstead, 1975.

931. Jacquin, William C., Timothy A. Barrow, and Guy D. Spiesman. "Legislature Gets General Purpose Staffing through Federal Grant." *State Government* 45 (Spring 1972): 89–94.

932. Jewell, Malcolm E., and Gerhard Loewenberg. "The State of United States Legislative Research." *Legislative Studies Quarterly* 6 (Feb. 1981): 1–25.

933. Jones, Harry W. "Bill-Drafting Services in Congress and the State Legislatures." *Harvard Law Review* 65 (Jan. 1952): 441–451.

934. Kammerer, Gladys M. "The Development of a Legislative Research Arm." *Journal of Politics* 12 (Nov. 1950): 652–667.

935. Kennedy, Leo F. *State Legislative Electronic Data Processing Applications*. Lexington, KY: Council of State Governments, 1970.

936. Kenton, Carolyn L. "Modern Legislative Staffing." *State Government* 47 (Summer 1974): 165–169.

937. Lederle, John W. "Legislative Personnel Given Careful Study." *Michigan Bar Journal* 28 (July 1949): 23–27.

938. Leek, John H. "The Legislative Reference Bureau in Recent Years." *American Political Science Review* 20 (Nov. 1926): 823–831.

939. Leek, John H. "Legislative Reference Work: A Comparative Study." Ph.D. dissertation, University of Pennsylvania, 1925.

940. Leek, John H. "Legislative Reference Work: A Summary." *Annals of the American Academy of Political and Social Science* 136 (Mar. 1928): 168–171.

941. *Legal Service for State Legislatures*. Chicago: Council of State Governments, 1960.

942. "Legislative Aids Outlined by Committee." *National Civic Review* 51 (Fall 1962): 83–84.

943. "Legislative Research in the States." *State Government* 25 (Oct. 1952): 233–236.

944. McKay, Fred J. "Legislative Services in State Government with Emphasis on Selected States." Ph.D. dissertation, American University, 1969.

945. Mason, Paul. "Legislative Bill Drafting." *California Law Review* 14 (May 1926): 299–310.

946. Meller, Norman. "The Policy Position of Legislative Service Agencies." *Western Political Quarterly* 5 (Mar. 1952): 109–123.

947. Menard, Albert R. "Legislative Bill Drafting." *Rocky Mountain Law Review* 23 (Dec. 1950): 127–144.

948. Mott, Rodney L. "Research Work of the American Legislators' Association." *American Political Science Review* 26 (Apr. 1932): 311–314.

949. National Municipal League. *Staff and Services for State Legislatures.* New York: National Municipal League, 1968.

950. Newkirk, Glenn. "Information Technology and State Legislatures." *State Legislatures* 5 (Jan. 1979): 13–15.

951. O'Rourke, Lawrence W. *Legislative Assistance: Some Staff Services Provided for Legislatures.* Los Angeles: University of California, Bureau of Governmental Research, 1951.

952. Price, Douglas. *Computer Simulation and Legislative "Professionalism": Some Quantitative Approaches to Legislative Evolution.* Washington, D.C.: American Political Science Association, 1970.

953. Reenstra-Bryant, Robin. "Government Information Gathering: The Search for Scientific and Technical Information in Five State Legislatures." Ph.D. dissertation, Massachusetts Institute of Technology, 1981.

954. Roberts, Albert B. "American State Legislatures: The Staff Environment." *Public Administration Review* 35 (Sept.-Oct. 1975): 501–504.

955. Sanstead, W. G. "From the Classroom . . . and into Politics." *State Government* 48 (Winter 1975): 14–17.

956. Simon, Lucinda. *A Legislator's Guide to Staffing Patterns.* Denver: National Conference of State Legislatures, 1980.

957. Simon, Lucinda. "Personnel Policy: Where Does Your Legislature Stand?" *State Legislatures* 5 (June 1979): 15–17.

958. Simon, Lucinda, and Jeri Zahorsky. "Are State Legislatures Equal Opportunity Employers?" *State Legislatures* 6 (Feb. 1980): 11–13.

959. *State Use of Electronic Data Processing*. Lexington, KY: Council of State Governments, 1974.

960. Talbott, Floyd C. "A Working Manual for the Legislative Draftsman." M.A. thesis, University of California, 1942.

961. Toll, Henry W. "The Proposed Interstate Legislative Reference Bureau." *American Political Science Review* 24 (Feb. 1930): 115–116.

962. U.S. Library of Congress, Congressional Research Service. *State Legislature Use of Information Technology*. Westport, CT: Greenwood Press, 1978.

963. University of Washington. Bureau of Public Administration. *Aids for Lawmakers: A Survey of Legislative Reference Services and Legislative Councils*. Seattle: University of Washington, Bureau of Public Administration, 1946.

964. Van der Vries, Bernice T. "Housekeeping in the Legislature." *State Government* 10 (Oct. 1937): 207–209.

965. Webb, Robert. "Legislative Modernization in the Computer Age." *Bureau of Governmental Research Bulletins* (Apr. 1967): 1–4.

966. Wigmore, John H. "Improving State Statute Law Publications." *American Bar Association Journal* 24 (Dec. 1938): 1020–1021.

967. Wissel, Peter, Robert O'Connor, and Michael King. "The Hunting of the Legislative Snark: Information Searches and Reforms in U.S. State Legislatures." *Legislative Studies Quarterly* 1 (May 1976): 251–267.

968. Witte, Edwin E. "Technical Services for State Legislators." *Annals of the American Academy of Political and Social Sciences* 195 (Jan. 1938): 137–143.

969. Worthley, John A. "Legislative Information Systems: A Review and Analysis of Recent Experience." *Western Political Quarterly* 30 (Sept. 1977): 418–430.

Policy Outputs

970. Anton, Thomas J. "The Legislature, Politics, and Public Policy, 1959." *Rutgers Law Review* 14 (Winter 1960): 269–289.

971. Arrington, W. Russell, and Richard E. Dunn. "Governmental Evolution and the Response of State Legislatures." *State Government* 43 (Summer 1970): 174–178.

972. Battle, Haron J. "State Involvement in the Urban Education Crisis." *Journal of Negro Education* 42 (Summer 1973): 315–321.

973. Bresnick, David. "Why Second-Tier Governments Won't Help the Powerless." *State and Local Government Review* 10 (Jan. 1978): 8–15.

974. Caldwell, Kenneth S. "Efficiency and Effectiveness Measurement in State and Local Government." *Governmental Finance* 2 (Nov. 1973): 19–26.

975. Chester, Edward W. *Issues and Responses in State Political Experience.* Totowa, NJ: Littlefield, Adams, 1968.

976. Clark, I. G. "State Legislation and Railroads of the Gulf Southwest." *Southwestern Social Science Quarterly* 41 (1960): 268–282.

977. Dawson, Richard E., and James A. Robinson. "Inter-Party Competition, Economic Variables, and Welfare Policies in the American States." *Journal of Politics* 25 (May 1963): 265–289.

978. Dye, Thomas R. *Politics, Economics, and the Public: Policy Outcomes in the American States.* Chicago: Rand-McNally, 1966.

979. Farabee, D. H., and L. Press. "Legislative Perspective on Public Mental Health Programs." *State Government* 50 (Autumn 1977): 203–208.

980. Feller, Irwin. "Issues in the Design of Federal Programs to Improve the Policy Management Capabilities of State Legislatures." *Public Administration Review* 35 (Dec. 1975): 780–785.

981. Francis, Wayne L., and Ronald E. Weber. "Legislative Issues in the 50 States: Managing Complexity Through Classification." *Legislative Studies Quarterly* 5 (Aug. 1980): 407–421.

982. Gary, Lawrence E. "Policy Decisions in the Aid to Families with Dependent Children Program: A Comparative State Analysis." *Journal of Politics* 35 (Nov. 1973): 886–923.

983. Gray, Virginia. "Innovation in the States: A Diffusion Study." *American Political Science Review* 67 (Dec. 1973): 1174–1185.

984. Gray, Virginia. "Models of Comparative State Politics: A Comparison of Cross-Sectional and Time Series Analysis." *American Journal of Political Science* 20 (May 1976): 235–256.

985. Gray, Virginia. "A Note on Competition and Turnout in the American States." *Journal of Politics* 38 (Feb. 1976): 153–158.

986. Hansell, Stafford. "Role of the Legislature in Collective Bargaining." *State Government* 49 (Autumn 1976): 221–223.

986A. Harrington, Joseph D. "Adoption and the State Legislatures." *Public Welfare* 42 (Spring 1984): 34–46.

987. Hart, Henry C. "Legislative Abdication in Regional Development." *Journal of Politics* 13 (Aug. 1951): 393–414.

988. Hazard, William R. "Schooling and the Law: Reflections on Social Change." *Education and Urban Society* 8 (May 1976): 307–332.

989. Hofferbert, Richard I. "The Relation Between Public Policy and Some Structural and Environmental Variables in the American States." *American Political Science Review* 60 (Mar. 1966): 73–82.

990. Hopkins, Anne H., and Ronald E. Weber. "Dimensions of Public Policies in the American States." *Polity* 8 (Spring 1976): 475–489.

991. Humphrey, Thomas F. "The States' Role in Policy Implementation: Transportation Policy." *Policy Studies Review* 1 (1982): 323–334.

992. Huwa, Randy, and Alan Rosenthal, eds. *Legislative Priorities for Policy Assistance*. New Brunswick, NJ: Rutgers University, Eagleton Institute of Politics, Center for State Legislative Research and Service, 1976.

993. Ingram, Helen M. "Future Policy Directions: Challenges for the States." *American Behavioral Scientist* 22 (Nov.-Dec. 1978): 311–320.

994. Jacobs, David. "Dimensions of Inequality and Public Policy in the States." *Journal of Politics* 42 (Feb. 1980): 291–306.

995. Jacobs, David. "On the Determinants of Class Legislation: An Ecological Study of Political Struggles Between Workers and Management." *Sociological Quarterly* 19 (Summer 1978): 469–480.

996. Jaros, D., and M. A. Baer. "Political Disaffection in the American States: Substantive and Symbolic Policy Determinants." *Social Science Quarterly* 57 (Dec. 1976): 579–588.

997. Jennings, Edward T. "Competition, Constituencies, and Welfare Policies in American States." *American Political Science Review* 73 (June 1979): 414–429.

998. Johnson, Marc A. "State Responsibilities for Rail Preservation." *State Government* 49 (Summer 1976): 148–154.

999. Johnston, Heather W. "Representation and Aspects of Public Policy in Four State Legislatures." Ph.D. dissertation, University of Iowa, 1972.

1000. Jones, Charles O. "State and Local Policy Analysis: A Review of Progress." In *Political Science and State and Local Government.* Washington, D.C.: American Political Science Association, 1973, pp. 27–54.

1001. Jones, E. B. "State Legislation and Hours of Work in Manufacturing." *Southern Economic Journal* 41 (Apr. 1975): 602–612.

1002. Kirk, Frank A. "State Policy Issues in New Towns and Large-Scale Developments." *Public Administration Review* 35 (May-June 1975): 246–249.

1003. Kirst, Michael W. "The States' Role in Education Policy Innovation." *Policy Studies Review* 1 (1982): 298–308.

1004. Klass, Gary M. "The Determination of Policy and Politics in the American States, 1948–1974." *Policy Studies Journal* 7 (Summer 1979): 745–752.

1005. Ledbetter, Cal L., and G. Robert Ross. "Reluctant Partners: Higher Education and State Legislatures." *State Legislatures* 4 (Mar.-Apr. 1978): 14–15.

1006. Lennertz, James E. "The Policy Consequences of State Legislative Appointment." Ph.D. dissertation, University of Pennsylvania, 1980.

1007. Masters, Nicholas A., Robert H. Salisbury, and Thomas H. Eliot. *State Politics and the Public Schools: An Exploratory Analysis.* New York: Knopf, 1964.

1008. Morrison, Peter A. "How Demographers Can Help Legislators." *Policy Analysis* 6 (Winter 1980): 85–98.

1009. Mushkin, S. J. "Policy Analysis in State and Community." *Public Administration Review* 37 (May 1977): 245–253.

1010. Nadworny, Milton J. "State 'Right-to-Work' Laws." *Current History* 49 (Aug. 1965): 85–90.

1011. Noell, J. "On the Administrative Sector of Social Systems: An Analysis of the Size and Complexity of Government Bureaucracies in the American States." *Social Forces* 42 (1976): 549–558.

1012. Oldfield, Jennifer D. "A Case Study of the Impact of Public Policy Affecting Women." *Public Administration Review* 36 (July-Aug. 1976): 385–389.

1013. Paulsen, Monrad, Graham Parker, and Lynn Adelman. "Child Abuse Reporting Laws—Some Legislative History." *George Washington Law Review* 34 (Mar. 1966): 482–506.

1014. Price, Charles M. "The Initiative: A Comparison State Analysis and Reassessment of a Western Phenomenon." *Western Political Quarterly* 28 (June 1975): 243–262.

1015. Regens, J. L. "State Policy Responses to the Energy Issue: An Analysis of Innovation." *Social Science Quarterly* 61 (June 1980): 44–57.

1016. Ritt, Leonard B. "The Policy Impact of Legislative Reform: A 50-State Analysis." In *Legislative Reform and Public Policy*, edited by Susan Welch and John G. Peters. New York: Praeger, 1977, pp. 189–200.

1017. Robinson, James A., ed. *State Legislative Innovation: Case Studies of Washington, Ohio, Florida, Illinois, Wisconsin, and California.* New York: Praeger, 1973.

1018. Roessner, J. D. "Federal Technology Policy: Innovation and Problem Solving in State and Local Governments." *Policy Analysis* 5 (Spring 1979): 181–201.

1019. Rose, Douglas D. "National and Local Forces in State Politics: The Implications of Multi-Level Policy Analysis." *American Political Science Review* 67 (Dec. 1973): 1162–1173.

1020. Sabatier, Paul A. "State and Local Government." *Policy Studies Journal* 1 (Summer 1973): 217–225.

1021. Savage, R. L. "Policy Innovativeness as a Trait of American States." *Journal of Politics* 40 (Feb. 1978): 212–224.

1022. Schneider, Mark, and David Swinton. "Policy Analysis in State and Local Government." *Public Administration Review* 39 (Jan.-Feb. 1976): 12–16.

1023. Sessums, T. Terrell. "Legislating a Growth Policy." *State Government* 47 (Spring 1974): 82–86.

1024. Shaffer, William R., and Ronald E. Weber. *Policy Responsiveness in the American States.* Beverly Hills, CA: Sage, 1974.

1025. Sharkansky, Ira. *The Maligned States: Policy Accomplishments, Problems, and Opportunities.* New York: McGraw-Hill, 1978.

1026. Sharkansky, Ira, and Richard I. Hofferbert. "Dimensions of State Politics, Economics, and Public Policy." *American Political Science Review* 63 (Sept. 1969): 867–879.

1027. Stavinsky, Leonard. "Education Policy: A Legislator's Overview." *State Legislatures* 6 (Sept. 1980): 11–14.

1028. Steindl, Frank G. "More on Minimum Wage and Political Clout." *Public Choice* 19 (Fall 1974): 137–138.

1029. Stevens, J. M., and R. D. Lee. "Patterns of Policy Analysis Use for State Governments: A Contingency and Demand Perspective." *Public Administration Review* 41 (Nov.-Dec. 1981): 636–644.

1030. Strouse, James C., and Philippe Jones. "Federal Aid: The Forgotten Variable in State Policy Research." *Journal of Politics* 36 (Feb. 1974): 200–207.

1031. Strouse, James C., and J. O. Williams. "Non-additive Model For State Policy Research." *Journal of Politics* 34 (May 1972): 648–657.

1032. Taeuber, Cynthia M., and Richard C. Taeuber. "Population and Public Policy." *State Government* 48 (Summer 1975): 183–188.

1033. Teitelbaum, Fred. "The Relative Responsiveness of State and Federal Aid to Distressed Cities." *Policy Studies Review* 1 (1982): 309–322.

1034. Thomas, Robert D. "Policy Issues and Intergovernmental Responsibility: A State Legislative Perspective on Change." *State and Local Government Review* 9 (May 1977): 54–59.

1035. Tilden, Richard A. "Incorporation by Reference of Federal Recovery Laws and Administration Regulation in State Acts." *George Washington Law Review* 3 (May 1935): 482–494.

Policy Outputs

1036. Uslaner, Eric M. "Comparative State Policy Formation, Interparty Competition, and Malapportionment: A New Look at V. O. Key's Hypotheses." *Journal of Politics* 40 (May 1978): 409–432.

1037. Uslaner, Eric M., and Ronald E. Weber. "The 'Politics' of Redistribution: Towards a Model of the Policy-Making Process in the American States." *American Politics Quarterly* 3 (Apr. 1975): 130–170.

1038. Wagner, Marvin H. "A Legislative Approach to Alcohol and Highway Safety." *State Government* 45 (Winter 1972): 51–54.

1039. Walker, Jack L. "The Diffusion of Innovations Among the American States." *American Political Science Review* 63 (Sept. 1969): 880–899.

1040. Weber, Ronald E., and William R. Shaffer. "Public Opinion and American State Policy-Making." *American Journal of Political Science* 16 (Nov. 1972): 683–699.

1041. Welch, Susan, and K. Thompson. "Impact of Federal Incentives on State Policy Innovation." *American Journal of Political Science* 24 (Nov. 1980): 715–729.

1042. West, E. G. "Vote Earning Versus Vote Losing Properties of Minimum Wage Laws." *Public Choice* 19 (Fall 1974): 133–136.

1043. Wheeler, Gerald R. "Evaluating Social Programs: The Case for a State GAO." *Policy Studies Journal* 3 (Summer 1975): 390–397.

1044. White, Leonard D. "Legislative Responsibility for the Public Service." *State Government* 18 (Nov. 1945): 195–199.

1045. Wilson, Paul E., and James H. Winkler. "The Response of State Legislation to Historic Preservation." *Law and Contemporary Problems* 36 (Summer 1971): 329–347.

1046. Yin, Robert K., et al. *Tinkering with the System: Technological Innovations in State and Local Services.* Lexington, MA: Lexington Books, 1977.

Part II
Studies on Individual Legislatures

Alabama

1047. Atkins, Leah. "The First Legislative Session: The General Assembly of Alabama, Huntsville, 1819." *Alabama Review* 23 (Jan. 1970): 30–44.

1048. Bernard, William D. "The Old Order Changes: Graves, Sparks, Folsom, and the Gubernatorial Election of 1912." *Alabama Review* 28 (July 1975): 163–184.

1049. Buttain, Joseph M. "Some Reflections on Negro Suffrage and Politics in Alabama—Past and Present." *Journal of Negro History* 47 (Apr. 1962): 127–138.

1050. Brown, Charles A. "A. H. Curtis: Alabama Legislator." *Negro History Bulletin* 25 (Feb. 1962): 99–101.

1051. Brown, Charles A. "John Dozier: Member of the General Assembly of Alabama." *Negro History Bulletin* 26 (Dec. 1962): 113, 128.

1052. Brown, Charles A. "Reconstruction Legislators in Alabama." *Negro History Bulletin* 26 (Mar. 1963): 198–199.

1053. Brown, Charles A. "William H. Councill: Alabama Legislator." *Negro History Bulletin* 26 (Feb. 1963): 171–173.

1054. Dobbins, Charles G. "Alabama Governors and Editors, 1930–1955: A Memoir." *Alabama Review* 29 (Apr. 1976): 135–154.

1055. "Establishment of the Alabama Territory." *Alabama Historical Quarterly* 24 (Spring 1962): 97–128.

1056. Farmer, Hallie. "Legislative Planning and Research in Alabama." *Journal of Politics* 9 (Aug. 1947): 429–438.

1057. Farmer, Hallie. *The Legislative Process in Alabama*. University: University of Alabama, Bureau of Public Administration, 1949.

1058. Flynt, Wayne. "Organized Labor, Reform and Alabama Politics, 1920." *Alabama Review* 23 (July 1970): 163–180.

1059. Harmon, Robert B. *Government and Politics in Alabama: An Information Source Survey*. Monticello, IL: Council of Planning Libraries, 1978.

1060. Havens, Murray C. *City Versus Farm? Urban-Rural Conflict in the Alabama Legislature*. University: University of Alabama, Bureau of Public Administration, 1957.

1061. Jones, Allen W. "Party Nominating Machinery in Ante-Bellum Alabama." *Alabama Review* 20 (Jan. 1967): 34–44.

1062. Larson, J. E. *Reapportionment in Alabama.* University: University of Alabama, Bureau of Public Administration, 1955.

1063. Lee, McDowell, H. E. Sterk, and Benjamin B. Williams. *The Role of the Senate in Alabama History.* Troy, AL: Troy State University Press, 1978.

1064. Martin, David L. *Alabama's State and Local Governments.* Dubuque, IA: Kendall/Hunt, 1975.

1065. Martin, Roscoe C. "Alabama Falls in Line: Sole State Quadrennial Legislative Session Yields to Biennial Sessions." *State Government* 13 (Mar. 1940): 43–44.

1066. Pow, Alex S. "Alabama's New Legislative Agencies." *Alabama Social Welfare* 11 (Aug. 1946): 5–6.

1067. Pow, Alex S. "Alabama's New Legislative Process in Action: Quadrennial Legislative Sessions Give Way to Biennial." *State Government* 16 (Dec. 1943): 246–247.

1068. Rodabaugh, Karl. "'Kolbites' Versus Bourbons: The Alabama Gubernatorial Election of 1892." *Alabama Historical Quarterly* 37 (Winter 1975): 275–321.

1069. Rogers, William W. "Agrarian Distress in the Seventies: The Mulberry Agricultural Club Versus Governor David P. Lewis." *Alabama Historical Quarterly* 33 (Fall-Winter 1971): 169–176.

1070. Sands, C. Dallas, and J. H. Brewer. "Time and Motion Study of the Alabama Legislature." *Alabama Law Review* 6 (Spring 1954): 157–185.

1071. Stanley, Harold W. *Senate vs. Governor, Alabama, 1971: Referents for Opposition in a One-Party Legislature.* University: University of Alabama Press, 1975.

1072. Stewart, William H. *The Alabama Constitutional Commission: A Pragmatic Approach to Constitutional Revision.* University: University of Alabama Press, 1975.

1073. Taylor, James S. "John M. Patterson and the 1958 Alabama Gubernatorial Race." *Alabama Review* 23 (July 1970): 226–234.

1074. Thomas, James D. *Adoption of Annual Legislative Sessions: The Case of Alabama.* University: University of Alabama, Bureau of Public Administration, 1976.

1075. Thomas, James D., and L. Franklin Blitz. *The Alabama Legislature: An Overview.* University: University of Alabama, Bureau of Public Administration, 1974.

1076. University of Alabama. Bureau of Public Administration. *The Legislative Process in Alabama: Recess and Interim Committees.* University: University of Alabama, Bureau of Public Administration, 1946.

1077. University of Alabama. Bureau of Public Administration. *The Legislative Process in Alabama: Standing Committees.* University: University of Alabama, Bureau of Public Administration, 1945.

1078. Vocino, Thomas, and James N. Hool. "Providing Academic Technical Assistance to a State Legislature: The Case of Alabama." *State and Local Government Review* 9 (Jan. 1977): 28–33.

1079. Woolfolk, Sarah V. "Amnesty and Pardon and Republicanism in Alabama." *Alabama Historical Quarterly* 26 (Summer 1964): 240–248.

1080. Woolfolk, Sarah V. "Carpetbaggers in Alabama: Tradition Versus Truth." *Alabama Review* 15 (Apr. 1962): 133–144.

1081. Wright, John P. "The Limited Quadrennial Legislative Session of Alabama." Ph.D. dissertation, Harvard University, 1932.

Alaska

1082. Atwood, Evangeline, and Robert N. DeArmond. *Who's Who in Alaskan Politics: A Biographical Dictionary of Alaskan Political Personalities, 1884–1974.* Portland, OR: Binford and Mort, 1977.

1083. Campbell, Ernest H. *The State Legislatures of Alaska, Oregon, and Washington.* Seattle: Northwest Regional American Assembly on State Legislatures in American Politics, 1966.

1084. Swap, C. Ralph. "The Capital Relocation Issue in Alaska." *Western Political Quarterly* 17 (June 1964): 213–234.

Arizona

1085. Arizona Legislative Council. *The Arizona Legislative Process and Bill Drafting Manual.* Phoenix: Arizona Legislative Council, 1961.

1086. "Arizona Restricts Population Representation." *National Municipal Review* 42 (Nov. 1953): 514.

1087. Brinegar, David F. "In Line of Duty: Governor Sidney P. Osborn's Last Year." *Journal of Arizona History* 16 (Autumn 1975): 226–252.

1088. Dengler, Louise W. "The Arizona Legislature and Twenty Years of Change." Ph.D. dissertation, University of Arizona, 1972.

1089. Fox, Kel M. "Longshot Governor: The Election of Bob Jones." *Journal of Arizona History* 19 (Winter 1978): 347–358.

1090. Harmon, Robert B. *Government and Politics in Arizona: An Information Source Survey.* Monticello, IL: Council of Planning Libraries, 1978.

1091. Mann, Dean E. "The Legislative Committee System in Arizona." *Western Political Quarterly* 14 (Dec. 1961): 925–941.

1092. Polinard, Jerry L. "An Analysis of the Inter-Party and Intra-Party Conflict in the Arizona State Legislative Redistricting Experience of 1966." Ph.D. dissertation, University of Arizona, 1970.

1093. Rice, Ross R. *An Annotated Bibliography of Arizona Politics and Government.* Tempe: Arizona State University, Center for Public Affairs, 1976.

1094. Riggs, Robert E. "The Legislative Process in Arizona." *Arizona Review of Business and Public Administration* 11 (Dec. 1962): 1–22.

1095. Rusco, Elmer R. *Voting Behavior in Arizona.* Reno: University of Nevada, Bureau of Governmental Research, 1967.

1096. Sanders, Ruby H. "How a Bill Becomes a Law in the Arizona House of Representatives." *Arizona Review of Business and Public Administration* 11 (Dec. 1962): 22–24.

1097. Van Petten, Donald. *The Constitution and Government of Arizona.* 2d ed. Phoenix: Sun Country, 1956.

1098. Wilson, Marjorie H. "Governor Hunt, the 'Beast' and the Miners." *Journal of Arizona History* 15 (Summer 1974): 119–138.

Arkansas

1099. Alexander, Henry M. "A School for State Legislators: Arkansas Lawmakers Have Opportunity for Preliminary Training at the Institute of Legislative Procedure." *State Government* 14 (Feb. 1941): 39–40.

1100. Anderson, Robert M. "Drafting a Legislative Act in Arkansas." *Arkansas Law Review* 2 (Fall 1948): 382–406.

1101. Craft, Ralph H. *Strengthening the Arkansas Legislature.* New Brunswick, NJ: Rutgers University Press, 1972.

1102. Crawford, Charles W. "From Classroom to State Capital: Charles H. Brough and the Campaign 1916." *Arkansas Historical Quarterly* 21 (Autumn 1962): 213–230.

1103. Dillard, Tom. "To the Back of the Elephant: Racial Conflict in the Arkansas Republican Party." *Arkansas Historical Quarterly* 33 (Spring 1974): 3–15.

1104. Gatewood, Willard G. "Negro Legislators in Arkansas, 1891: A Document." *Arkansas Historical Quarterly* 31 (Autumn 1972): 220–233.

1105. Harmon, Robert B. *Government and Politics in Arkansas: An Information Source Survey.* Monticello, IL: Council of Planning Libraries, 1976.

1106. Ledbetter, Cal L. "Legislative Improvement in Arkansas." *State Government* 46 (Spring 1973): 109–114.

1107. Moyers, David. "From Quackery to Qualification: Arkansas Medical and Drug Legislation, 1881–1909." *Arkansas Historical Quarterly* 35 (Spring 1976): 3–26.

1108. O'Connor, Patrick F. "Voting Structure in a One-Party Legislature: The Arkansas House of Representatives Over Five Sessions." Ph.D. dissertation, Indiana University, 1973.

1109. Smith, Harold T. "The Know-Nothings in Arkansas." *Arkansas Historical Quarterly* 34 (Winter 1975): 291–303.

1110. Treon, John A. "Politics and Concrete: The Building of the Arkansas State Capital, 1899–1917." *Arkansas Historical Quarterly* 31 (Summer 1972): 99–133.

1111. White, Lonnie J. "The Fall of Governor John Pope." *Arkansas Historical Quarterly* 23 (Spring 1964): 74–84.

California

1112. Adickes, R. "California Reapportionment: A New Amendment." *Southern California Law Review* 40 (Summer 1967): 664–668.

1113. Antognini, Richard. "The Role of A. P. Giannini in the 1934 California Gubernatorial Election." *Southern California Quarterly* 57 (Spring 1975): 53–86.

1114. Baird, Lawrence M. "The Use of Scientific and Technical Information and Advice by the California Legislature: A Survey of

Current Policies and Proposals for Improvement." Ph.D. dissertation, University of Southern California, 1979.

1115. Barclay, Thomas S. "Bifurcation Out West: The Split-Session in California." *State Government* 5 (Apr. 1932): 5–6.

1116. Barclay, Thomas S. "Reapportionment in California." *Pacific Historical Review* 5 (June 1936): 93–129.

1117. Barclay, Thomas S. "The Reapportionment Struggle in California in 1948." *Western Political Quarterly* 4 (June 1951): 313–324.

1118. Barclay, Thomas S. "The Split Session of the California Legislature." *California Law Review* 20 (Nov. 1931): 42–58.

1119. Barrett, Edward L. *The Tenney Committee: Legislative Investigation of Subversive Activities in California.* Ithaca: Cornell University Press, 1951.

1120. Beek, Joseph A. *The California Legislature.* Sacramento: California State Senate, 1960.

1121. Bell, Charles G., and Charles M. Price. *California Government Today: Politics of Reform.* Homewood, IL: Dorsey Press, 1980.

1122. Bell, Charles G., and Charles M. Price. *The First Term: A Study of Legislative Socialization.* Beverly Hills, CA: Sage, 1975.

1123. Bemis, George W. "Regionalism and Sectionalism in the California Legislature, 1911–1926." Ph.D. dissertation, University of California, 1934.

1124. Berwanger, Eugene H. "The 'Black Law' Question in Ante-Bellum California." *Journal of the West* 6 (Apr. 1967): 205–220.

1125. Best, Wallace H. *Initiative and Referendum Politics in California.* Los Angeles: University of Southern California, 1955.

1126. BeVier, Michael J. *Politics Backstage: Inside the California Legislature.* Philadelphia: Temple University Press, 1979.

1127. Binford, Robert K. "Party Cohesion in the California State Assembly, 1953–1963." M.A. thesis, Stanford University, 1964.

1128. Blackford, Mansel G. "Banking and Bank Legislation in California, 1890–1915." *Business History Review* 47 (Winter 1973): 482–507.

1129. Blair, George S., and Houston I. Flournoy. *Legislative Bodies in California.* Belmont, CA: Dickenson, 1967.

California

1130. Bowles, Brinton D. "Educational Pressure Groups and the Legislative Process in California, 1945–1966." Ph.D. dissertation, Claremont Graduate School, 1967.

1131. Bowles, Brinton D. "Local Government Participation as a Route of Recruitment to the State Legislature in California and Pennsylvania, 1900–1962." *Western Political Quarterly* 19 (Sept. 1966): 491–503.

1132. Buchanan, William. *Legislative Partisanship: The Deviant Case of California*. Berkeley: University of California Press, 1963.

1133. Burk, Robert E. "Cross-Filing in California Elections, 1914–1946." M.A. thesis, University of California, 1947.

1134. Burke, Norris J. "Legislative Delegation of Power in California." Ph.D. dissertation, Harvard University, 1950.

1135. Byrne, Paul L. "Functions of the Standing and Interim Committees of Our Legislature." *California—Magazine of the Pacific* 50 (Dec. 1960): 14–33.

1136. California State Chamber of Commerce. *Proposals for a Unicameral Legislature in California*. San Francisco: California State Chamber of Commerce, 1937.

1137. California State Chamber of Commerce. *Salaries of State Legislators*. San Francisco: California State Chamber of Commerce, 1948.

1138. Capell, Elizabeth A. *The Growth of California State Government, 1845 to 1975*. Berkeley: University of California, Institute of Governmental Studies, 1977.

1139. Casjens, Robert S. "The California Senate: The Impact of Reapportionment on Its Educational Policy Decisions." Ph.D. dissertation, Claremont Graduate School, 1974.

1140. Citizens' Committee for Equal Representation in the California State Senate. *California's Need for Senate Reapportionment: Does Your Vote Count?* Sacramento: Citizens' Committee for Equal Representation in the California State Senate, 1947.

1141. Cloner, Alexander. "Legislative Compensation in California: An Appraisal of Alternative Salary Criteria." Ph.D. dissertation, University of Southern California, 1962.

1142. Cloner, Alexander, and Richard Gable. "The California Legislator and the Problem of Compensation." *Western Political Quarterly* 12 (Sept. 1959): 712–726.

1143. Collings, R. A. "California's New Lobby Control Act." *California Law Review* 38 (Aug. 1950): 478–497.

1144. Commonwealth Club of California. "How Should Legislative Investigating Committees Operate?" *Transactions* 45 (July 1951): 154–178.

1145. Commonwealth Club of California. "A Legislative Advisory Board?" *Transactions* 39 (Mar. 1945): 155–180.

1146. Commonwealth Club of California. *The Legislature of California: Its Membership, Procedure, and Work*. San Francisco: Commonwealth Club of California, 1943.

1147. Constantini, Edmond. "Interparty Attitude Conflict: Democratic Party Leadership in California." *Western Political Quarterly* 16 (Dec. 1963): 956–972.

1148. Constantini, Edmond, and K. H. Craik. "Personality and Politicians: California Party Leaders, 1960–1976." *Journal of Personality and Social Psychology* 38 (Apr. 1980): 641–661.

1149. Cattrell, Edwin A. "Twenty-Five Years of Direct Legislation in California." *Public Opinion Quarterly* 3 (Jan. 1939): 30–45.

1150. Crouch, Winston W. *The Initiative and Referendum in California*. Los Angeles: Haynes Foundation, 1950.

1151. Crouch, Winston W., John C. Bollens, and Stanley Scott. *California Government and Politics*. 7th ed. Englewood Cliffs, NJ: Prentice-Hall, 1981.

1152. Culver, John H., and John C. Syer. *Power and Politics in California*. New York: Wiley, 1980.

1153. Danziger, James N. "California's Proposition 13 and the Fiscal Limitations Movement in the United States." *Political Studies* 28 (Dec. 1980): 599–612.

1154. Davies, Race D. "Policy Content and Political Behavior: Policymaking in the California State Legislature." Ph.D. dissertation, University of California, Davis, 1974.

1155. Davis, Raymond G. "The Administration of Politics: Staff Structures in the California Legislature." Ph.D. dissertation, University of California, Davis, 1972.

1156. DeAngelis, Eugene P. "The Political Feasibility of Unicameralism in California." M.A. thesis, Claremont College, 1950.

California 91

1157. Doubleday, D. Jay. *Legislative Review of the Budget in California*. Berkeley: University of California, Institute of Governmental Studies, 1967.

1158. Driscoll, James D. *California's Legislature, 1974*. Sacramento: California Legislature, Assembly, 1973.

1159. Dvorin, Eugene P., and Arthur J. Misner, eds. *California Politics and Policies: Original Essays by Richard Harvey and Others*. Reading, MA: Addison-Wesley, 1966.

1160. Engelbert, Ernest A. "Legislative Reorganization in California." *State Government* 36 (Winter 1963): 58–64.

1161. Findley, James C. "Cross-Filing and the Progressive Movement in California Politics." *Western Political Quarterly* 11 (Sept. 1959): 699–712.

1162. Franklin, William E. "The Religious Order of Peter H. Burnett, California's First American Governor." *California Historical Quarterly* 45 (June 1966): 125–131.

1163. Freitas, Carol Ann. "Interim Committee Investigations in the California State Legislature." M.A. thesis, University of California, 1959.

1164. Gallagher, J. F. *Apportionment in California Counties: The Impact of Judicial Decisions*. Davis: University of California, Institute of Governmental Affairs, 1964.

1165. Gallagher, J. F. *Supervisional Districting in California Counties: 1960–1963*. Davis: University of California, Institute of Governmental Affairs, 1963.

1166. Gordon, Dudley. "California's First Half-Century of Statehood, 1850–1900." *Southern California Quarterly* 53 (Summer 1971): 133–146.

1167. Grant, J. A. C. "The Bicameral Principle in the California Legislature." Ph.D. dissertation, Stanford University, 1927.

1168. Grant, J. A. C. "Judicial Control of Legislative Procedure in California." *Stanford Law Review* 1 (Apr. 1949): 428–451.

1169. Greenberg, David, Al Lipson, and Bernard Rostker. "Technical Success, Political Failure: The Incentive Pay Plan for California Job Agents." *Policy Analysis* 2 (Fall 1976): 545–576.

1170. Greenfield, M., P. Ford, and D. R. Emery. *Legislative Reapportionment: California in National Perspective.* Berkeley: University of California, Bureau of Public Administration, 1959.

1171. Grody, Harvey P. "The California Legislature and Comprehensive Water Resources Development: 1941–1959." Ph.D. dissertation, University of California, Los Angeles, 1971.

1172. Hardy, Leroy C. *California Government.* New York: Harper and Row, 1964.

1173. Hardy, Leroy C., and Charles P. Sohner. "Constitutional Challenge and Political Response: California Reapportionment, 1965." *Western Political Quarterly* 23 (Dec. 1970): 733–751.

1174. Harmon, Robert B. *Government and Politics in California: An Information Source Survey.* Monticello, IL: Council of Planning Libraries, 1978.

1175. Harris, Joseph P. *California Politics.* Stanford: Stanford University Press, 1955.

1176. Harvey, Richard B. *The Dynamics of California Government and Politics.* Belmont, CA: Wadsworth, 1970.

1177. Harvey, Richard B. "Governor Earl Warren of California: A Study in 'Non-Partisan' Republican Politics." *California Historical Quarterly* 46 (Mar. 1967): 33–51.

1178. Hayden, Richard D. "A History and Analysis of the Election of Assemblymen from California's Fourth District from 1932–1952." M.A. thesis, Chico State College, 1953.

1179. Hendrick, Irving G. "Academic Revolution in California: A History of Events Leading to the Passage and Implementation of the 1961 Fisher Bill on Teacher Certification." *Southern California Quarterly* 49 (Summer 1967): 127–166.

1180. Hennings, Robert E. "California Democratic Politics in the Period of Republican Ascendancy." *Pacific Historical Review* 31 (Aug. 1962): 267–280.

1181. Hichborn, Franklin. *Story of the Session of the California Legislature of 1909.* San Francisco: Press of the James H. Barry Co., 1909.

1182. Hichborn, Franklin. *Story of the Session of the California Legislature of 1911.* San Francisco: Press of the James H. Barry Co., 1911.

California

1183. Hichborn, Franklin. *Story of the Session of the California Legislature of 1913.* San Francisco: Press of the James H. Barry Co., 1913.

1184. Hichborn, Franklin. *Story of the Session of the California Legislature of 1915.* San Francisco: Press of the James H. Barry Co., 1916.

1185. Hill, Gladwin. *Dancing Bear: An Inside Look at California Politics.* Cleveland: World, 1968.

1186. Hoopes, David C. "Policy-Making by the Joint Committee on Reorganization of Large Urban Unified School Districts of the California Legislature, 1969–1970: A Case Study." Ph.D. dissertation, University of Southern California, 1971.

1187. Hopper, Stanley. "Fragmentation of the California Republican Party in the One-Party Era, 1893–1932." *Western Political Quarterly* 28 (June 1975): 372–386.

1188. Hushaw, Charles W. "The Committee System of the California Legislature." M.A. thesis, University of California, 1959.

1189. Hutchinson, W. H. "Prologue to Reform, the California Anti-Railroad Republicans, 1899–1905." *Southern California Quarterly* 44 (Sept. 1962): 175–218.

1190. Hyink, Bernard L., Seyom Brown, and Ernest W. Thacker. *Politics and Government in California.* 10th ed. New York: Harper and Row, 1979.

1191. "Interim Legislative Committees." *Tax Digest* 26 (Jan. 1948): 16–17.

1192. Jacobs, Clyde E., and Alvin D. Sokolow. *California Government: One Among Fifty.* 2d ed. New York: Macmillan, 1970.

1193. Jensen, James E. "A Study of Influence in Education Committees of the California State Legislature." Ed.D. dissertation, University of California, Berkeley, 1965.

1194. Johnson, Kenneth M. "California's Constitution of 1879: An Unpaid Debt." *California Historical Quarterly* 49 (June 1970): 135–141.

1195. Johnson, William C. "The Political Party System in the 1959–1960 California Legislature." M.A. thesis, University of California, 1960.

1196. Kenny, R. W. "The California Legislature's Contribution to the War Effort." *State Bar Journal of California* 18 (May-June 1943): 195–205.

1197. Kirwin, Alice. *A Source Book on the California Legislature 1849–1962.* Sacramento: California Legislative Reference Service, 1965.

1198. Kleps, Ralph N. "The Revision and Codification of California Statutes, 1849–1953." *California Law Review* 42 (Dec. 1954): 766–802.

1199. Larsen, Christian L. "The Use of Special Committees and Commissions by the California Legislature." Ph.D. dissertation, University of California, Berkeley, 1937.

1200. League of Women Voters of California. *Committees of the California State Legislature.* Berkeley: League of Women Voters of California, 1948.

1201. Lee, Eugene C., ed. *The California Governmental Process: Problems and Issues.* Boston: Little, Brown, 1966.

1202. Lee, Eugene C. *The Presiding Officer and Rules Committee in Legislatures of the United States, with Special Reference to California.* Berkeley: University of California, Bureau of Public Administration, 1952.

1203. "Legislative Partisanship, Constituency and Malappointment: The Case of California." *American Political Science Review* 66 (Dec. 1972): 1234–1245.

1204. *Legislators and Party Loyalty: The Impact of Reapportionment in California.* Washington, D.C.: University Press of America, 1978.

1205. "Legislatures and Legislators—Statutes—California Legislative Aids." *California Law Review* 39 (June 1951): 288–294.

1206. Leister, D. R. *California Politics and Problems, 1964–1968: A Selective Bibliography.* Berkeley: University of California, Institute of Governmental Studies, 1969.

1207. Leiter, William M., comp. *California Government: Issues and Institutions.* Pacific Palisades, CA: Goodyear, 1971.

1208. Leuthold, David A. *California Politics and Problems, 1900–1963: A Selective Bibliography.* Berkeley: University of California, Institute of Governmental Studies, 1965.

California 95

1209. Levit, Victor B. "California Legislative Materials." *Stanford Law Review* 4 (Apr. 1952): 367–380.

1210. Levit, Victor B. "Legislative Materials in California." *American Bar Association Journal* 49 (June 1963): 597–598.

1211. Lincoln, L. H. "California'a Legislative Internship Program." *State Government* 31 (Jan. 1958): 12–13.

1212. Lipson, Albert J. "Legislative Grantsmanship—California Style." *State Government* 44 (Winter 1971): 31–36.

1213. McHenry, Dean E. "Legislative Personnel in California." *Annals of the American Academy of Political and Social Science* 195 (Jan. 1938): 45–52.

1214. McHenry, Dean E. "The Legislative Power to Investigate on the Anvil: California Legislature Loses and Regains Investigative Authority." *State Government* 15 (May 1942): 105–106.

1215. McHenry, Dean E. *A New Legislature for Modern California.* Los Angeles: Haynes Foundation, 1949.

1216. McHenry, Dean E. "Urban vs. Rural in California." *National Municipal Review* 35 (July 1946): 350–354.

1217. Mann, Dean E. *The Citizen and the Bureaucracy: Complaint-Handling Procedures of Three California Legislators.* Berkeley: University of California, Institute of Governmental Studies, 1968.

1218. Melcher, Daniel P. "The Politics of Discontent: California Politics, 1920–1932." Ph.D. dissertation, University of California, San Diego, 1975.

1219. Morlan, Robert L., and Leroy C. Hardy. *Politics in California.* Belmont, CA: Dickenson, 1968.

1220. Mueller, John E. "Voting on the Propositions: Ballot Patterns and Historical Trends in California." *American Political Science Review* 63 (Dec. 1969): 1197–1212.

1221. Nash, Gerald D. "The Influence of Labor on State Policy 1860–1920: The Experience of California." *California Hsitorical Quarterly* 42 (Sept. 1963): 241–257.

1222. Nathan, Harriet, ed. *Attitudes, Innovation, and Public Policy: A Symposium for the California Legislature.* Berkeley: University of California, Institute of Governmental Studies, 1968.

1223. Newton, Martha R. *Legislative Information in California.* Stanford: Stanford University, 1942.

1224. Ohnimus, Arthur A. "History of California State Legislature." *California—Magazine of the Pacific* 50 (Dec. 1960): 12, 29.

1225. Ohnimus, Arthur A. *The Legislature of California.* Sacramento: California State Legislature, 1959.

1226. Oshita, Edward J. "Liquor Control in California and Certain of Its Political Legislative Aspects." M.A. thesis, University of the Pacific, 1958.

1227. Owens, John R. *Trends in Campaign Spending in California, 1958–1970: Tests of Factors Influencing Costs.* Princeton, NJ: Citizens' Research Foundation, 1973.

1228. Owens, John R., Edmond Constantini, and Louis F. Weschler. *California Politics and Parties.* New York: Macmillan, 1970.

1229. Owens, John R., and Edward Olson. "Campaign Spending and the Electoral Process in California, 1966–1974." *Western Political Quarterly* 30 (Dec. 1977): 493–512.

1230. Padilla, Fernando V. "Legislative Gerrymandering of California Chicanos." Ph.D. dissertation, University of California, Santa Barbara, 1977.

1231. Petersen, Eric F. "The Adoption of the Direct Primary in California." *Southern California Quarterly* 54 (Winter 1972): 363–378.

1232. Petersen, Eric F. "The End of an Era: California's Gubernatorial Election of 1894." *Pacific Historical Review* 38 (May 1969): 141–156.

1233. Pickerell, Albert G., and Edward L. Feder. *Open Public Meetings of Legislative Bodies—California's Brown Act.* Berkeley: University of California, Bureau of Public Administration, 1957.

1234. Price, Charles M. "Voting Alignments in the California Legislature: A Roll Call Analysis of the 1957–1959–1961 Sessions." Ph.D. dissertation, University of Southern California, 1965.

1235. Price, Charles M., and Charles G. Bell. "Socializing California Freshman Assemblymen: The Role of Individuals and Legislative Sub-Groups." *Western Political Quarterly* 23 (Mar. 1970): 166–179.

1236. Putnam, Jackson K. *Modern California Politics, 1917–1980.* San Francisco: Boyd and Fraser, 1980.

California

1237. Putnam, Jackson K. "The Persistence of Progressivism in the 1920's: The Case of California." *Pacific Historical Review* 35 (Nov. 1966): 395–412.

1238. Radin, Max. "Popular Legislation in California." *Minnesota Law Review* 23 (Apr. 1939): 559–584.

1239. Rich, William P. "Legislative Budget Committee." *Tax Digest* 21 (Jan. 1943): 10–11.

1240. Robeck, Bruce W. "Committee Assignments in the California Senate: Seniority, Party, or Ideology?" *Western Political Quarterly* 24 (Sept. 1971): 527–539.

1241. Robeck, Bruce W. *Legislators and Party Loyalty: The Impact of Reapportionment in California*. Washington, D.C.: University Press of America, 1979.

1242. Robeck, Bruce W. "Urban-Rural and Regional Voting Patterns in the California Senate Before and After Reapportionment." *Western Political Quarterly* 23 (Dec. 1970): 785–794.

1243. Rogin, Michael W. "California Populism and the 'System of 1896.'" *Western Political Quarterly* 22 (Mar. 1969): 179–196.

1244. Rogin, Michael W. "Progressivism and the California Electorate." *Journal of American History* 55 (Sept. 1968): 297–314.

1245. Rosenbaum, Walter A. "Legislative Participation in California Direct Legislation, 1940–1960." Ph.D. dissertation, Princeton University, 1964.

1246. Ross, Michael J. *California: Its Government and Politics*. Scituate, MA: Duxbury Press, 1979.

1247. Sabatier, Paul A. *The Sacramento Connection: Linking the Legislature with the University*. Davis: University of California, Institute of Governmental Affairs, 1978.

1248. Salzman, Ed, comp. *California Journal Almanac of State Government and Politics*. Sacramento: Center for Research and Education in Government, 1975.

1249. Samish, Arthur H., and Bob Thomas. *The Secret Boss of California: The Life and High Times of Art Samish*. New York: Crown, 1971.

1250. Schuck, Victoria. "The Legislative Process in California." M.A. thesis, Stanford University, 1931.

1251. Scobie, Ingrid W. "Jack B. Tenney and the 'Parasitic Menace': Anti-Communist Legislation in California 1940–1949." *Pacific Historical Review* 43 (May 1974): 188–211.

1252. Scott, Stanley. *Streamlining State Legislatures: Report on a Conference Held at the University of California, Berkeley, October 27–29, 1955.* Berkeley: University of California, Bureau of Public Administration, 1956.

1253. Segal, Morley. "The Role and Function of the Legislative Staff in the California Assembly." Ph.D. dissertation, Claremont Graduate School, 1965.

1254. Sherwood, Frank P., and Richard Gable. *The California System of Governments.* Belmont, CA: Dickenson, 1968.

1255. Shover, John L. "Was 1928 a Critical Election in California?" *Pacific Northwest Quarterly* 58 (Oct. 1967): 196–204.

1256. Sohner, Charles P. *California Government and Politics Today.* 2d ed. Glenview, IL: Scott, Foresman, 1976.

1257. Sokolow, Alvin D. *Committee Assignments and Changing Leadership Structures in the California Senate: A Survey of Four Regimes.* Davis: University of California, Institute of Governmental Affairs, 1971.

1258. Sokolow, Alvin D. *The Committee Structure of the California Senate.* Davis: University of California, Institute of Governmental Affairs, 1970.

1259. Sokolow, Alvin D., and Richard Brandsma. *Leadership Strategy and Legislative Committee Assignments: California After Reapportionment.* Davis: University of California, Institute of Governmental Affairs, 1969.

1260. Sokolow, Alvin D., and Richard W. Brandsma. "Partisanship and Seniority in Legislative Committee Assignments: California After Reapportionment." *Western Political Quarterly* 24 (Dec. 1971): 740–760.

1261. "Sources of California Law." *Journal of the State Bar of California* 33 (Jan.-Feb. 1958): 37–43.

1262. Staniford, Edward F. *Legislative Assistance.* Berkeley: University of California, Bureau of Public Administration, 1957.

1263. "States Act to Cure Unfair Districting." *National Municipal Review* 37 (May 1948): 259–260.

1264. Steck, E. "California Legislation: Sources Unlimited." *Pacific Law Journal* 6 (July 1975): 536–564.

1265. Stowe, Noel J. *California Government: The Challenge of Change.* Beverly Hills, CA: Glencoe, 1975.

1266. Sumner, Bruce W. "Constitutional Revision in California." *State Government* 40 (Autumn 1967): 224–230.

1267. Turner, Henry A., and John A. Vieg. *The Government and Politics of California.* 3d ed. New York: McGraw-Hill, 1967.

1268. University of California. Institute of Governmental Studies. *Research and Service: A Fifty Year Record.* Berkeley: University of California, 1971.

1269. Unruh, Jesse M. "The California Ombudsman." *Journal of the Constitutional and Parliamentary Studies* 1 (Apr.-June 1967): 13–20.

1270. "Validity of the Creation of Interim Committees by Resolution." *California Law Review* 28 (Jan. 1940): 229–232.

1271. Van Alstyne, Arvo, and Mitchell J. Ezer. "Legislative Research in California: The Uncharted Wilderness." *Los Angeles Bar Bulletin* 35 (Mar. 1960): 145–157.

1272. Walker, Robert A., and Floyd A. Cave. *How California Is Governed.* New York: Dryden Press, 1956.

1273. "The Work of the 1947 California Legislature." *Southern California Law Review* 21 (Dec. 1947): 1–35.

1274. "The Work of the 1949 California Legislature." *Southern California Law Review* 23 (Dec. 1949): 1–47.

1275. Wyner, Alan J. "Legislative Reform and Politics in California: What Happened, Why, and So What?" In *State Legislative Innovation: Case Studies of Washington, Ohio, Florida, Illinois, Wisconsin, and California*, edited by James A. Robinson. New York: Praeger, 1973, pp. 46–100.

1276. Young, C. C. *The Legislature of California: Its Membership, Procedure and Work.* San Francisco: Commonwealth Club of California, 1943.

Colorado

1277. "Apportionment of Colorado's State Representatives—1933, 1940, 1950." *Colorado Taxpayer* 3 (Dec. 1952): 4.

1278. Bakken, Gordon M. "The Development of Law in Colorado, 1861–1912." *Colorado Magazine* 53 (Winter 1976): 63–78.

1279. Delorme, Roland L. "Colorado's Mugwumps Interlude: The State Voters' League, 1905–1906." *Journal of the West* 7 (Oct. 1968): 522–530.

1280. Furniss, Susan W. "The Response of the Colorado General Assembly to Metropolitan Reform in the Denver Metropolitan Area: 1961–1970." Ph.D. dissertation, University of Colorado, 1970.

1281. Furniss, Susan W. "The Response of the Colorado General Assembly to Proposals for Metropolitan Reform." *Western Political Quarterly* 26 (Dec. 1973): 747–765.

1282. Gomez, Rudolph. "Urban and Rural Voting in the Colorado General Assembly: 1902–1960." Ph.D. dissertation, University of Colorado, 1963.

1283. Gregson, Ronald E. "Sunset in Colorado: The Second Round." *State Government* 53 (Spring 1980): 58–62.

1284. Harmon, Robert B. *Government and Politics in Colorado: An Information Source Survey.* Monticello, IL: Vance Bibliographies, 1978.

1285. Henhoe, Kenneth W. "The Committee System of the Colorado State Legislature." M.A. thesis, University of Colorado, 1937.

1286. Henry, Hubert D. "The Desirability of Change in Colorado's Legislative Organization and Procedure." *Dicta* 23 (June 1946): 119–133.

1287. Henry, Hubert D. "The Thirty-Seventh General Assembly." *Dicta* 26 (May 1949): 105–115.

1288. Hjelm, Victor S. "The Colorado State Legislator: Tenure and Turnover." Ph.D. dissertation, University of Colorado, 1967.

1289. Hjelm, Victor S., and Joseph P. Pisciotte. "Profiles and Careers of Colorado State Legislators." *Western Political Quarterly* 21 (Dec. 1968): 698–722.

1290. Hornbein, Marjorie. "Three Governors in a Day." *Colorado Magazine* 45 (Summer 1968): 243–260.

1291. Keating, Edward. *The Gentleman from Colorado: A Memoir.* Denver: Sage Books, 1964.

1292. Lorch, Robert S. *Colorado's Government.* Boulder: Colorado Associated University Press, 1976.

1293. McCarthy, G. Michael. "Colorado's Populist Leadership." *Colorado Magazine* 48 (Winter 1971): 30–42.

1294. McCarthy, G. Michael. "The People's Party in Colorado: A Profile of Populist Leadership." *Agricultural History* 47 (Apr. 1973): 146–155.

1295. McCarthy, G. Michael. "Retreat from Responsibility: The Colorado Legislature in the Conservation Era, 1876–1908." *Rocky Mountain Social Science Journal* 10 (Apr. 1973): 27–36.

1296. Martin, Curtis, and Rudolph Gomez. *Colorado Government and Politics.* 4th ed. Boulder, CO: Pruitt, 1976.

1297. Martin, Curtis, and Wallace Stealey, comp. *Readings in Colorado Government and Politics.* Boulder: University of Colorado, Bureau of Governmental Research and Service, 1967.

1298. Morris, John R. "The Women and Governor Waite." *Colorado Magazine* 44 (Winter 1967): 11–19.

1299. Pisciotte, Joseph P. "The Colorado State Legislator: Entry into the Legislative Process." Ph.D. dissertation, University of Colorado, 1967.

1300. University of Colorado, Bureau of Governmental Research and Service. *A Selected Bibliography of Colorado State and Local Government.* Boulder: University of Colorado, Bureau of Governmental Research and Service, 1964.

1301. Ware, Alan. "End of Party Politics? Activist-Office-Seeker Relationships in the Colorado Democratic Party." *British Journal of Political Science* 9 (Apr. 1979): 237–255.

1302. Wickens, James F. "Tightening the Colorado Purse Strings." *Colorado Magazine* 46 (Fall 1969): 271–288.

Connecticut

1303. Beasley, James R. "Emerging Republicanism and the Standing Order: The Appropriation Act Controversy in Connecticut, 1793–1795." *William and Mary Quarterly* 29 (Oct. 1972): 587–610.

1304. Buckley, William E., and Charles E. Perry. *Connecticut, the State and Its Government.* rev. ed. New York: Oxford Book Co., 1948.

1305. "Connecticut Adapts Legislative Council." *National Municipal Review* 26 (May 1937): 253.

1306. Connecticut Citizens Conference on the General Assembly. *A Modern Legislature Is Up to You.* Hartford: Connecticut Citizens Conference on the General Assembly, 1969.

1307. Connecticut Public Expenditures Council. *Districting and Redistricting the Connecticut Senate.* Hartford: Connecticut Public Expenditures Council, 1961.

1308. Connecticut Public Expenditures Council. *Further Improvements in Legislative Procedure, 1947.* Hartford: Connecticut Public Expenditures Council, 1947.

1309. Connecticut Public Expenditures Council. *Proposed Improvements in Legislative Procedure.* Hartford: Connecticut Public Expenditures Council, 1944.

1310. Connecticut Public Expenditures Council. *The Structure of Connecticut's State Government.* Hartford: Connecticut Public Expenditures Council, 1968.

1311. Cornell, J. A. "Power of Connecticut Legislature Over Courts." *Connecticut Bar Journal* 17 (Apr. 1943): 123–166.

1312. Daniels, Bruce C. "Democracy and Oligarchy in Connecticut Towns: General Assembly Officeholding, 1701–1790." *Social Science Quarterly* 56 (Dec. 1975): 460–476.

1313. Davis, I. Ridgeway. *The Effects of Reapportionment on the Connecticut Legislature: Decade of the Sixties.* New York: National Municipal League, 1972.

1314. "Establishment vs. Free Exercise—Exclusion of Clergy from State Legislative Office Upheld." *Connecticut Law Review* 10 (Winter 1978): 470–486.

1315. Hall, Frances P. *The Connecticut General Assembly: Proposals for Reform.* New York: New School for Social Research, 1968.

1316. Harmon, Robert B. *Government and Politics in Connecticut: An Information Source Survey.* Monticello, IL: Vance Bibliographies, 1978.

1317. Haugherty, James H. *An Outline of Government in Connecticut.* Hartford: Case, Parkwood, and Brainard, 1945.

1318. Humphrey, E. F. "Connecticut's Colonial Committee System." *Connecticut Bar Journal* 10 (Oct. 1936): 239–247.

1319. Lockard, Duane. "Connecticut: The Politics of Competition, and Connecticut—Legislative Politics and Party Competition." In

Connecticut

New England State Politics. Princeton: Princeton University Press, 1959, pp. 226–269.

1320. Lockard, Duane. *Connecticut's Challenge Primary: A Study in Legislative Politics*. New York: Holt, 1959.

1321. Lockard, Duane. "Legislative Politics in Connecticut." *American Political Science Review* 48 (Mar. 1954): 166–173.

1322. Lockard, Duane. "The Role of Party in the Connecticut General Assembly, 1931–1951." Ph.D. dissertation, Yale University, 1952.

1323. Mars, David. "The Connecticut Mock Legislature." *State Government* 28 (June 1955): 137–140.

1324. Moffett, Anthony J. *Nobody's Business: The Political Intruder's Guide to Everyone's State Legislature*. Riverside, CT: Chatham Press, 1973.

1325. Murray, Mary. "Connecticut's Depression Governor: Wilbur L. Cross." *Connecticut History* 16 (Aug. 1975): 44–64.

1326. Naylor, M. A. "The General Assembly and Its Legislative Reference Service." *Connecticut Bar Journal* 20 (Aug. 1946): 1024–1026.

1327. Ogle, David B. "Joint Committee Operations and Bill Procedures in Connecticut." *State Government* 47 (Summer 1974): 170–174.

1328. Ogle, David B. *Strengthening the Connecticut Legislature*. New Brunswick, NJ: Rutgers University Press, 1970.

1329. Ransom, David F. "James G. Batterson and the New State House." *Connecticut Historical Society Bulletin* 45 (Jan. 1980): 1–15.

1330. Riege, John H. "Representation in the General Assembly: Some Aspects of the Present System." *Connecticut Bar Journal* 22 (June 1948): 135–148.

1331. Rodnick, David. "Group Frustrations in Connecticut." *American Journal of Sociology* 47 (Sept. 1941): 155–166.

1332. Satter, Robert. "The Role of Connecticut's Legislative Counsel: A Case Study." *State Government* 53 (Autumn 1980): 185–187.

1333. Smith, Edwin O. "A Memorandum Concerning Sessions of the General Assembly." *Connecticut Bar Journal* 20 (Oct. 1946): 332–342.

1334. *The Structure of Connecticut's State Government*. Hartford: Connecticut Public Expenditures Council, 1955.

1335. Tilson, J. Q. "Recent Changes in Legislative Procedure." *Connecticut Bar Journal* 19 (Apr. 1945): 54–66.

1336. University of Connecticut. Institute of Public Service. *Law Making in Connecticut: An Explanation of the Procedure Followed in Enacting Bills into Law.* Storrs: University of Connecticut, Institute of Public Service, 1951.

1337. Valenti, J. J., and R. T. Galiette. *The Problem of Representation: A Review of Connecticut's General Assembly.* New Haven: League of Independent Voters, 1963.

1338. "We Recommend: Taxpayers Group Shows Connecticut the Way to Better Government." *Tax Outlook* (Aug. 1955): 6–10.

Delaware

1339. Dolan, Paul. *The Government and Administration of Delaware.* New York: Crowell, 1956.

1340. Peltier, David P. "Party Development and Voter Participation in Delaware, 1792–1811." *Delaware History* 14 (Oct. 1970): 77–97.

1341. Schwartz, Sally. "The Old State House: A Study of Its Origins and Construction." *Delaware History* 17 (Spring-Summer 1977): 179–190.

Florida

1342. Baker, M. L. "The Legislature Has Done Its Work—Some Changes of Interest to Lawyers." *Florida Law Journal* 15 (July 1941): 259–261.

1343. Bartley, Ernest R. *The Legislative Process in Florida.* Gainesville: University of Florida, Public Administration Clearing Service, 1950.

1344. Beardsley, Janet. "Florida: The Transformation of a Legislature." *State Legislatures* 7 (Jan. 1981): 19–22.

1345. Beth, Loren P., and William Havard. "Committee Stacking and Political Power in Florida." *Journal of Politics* 23 (Feb. 1961): 157–183.

1346. Carter, Edward F. "The Unicameral Legislative System." *Florida Law Journal* 21 (May 1947): 112–115.

Florida　　　　　　　　　　　　　　　　　　　　　　　　　　　　　　　　　　105

1347. Carver, Joan S. "Women in Florida." *Journal of Politics* 41 (Aug. 1979): 941–955.

1348. Catterson, Lorace E. *The Legislative Process in Florida.* Tallahassee: Florida State University, 1951.

1349. Caver, Manning J., et al. *Should Florida Adopt the Proposed Constitution?* Gainesville: University of Florida, Public Administration Service, 1968.

1350. Citizens Constitution Committee of Florida. *Florida's Constitution: Need for Change in the Legislative Article.* St. Petersburg: Citizens Constitution Committee of Florida, 1951.

1351. Colburn, David R., and Richard K. Scher. "Race Relations and Florida Gubernatorial Politics Since the *Brown* Decision." *Florida Historical Quarterly* 55 (Oct. 1976): 153–169.

1352. Dauer, Manning J., and Gladys Kammerer. *Legislative Power to Revise Constitution.* Gainesville: University of Florida, Public Administration Clearing Service, 1964.

1353. Dixon, K. H. "Reapportionment and Reform: The Florida Experience." *National Civic Review* 62 (Nov. 1973): 548–553.

1354. Dovell, J. E. "Apportionment in State Legislatures: Its Practice in Florida." *Economic Leaflets* 7 (Feb. 1948): 1–4.

1355. Doyle, Wilson K., Angus Laird, and S. Weiss. *The Government and Administration of Florida.* New York: Crowell, 1954.

1356. Echols, Margaret T., and Austin Ranney. "The Impact of Interparty Competition Reconsidered: The Case of Florida." *Journal of Politics* 38 (Feb. 1976): 142–152.

1357. Feibelman, Herbert U. "Shall We Abolish the Bicameral Legislature?" *Florida Law Journal* 8 (Nov. 1934): 168–170.

1358. Florida Institute of Government. *Orientation Course for New House Members.* Gainesville: Florida Institute of Government, 1949.

1359. Flory, Claude R. "Marcellus L. Stearns, Florida's Last Reconstruction Governor." *Florida Historical Quarterly* 44 (Jan. 1966): 181–192.

1360. Flynt, Wayne. "William V. Knott and the Gubernatorial Campaign of 1916." *Florida Historical Quarterly* 51 (Apr. 1973): 423–430.

1361. Grobman, Hulda. *Alternatives in a Revision of Florida's Constitution: The Legislative Article (Article 3).* St. Petersburg: Citizens Constitution Committee of Florida, 1951.

1362. Havard, William C. *Your Florida Government.* Gainesville: University of Florida, Public Administration Clearing Service, 1959.

1363. Havard, William C., and Loren P. Beth. *The Politics of Mis-Representation: Rural-Urban Conflict in the Florida Legislature.* Baton Rouge: Louisiana State University Press, 1962.

1364. Havard, William C., and L. P. Beth. *Representative Government and Reapportionment: A Case Study of Florida.* Gainesville: University of Florida, Public Administration Clearing Service, 1960.

1365. Hester, Lewis A. "An Exploratory Study of the Florida Legislature's View of the Rule of the Executive Branch of Government in the Enactment of Administrative Bills." M.A. thesis, Florida State University, 1960.

1366. Horowitz, Sol D., and Frank Strahan. "The Unicameral Legislative System." *Florida Law Journal* 10 (July 1936): 239–243.

1367. Hume, Richard L. "Membership of the Florida Constitutional Convention of 1868: A Case Study of Republican Factionalism in the Reconstruction South." *Florida Historical Quarterly* 51 (July 1972): 1–21.

1368. Johnson, Dozier. "The Florida Legislature Appropriations System." *State Government* 49 (Winter 1976): 43–46.

1369. "Legislative Efforts to Amend the Florida Constitution: The Implications of Smathers vs. Smith." *Florida State University Law Review* 5 (Fall 1977): 747–808.

1370. Leroy, David J., and Leslie F. Smith. "Perceived Ethicality of Some TV News Production Techniques by a Sample of Florida Legislators." *Speech Monographics* 40 (Nov. 1973): 326–329.

1371. Levine, E. Lester, and William H. Creamer. *The Florida Legislature: A Bibliography.* Gainesville: University of Florida, Public Administration Clearing House, 1970.

1372. Lyle, Mary L. "The 1980 Florida Legislative System and the Passage of an Omnibus Postsecondary Education Bill." Ph.D. dissertation, University of Florida, 1981.

1373. McDonell, Victoria H. "Rise of the 'Businessman's Politician': The 1924 Florida Gubernatorial Race." *Florida Historical Quarterly* 52 (July 1973): 39–50.

1374. Morris, Allen, and Amelia Rea Maguire. "Beginnings of Popular Government in Florida." *Florida Historical Quarterly* 57 (July 1978): 19–38.

Florida

1375. Morris, Allen, and Amelia Rea Maguire. "The Unicameral Legislature in Florida." *Florida Historical Quarterly* 58 (Jan. 1980): 303–314.

1376. "Multi-Member Legislative Districts: Requiem for a Constitutional Burial." *University of Florida Law Review* 29 (Summer 1977): 703–729.

1377. Parsons, Malcolm B. "Quasi-Partisan Conflict in a One-Party Legislative System: The Florida Senate, 1947–61." *American Political Science Review* 56 (Sept. 1962): 605–614,

1378. Rackleff, Robert B. "Anti-Catholicism and the Florida Legislature, 1911–1919." *Florida Historical Quarterly* 50 (Apr. 1972): 352–365.

1379. Richardson, Joe M. "Jonathan C. Gibbs: Florida's Only Negro Cabinet Member." *Florida Historical Quarterly* 42 (Apr. 1964): 353–368.

1380. Roady, Elston, and Carl D. McMurray. *Republican Campaign Financing in Florida, 1963–1967.* Princeton, NJ: Citizens' Research Foundation, 1969.

1381. Roberts, Derrell C. "Social Legislation in Reconstruction Florida." *Florida Historical Quarterly* 43 (Apr. 1965): 349–360.

1382. Rogers, W. H. "What We May Learn from Our Experience with the 1935 Legislature." *Florida Law Journal* 10 (Jan. 1936): 3–9.

1383. Schuck, Victoria. "Dissecting Florida's Legislature: Analysis of Personnel." *State Government* 13 (Mar. 1940): 45–47.

1384. Shofner, Jerrell H. "Custom, Law, and History: The Enduring Influence of Florida's 'Black Code.'" *Florida Historical Quarterly* 55 (Jan. 1977): 277–298.

1385. Shofner, Jerrell H. "A Note on Governor George F. Drew." *Florida Historical Quarterly* 48 (Apr. 1970): 412–414.

1386. Shofner, Jerrell H. "Political Reconstruction in Florida." *Florida Historical Quarterly* 45 (Oct. 1966): 145–170.

1387. Smith, C. Lynwood. *Strengthening the Florida Legislature.* New Brunswick, NJ: Rutgers University Press, 1970.

1388. Todd, John R. "Reapportionment and Legislative Outputs: A Florida Case Study." Ph.D. dissertation, University of Florida, 1971.

1389. Turnbull, Augustus B. "Staff Impact on Policy Development in the Florida Legislature." *Policy Studies Journal* 5 (Summer 1977): 450–454.

1390. University of Florida. Public Administration Clearing Service. *Florida's Population, 1920–1950: The Urban Trend and Political Representation.* Gainesville: University of Florida, Public Administration Clearing Service, 1952.

1391. University of Florida. Public Administration Clearing Service. "Research for the Legislature in Florida." *Studies in Florida Administration* 1 (1949): 93–101.

1392. Wagy, Thomas R. "Governor LeRoy Collins of Florida and the Little Rock Crisis of 1957." *Arkansas Historical Quarterly* 38 (Summer 1979): 99–115.

1393. Wagy, Thomas R. "Governor LeRoy Collins of Florida and the Selma Crisis of 1965." *Florida Historical Quarterly* 57 (Apr. 1979): 403–420.

1394. Weiss, S. S. "Legislative Council and Reference Bureau." *Florida Law Journal* 25 (Feb. 1951): 57–59.

1395. Whitfield, J. B. "The President of the Senate and Gubernatorial Succession." *Florida Law Review* 19 (Mar. 1945): 116–118.

1396. Worman, Michael A. "Personal Aides in the Florida State Legislative Process." Ph.D. dissertation, Florida State University, 1972.

1397. Worthley, John A., and Jack Overstreet. "Modern Technology Applied to Traditional Political Functions: The Florida Senate Ombudsman Program." *Polity* 11 (Winter 1978): 280–289.

Georgia

1398. Cornelius, William G. "The County Unit System of Georgia." *Western Political Quarterly* 14 (Dec. 1961): 942–960.

1399. Coulter, E. Merton. "Aaron Alporia Bradley, Georgia Negro Politician During Reconstruction Times." *Georgia Historical Quarterly* 51 (Mar. 1967): 15–41.

1400. Coulter, E. Merton. "Tunis G. Campbell, Negro Reconstructionist in Georgia." *Georgia Historical Quarterly* 51 (Dec. 1967): 401–424.

1401. Elson, Charles Myer. "The Georgia Three-Governor Controversy of 1947." *Atlanta History Bulletin* 20 (Fall 1976): 72–95.

1402. Gosnell, Cullen B. "Rotten Boroughs in Georgia." *National Municipal Review* 20 (July 1931): 395–397.

1403. Gosnell, Cullen B., and C. David Anderson. *The Government and Administration of Georgia.* New York: Crowell, 1956.

1404. Harmon, Robert B. *Government and Politics in Georgia: An Information Source Survey.* Monticello, IL: Vance Bibliographies, 1978.

1405. Hawkins, B. W., and C. Whelchel. "Reapportionment and Urban Representation in Legislative Influence Positions: The Case of Georgia." *Urban Affairs Quarterly* 3 (Mar. 1968): 69–80.

1406. Huff, Lawrence. "Joseph Addison Turner's Role in Georgia Politics, 1851–1860." *Georgia Historical Quarterly* 50 (Mar. 1966): 1–13.

1407. Jackson, Edwin L. *Handbook for Georgia Legislators.* 8th ed. Athens: University of Georgia, Institute of Government, 1980.

1408. McDaniel, Ruth Currie. "Black Power in Georgia: William A. Pledger and the Takeover of the Republican Party." *Georgia Historical Quarterly* 62 (Fall 1978): 225–239.

1409. McDuffie, James M. "An Examination of the Reciprocal Perceptions of Legislators and Executives in Georgia State Government." D.P.A. dissertation, University of Georgia, 1980.

1410. Murray, Richard M., ed. "'One Man, One Vote'—1860 Style." *Georgia Historical Quarterly* 53 (Dec. 1969): 518–521.

1411. Nightingale, Bernard. "The Legislative Program and the Georgia General Assembly." *Georgia Local Government Journal* 3 (Nov. 1953): 15–19.

1412. Pepper, H. C. *The Legislative Process in Georgia.* Atlanta: University of Georgia, School of Business Administration, Atlanta Division, Division of Research, 1955.

1413. Pound, Merritt B. *The State Legislature: Two Houses or One?* Athens: University of Georgia, Division of Publications, 1938.

1414. Pound, Merritt B., and J. Thomas Askew. *The Government of Georgia.* Oklahoma City: Harlow, 1959.

1415. Roberts, Derrell C. "Governor Joseph E. Brown of Georgia and the Texas and Pacific Railroad." *West Texas Historical Association Yearbook* 46 (1970): 184–186.

1416. Saye, Albert B. "The Extent of State Legislative Power." *Georgia Bar Journal* 12 (Nov. 1949): 147–152.

1417. Saye, Albert B. *Georgia Government and History*. Evanston, IL: Peterson, 1957.

1418. Shaeffer, John N. "Georgia's 1789 Constitution: Was It Adopted in Defiance of the Constitutional Amending Process?" *Georgia Historical Quarterly* 61 (Winter 1977): 329–341.

1419. Sharkansky, Ira. "Reapportionment and Roll Call Voting: The Case of the Georgia Legislature." *Social Science Quarterly* 51 (June 1970): 129–137.

1420. Skelton, Lynda W. "The States Rights Movement in Georgia, 1825–1850." *Georgia Historical Quarterly* 50 (Dec. 1966): 391–412.

1421. Thomason, Hugh M. "The Legislative Process in Georgia." Ph.D. dissertation, Emory University, 1961.

1422. University of Georgia. Institute of Government. *Strengthening the Georgia General Assembly: Research Papers*. Athens: University of Georgia, Institute of Government, 1970.

1423. Walton, Brian G. "Georgia's Biennial Legislatures, 1840–1860, and Their Elections to the U.S. Senate." *Georgia Historical Quarterly* 61 (Summer 1977): 140–155.

Hawaii

1424. *Hawaii Legislators' Handbook*. 8th ed. Rev. by Richard F. Kahle. Honolulu: Legislative Reference Bureau, 1983.

1425. Lau, K. K. *Reapportionment of the Territorial Legislature*. Honolulu: University of Hawaii, Legislative Reference Bureau, 1958.

1426. Meller, Norman, and Robert Kamins. "The Short-Form Bill in Hawaii." *State Government* 3 (June 1958): 116–119.

1427. Okaji, Dick H. "The Legislature of the Territory of Hawaii: Its Organization, Structure, Procedure, Powers and Functions." M.A. thesis, University of Missouri, 1951.

1428. Spitz, Allan. "The Transplantation of American Democratic Institutions: The Case of Hawaii." *Political Science Quarterly* 82 (Sept. 1967): 386–398.

Idaho

1429. Garoury, William J. "From Statehouse to Bull Pen: Idaho Populism and the Coeur d'Alene Troubles of the 1890's." *Pacific Northwest Quarterly* 58 (Jan. 1967): 14–22.

1430. Huckshorn, Robert J., et al. *The Idaho Legislature.* Moscow: University of Idaho, Bureau of Public Affairs Research, 1960.

1431. Kinney, Richard S. "Decisions and Roles of Executive and Legislative Officials in the Idaho State Budgetary Process." Ph.D. dissertation, University of Notre Dame, 1980.

1432. Lewis, William O. *Staff Agencies for the Idaho Legislature.* Moscow: University of Idaho, Bureau of Public Affairs Research, 1962.

1433. Limbaugh, Ronald H. "The Carpetbag Image: Idaho Governors in Myth and Reality." *Pacific Northwest Quarterly* 60 (Apr. 1969): 77–83.

1434. Lujan, Herman D. "The Rural Electorate in Idaho." *Rocky Mountain Social Science Journal* 5 (Oct. 1968): 97–105.

1435. Malone, Michael J. "C. Ben Ross: Idaho's Cowboy Governor." *Idaho Yesterdays* 10 (Winter 1966–1967): 2–9.

1436. The Montana-Idaho Assembly on State Legislatures. *Profiles: The Idaho Legislature, the Montana Legislative Assembly.* Missoula: University of Montana, 1966.

1437. Smylie, Robert E. "The Pre-Legislative Budget in Idaho." *State Government* 31 (May 1958): 83–84.

1438. "Territorial Governors of Idaho." *Idaho Yesterdays* 7 (Spring 1963): 14–23.

Illinois

1439. Andrews, James H. *Private Groups in Illinois Government.* Urbana: University of Illinois, Institute of Government and Public Affairs, 1965.

1440. Anton, Thomas J. *The Politics of State Expenditure in Illinois.* Urbana: University of Illinois Press, 1966.

1441. "Apportionment Passes Illinois Legislature." *National Municipal Review* 42 (Oct. 1953): 458.

1442. Bernardini, C. R. "Legislative Investigations in Illinois: Due Process of Law or Procedural Vacuum? A Proposal." *Chicago Bar Record* 56 (Mar.-Apr. 1975): 282–286.

1443. Blair, George S. "The Case for Cumulative Voting in Illinois." *Northwestern University Law Review* 47 (July-Aug. 1952): 344–357.

1444. Blair, George S. *Cumulative Voting: An Effective Electoral Device in Illinois Politics.* Urbana: University of Illinois Press, 1960.

1445. Blair, George S. "Cumulative Voting: Patterns of Party Allegiance and Rational Choice in Illinois State Legislative Contests." *American Political Science Review* 52 (Mar. 1958): 123–130.

1446. Bogert, G. T., and W. S. Singer. "Legislative Apportionment in Illinois: Mandate and Opportunity." *Chicago Bar Record* 49 (June 1968): 378–383.

1447. Borit, G. S. "Lincoln and Taxation During His Legislative Years." *Journal of the Illinois State Historical Society* 61 (Autumn 1968): 365–373.

1448. Buenker, John D. "The Illinois Legislature and Prohibition, 1907–1919." *Journal of the Illinois State Historical Society* 62 (Winter 1969): 363–384.

1449. Carlson, Theodore L. *Illinois Government and Institutions, with Correlative Materials on the Declaration of Independence, the Constitution of the United States of America and the Constitution of Illinois.* Boston: Allyn and Bacon, 1962.

1450. Carpentier, Charles F. "Prairie State's Elephant: History of the Republican Party in Illinois." *Illinois History* 15 (Apr. 1962): 147–150.

1451. Cassidy, John Thomas. "The Issue of Freedom in Illinois: Under Gov. Edward Coles, 1822–1826." *Journal of the Illinois State Historical Society* 57 (Autumn 1964): 284–288.

1452. Civic Federation of Chicago. *How the Illinois Legislature Operates.* Chicago: Civic Federation of Chicago, 1944.

1453. Civic Federation of Chicago. *The Illinois General Assembly.* Chicago: Civic Federation of Chicago, 1954.

1454. Crane, Edgar G., ed. *Illinois: Political Processes and Governmental Performance.* Dubuque, IA: Kendall/Hunt, 1980.

1455. Derge, David R., Jr. "The Power Position of the Cook County Delegation in the Illinois General Assembly, 1949–1953, as Tested by

Illinois 113

Roll-Call Votes and Committee Positions." Ph.D. dissertation, Northwestern University, 1955.

1456. Dodd, Walter F., and Sue Hutchinson Dodd. *Government in Illinois*. Chicago: University of Chicago Press, 1923.

1457. Duncan, Michael P. *Functioning of the Illinois House Committee System*. Springfield: Illinois Legislative Council, 1965.

1458. Elazar, Daniel J. "Gubernatorial Power and the Illinois and Michigan Canal: A Study of Political Development in the Nineteenth Century." *Journal of the Illinois State Historical Society* 58 (Winter 1965): 396–423.

1459. Elson, Alex. "Constitutional Revision and Reorganization of the General Assembly." *Illinois Law Review* 33 (May 1938): 15–31.

1460. Fahrnkopf, Nancy. *State and Local Government in Illinois: A Bibliography, 1954–1964*. Urbana: University of Illinois, Institute of Government and Public Affairs, 1965.

1461. Garvey, Neil F. *The Government and Administration of Illinois*. New York: Crowell, 1958.

1462. Gove, Samuel K. *Illinois State Government: A Look Ahead*. Urbana, University of Illinois, Institute of Government and Public Affairs, 1957.

1463. Gove, Samuel K. "The Implications of Legislative Reform in Illinois." In *Legislative Reform and Public Policy*, edited by Susan Welch and John G. Peters. New York: Praeger, 1977, pp. 174–187.

1464. Gove, Samuel K. *The Legislature Redistricts Illinois*. Urbana: University of Illinois, Institute of Government and Public Affairs, 1956.

1465. Gove, Samuel K. "Policy Implications of Legislative Reorganization in Illinois." In *State Legislative Innovation: Case Studies of Washington, Ohio, Florida, Illinois, Wisconsin, and California*, edited by James A. Robinson. New York: Praeger, 1973, pp. 101–135.

1466. Gove, Samuel K. *Reapportionment and the Cities: The Impact of Reapportionment on Urban Legislation in Illinois*. Chicago: Loyola University, Center for Research in Urban Government, 1968.

1467. Gove, Samuel K. "Reorganization in Illinois." *National Civic Review* 42 (Nov. 1953): 502–506.

1468. Gove, Samuel K., Richard W. Carlson, and Richard J. Carlson. *The Illinois Legislature.* Urbana: University of Illinois Press, 1976.

1469. Gove, Samuel K., and Richard J. Carlson. *An Introduction to the Illinois Assembly.* Urbana: University of Illinois, Institute of Government and Public Affairs, 1972.

1470. Gove, Samuel K., and Gilbert Y. Steiner. *The Illinois Legislative Process.* Urbana: University of Illinois, Institute of Government and Public Affairs, 1954.

1471. Greene, Evarts. *The Government of Illinois: Its History and Administration.* New York: Macmillan, 1904.

1472. Hall, William K., ed. *Illinois Government and Politics: A Reader.* Dubuque, IA: Kendall/Hunt, 1975.

1473. Harmon, Robert B. *Government and Politics in Illinois: An Information Source Survey.* Monticello, IL: Vance Bibliographies, 1978.

1474. Hatch, Richard A. "Reporters and Legislators in Illinois: Their Roles and How They Interact." Ph.D. dissertation, University of Illinois, 1969.

1475. Hedlund, Ronald D. "The Recruitment of Lobbyists: The Case of Illinois." M.A. thesis, University of Iowa, 1964.

1476. Howard, Victor B. "The Illinois Republican Party: Part I, A Party Organizer for the Republicans in 1854." *Journal of the Illinois State Historical Society* 64 (Summer 1971): 125–160.

1477. Howard, Victor B. "The Illinois Republican Party: Part II, The Party Becomes Conservative, 1855–1856." *Journal of the Illinois State Historical Society* 64 (Autumn 1971): 285–311.

1478. Hyneman, Charles S., et al. "Legislative Experience of Illinois Lawmakers." *University of Chicago Law Review* 3 (Dec. 1935): 104–118.

1479. Illinois Commission on the Organization of the General Assembly. *Improving the State Legislature: A Report.* Urbana: University of Illinois Press, 1967.

1480. *Illinois Elections: Parties, Patterns, Reapportionment, Consolidation.* Springfield, IL: Sangamon State University, 1979.

1481. Illinois General Assembly. Efficiency and Economy Committee. *Report of the Efficiency and Economy Committee Created Under*

Illinois 115

the Authority of the Forty-Eighth General Assembly, State of Illinois. Chicago: Windemere Press, 1915.

1482. "Illinois Governors, 1818–1857." *Illinois History* 15 (Mar. 1962): 132–133.

1483. *Illinois: Political Processes and Government Performance*, edited by Edgar G. Crane. Dubuque, IA: Kendall/Hunt, 1980.

1484. Jensen, Richard. "The Religious and Occupational Roots of Party Identification: Illinois and Indiana in the 1870's." *Civil War History* 16 (Dec. 1970): 325–343.

1485. Juergensmeyer, J. E. *The Campaign for the Illinois Reapportionment Amendment*. Urbana: University of Illinois, Institute of Government and Public Affairs, 1957.

1486. Keefe, William J. "Party Government and Lawmaking in Illinois General Assembly." *Northwestern University Law Review* 47 (Mar.-Apr. 1952): 55–71.

1487. Keefe, William J. "A Study of the Role of Political Parties in the Legislative Process, Illinois General Assembly." Ph.D. dissertation, Northwestern University, 1952.

1488. Kenney, David. *Basic Illinois Government: A Systematic Explanation*. Carbondale: Southern Illinois University Press, 1970.

1489. Kent, James P. "Legislative Fiscal Staffing in Illinois." In *The Political Pursestrings*, edited by Alan P. Balutis and Daron K. Butler. New York: Wiley, 1975, pp. 91–101.

1490. Kneier, Charles M. "Illinois Legislative Council Completes Its First Year." *National Municipal Review* 28 (Sept. 1939): 640–645.

1491. Kulinski, James H. "Cumulative and Plurality Voting: An Analysis of Illinois' Unique Electoral System." *Western Political Quarterly* 26 (Dec. 1973): 726–746.

1492. League of Women Voters of Illinois. *The Problem of Legislative Reapportionment in Illinois: A Comprehensive Study of State Government, the Second Year's Work, 1950–1951*. Chicago: League of Women Voters of Illinois, 1951.

1493. League of Women Voters of Illinois. *Should Your Illinois General Assembly Have Annual Sessions?* Chicago: League of Women Voters of Illinois, 1964.

1494. Littlewood, Thomas B. *Bipartisan Coalition in Illinois*. New York: McGraw-Hill, 1962.

1495. McDowell, James L. "Changes in the Apportionment System: The Illinois General Assembly, 1963–1967." Ph.D. dissertation, University of Illinois, 1972.

1496. McGriggs, Lee Augustus. *Black Legislative Politics in Illinois: A Theoretical and Structural Analysis.* Washington, D.C.: University Press of America, 1977.

1497. Moore, Blaine F. *The History of Cumulative Voting and Minority Representation in Illinois, 1870–1919.* Rev. ed. Urbana: University of Illinois, 1920.

1498. Nichols, George A. "Legislative Bill-Drafting in Illinois." *Illinois Bar Journal* 41 (Dec. 1952): 136–140.

1499. Padover, Saul K. "Altgeld of Illinois '... Eagle Forgotten.'" *American-German Review* 32 (June-July 1966): 5–8.

1500. Powell, Paul. "Prairie State's Donkey: History of the Democratic Party in Illinois." *Illinois History* 15 (Mar. 1962): 123–125.

1501. Ranney, Austin. *Illinois Politics.* New York: New York University Press, 1960.

1502. Saltiel, Edward P. "The Illinois Legislative Council." *Public Aid in Illinois* 15 (Oct. 1948): 4–6, 15.

1503. Sawyer, Jack, and Duncan MacRae. "Game Theory and Cumulative Voting in Illinois: 1902–1954." *American Political Science Review* 56 (Dec. 1962): 936–946.

1504. Shankman, Arnold. "Partisan Conflicts, 1839–1841 and the Illinois Constitution." *Journal of the Illinois State Historical Society* 63 (Winter 1970): 337–367.

1505. Sigale, Merwin K. "Press Coverage of the Illinois Legislature." M.A. thesis, University of Illinois, 1960.

1506. Simon, Paul. *Lincoln's Preparation for Greatness: The Illinois Legislative Years.* Norman: University of Oklahoma Press, 1965.

1507. Spencer, Richard C., Jack Isakoff, and Samuel K. Gove. *Lawmaking in the Illinois General Assembly.* Springfield: Illinois Legislative Council, 1963.

1508. Steiner, Gilbert Y. "Legislative Power Blocs." *Illinois Government* (Oct. 1963): 1–4.

1509. Steiner, Gilbert Y., and Samuel K. Gove. *Legislative Politics in Illinois.* Urbana: University of Illinois Press, 1960.

1510. Thomason, William R. "State Legislative Councils with Special Reference to Illinois." M.A. thesis, University of Illinois, 1954.

1511. Toussaint, George W. "Shifting Majorities in the Illinois Senate, 1955–61." M.A. thesis, University of Iowa, 1963.

1512. Tucker, Joseph P. "The Administration of a State Patronage System: The Democratic Party in Illinois." *Western Political Quarterly* 22 (Mar. 1969): 79–84.

1513. Van der Slick, Jack R., Samuel J. Pernacciaro, and David Kenney. "Patterns of Partisanship in a Nonpartisan Representational Setting: The Illinois Constitutional Convention." *American Journal of Political Science* 18 (Feb. 1974): 95–116.

1514. Waller, Robert A. "Norman L. Jones versus Len Small in the Illinois Gubernatorial Campaign of 1924." *Journal of the Illinois State Historical Society* 72 (Aug. 1979): 162–178.

1515. Wiggins, Charles W., and Janice Petty. "Cumulative Voting and Electoral Competition: The Illinois House." *American Politics Quarterly* 7 (July 1979): 345–365.

1516. Wimberly, W. C. "The Direct Primary in Illinois." Ph.D. dissertation, University of Illinois, 1957.

1517. Wood-Simons, May. "Operation of the Bicameral System in Illinois and Wisconsin." *Illinois Law Review* 20 (Mar. 1926): 674–686.

1518. Ziegler, Martha J. "Legislative Investigating Committees and Interim Commissions in Illinois Since 1900." Ph.D. dissertation, Northwestern University, 1934.

Indiana

1519. Bicker, William E. "The Assembly Party: Change and Consistency in Legislative Voting Behavior in the Indiana House, 1923–1963." Ph.D. dissertation, Indiana University, 1969.

1520. Bremmer, John A. *Legislative Procedure in the General Assembly of the State of Indiana.* Indianapolis: Indiana Legislative Council, 1972.

1521. Bridge, Franklin M. "The Making of Public Policy in the 1949 Indiana General Assembly." Ph.D. dissertation, Northwestern University, 1952.

1522. Calhoun, Charles W. "'Incessant Noise and Tumult': Walter Q. Gresham and the Indiana Legislature During the Secession Crisis." *Indiana Magazine of History* 74 (Sept. 1978): 223–251.

1523. Conway, Mary M. "Party and Constituency in the 1963 Indiana General Assembly: A Case Study of Party Responsibility." Ph.D. dissertation, Indiana University, 1965.

1524. Derge, David R. "The Lawyer in the Indiana General Assembly." *American Journal of Political Science* 6 (Feb. 1962): 19–53.

1525. Francis, Wayne L. "Interaction and Influence in the Indiana General Assembly." Ph.D. dissertation, Indiana University, 1961.

1526. Hadley, David J. "Legislative Role Orientations and Support for Party and Chief Executive in the Indiana House." *Legislative Studies Quarterly* 2 (Aug. 1977): 309–335.

1527. Hadley, David J. "Role Orientations and Roll-Call Voting: A Computer Simulation Analysis of the Indiana House of Representatives." Ph.D. dissertation, Indiana University, 1974.

1528. Hamilton, H. D., J. E. Beardsley, and C. C. Coates. "Legislative Reapportionment in Indiana: Some Observations and a Suggestion." *Notre Dame Lawyer* 35 (May 1960): 368–404.

1529. Hofstetter, C. Richard. "Malapportionment and Roll-Call Voting in Indiana, 1923–1963: A Computer Simulation." *Journal of Politics* 33 (Feb. 1971): 92–111.

1530. House, Albert V. "The Democratic State Central Committee of Indiana in 1880: A Case Study in Party Tactics and Finance." *Indiana Magazine of History* 58 (Sept. 1962): 179–210.

1531. Hoy, Suellen M. "Governor Samuel M. Ralston and Indiana's Centennial Celebration." *Indiana Magazine of History* 71 (Sept. 1975): 245–266.

1532. Hyneman, Charles S. "Tenure and Turnover in the Indiana General Assembly." *Indiana Law Journal* 32 (Summer 1957): 489–514.

1533. Hyneman, Charles S. "Tenure and Turnover of the Indiana General Assembly." *American Political Science Review* 32 (Feb., Apr. 1938): 51–67, 311–331.

1534. Hyneman, Charles S., and H. Lay. "A Statistical Study of Successive Indiana Legislatures from 1925–33." *American Political Science Review* 32 (Feb. 1938): 51–67.

1535. Indiana Legislative Council. *A Legislator's Handbook.* Indianapolis: Indiana Legislative Council, Research Department, 1973.

1536. Indiana University. Institute of Politics. *Indiana's Representatives: A Study of Background Interests and Political Trends.* Bloomington: Indiana University, Institute of Politics, 1943.

1537. Kahn, Melvin A. "Labor and the Law Making Process: The Case of Indiana." Ph.D. dissertation, Indiana University, 1969.

1538. Kessler, James B., ed. *Empirical Studies of Indiana Politics: Studies of Legislative Behavior.* Bloomington: Indiana University Press, 1970.

1539. Kessler, James B. *Pre-Legislative Conferences.* Bloomington: Indiana University, Bureau of Government Research, 1960.

1540. Key, V. O., and Frank Munger. "Social Determinism and Electoral Decision: The Case of Indiana." In *American Voting Behavior,* edited by Eugene Burdick and Arthur J. Brodbeck. Glencoe, IL: Free Press, 1959, pp. 281–299.

1541. Littell, Noble K. *One Hundred Men: A Legislative History of Morgan County, Indiana.* Martinsville, IN: n.p., 1970.

1542. Lovrich, Nicholas P., Byron W. Daynes, and Laura Ginger. "Public Policy and the Effects of Historical-Cultural Phenomena: The Case of Indiana." *Publius* 10 (Spring 1980): 111–125.

1543. McDowell, James L. *The Emperor's New Clothes? Legislative Reform in Indiana: A Report from the Center for Government Services.* Terre Haute: Indiana State University, Department of Political Science, 1976.

1544. McDowell, James L. "Legislative Reform in Indiana: The Promise and the Product." In *Legislative Reform and Public Policy,* edited by Susan Welch and John G. Peters. New York: Praeger, 1977, pp. 157–173.

1545. McPheron, Edwin B., and George B. Roberts. *Apportionment and Reapportionment in Indiana.* Bloomington: Indiana University, Bureau of Government Research, 1957.

1546. Moore, David W. "Legislative Effectiveness and Majority Party Size: A Test in the Indiana House." *Journal of Politics* 31 (Nov. 1969): 1063–1079.

1547. Nolan, Val. "Unicameralism and the Indiana Constitutional Convention of 1850." *Indiana Law Journal* 26 (Spring 1951): 349–359.

1548. Pierce, Melvin. "Third House in Indiana." *National Civic Review* 40 (Oct. 1951): 473–549.

1549. Scholten, Pat C. "A Public 'Jollification': The 1859 Women's Rights Petition Before the Indiana Legislature." *Indiana Magazine of History* 72 (Dec. 1976): 347–359.

1550. Shepherd, Rebecca A., comp. and ed. *A Biographical Directory of the Indiana General Assembly.* Indianapolis: Indiana Historical Bureau, 1980–.

1551. Sikes, Pressly S. *Indiana State and Local Government.* Bloomington: Principia Press, 1946.

1552. Sikes, Pressly S. "Special Interim Commissions in the Indiana Legislative Process." *American Political Science Review* 36 (Oct. 1942): 906–915.

1553. Teune, Henry J. "Indiana Legislative Candidates' Attitudes Towards Interest Groups." Ph.D. dissertation, Indiana University, 1961.

1554. Wallace, L. J. "Legislative Apportionment In Indiana: A Case History." *Indiana Law Journal* 42 (Fall 1966): 6–76.

1555. Wathen, Richard B. *Wathen's Law.* Chicago: Regnery Gateway, 1981.

1556. Wilbern, York Y., and D. H. Clark. "Prelegislative Conferences in Indiana." *State Government* 32 (Winter 1959): 43–46.

Iowa

1557. Bower, Robert K. "Frontier Stone: The Story of Iowa's Old Capital." *Palimpsest* 57 (July-Aug. 1976): 98–120.

1558. DeWitt, Paul B. "A Technical Drafting Service for the General Assembly." *Iowa Bar Review* 4 (May 1938): 95–102.

1559. Dykstra, Robert R., and Russell M. Ross. "Toward Adjournment: The Second Session of the 65th General Assembly." *Palimpsest* 55 (Nov.-Dec. 1974): 184–189.

1560. Gold, David, and John Schmidhauser. "Urbanization and Party Competition: The Case of Iowa." *Midwest Journal of Political Science* 4 (Feb. 1960): 62–75.

Iowa

1561. Hahn, Harlan. "Turnover in Iowa State Party Conventions: An Exploratory Study." *American Journal of Political Science* 11 (Feb. 1967): 98–105.

1562. Hedlund, Ronald D. "Legislative Socialization and Role Orientations: A Study of the Iowa Legislature." Ph.D. dissertation, University of Iowa, 1967.

1563. Horack, Frank E. "The Sifting Committee as a Legislative Expedient." *Iowa Journal of History and Politics* 32 (Oct. 1934): 291–311.

1564. Hyneman, Charles S., and Edmond F. Ricketts. "Tenure and Turnover of the Iowa Legislature." *Iowa Law Review* 24 (May 1939): 673–696.

1565. Iowa State College. Advisory Council for Iowa Economic Studies. *Helping Iowa's Legislature*. Ames: Iowa State College, Advisory Council for Iowa Economic Studies, 1949.

1566. Junkins, Lowell L. "Changes in Legislative Procedure: The Iowa Experiment." *State Government* 51 (Winter 1978): 173–179.

1567. *Legislative Sub-Districting: Applying a Technique and Identifying Alternatives—A Case Study in Iowa*. Des Moines, IA: Bureau of Governmental Research, 1966.

1568. Leiden, Carl. "Legislative Districting in Iowa." Ph.D. dissertation, University of Iowa, 1949.

1569. Nye, Frank T. "Reapportionment in Iowa." *Palimpsest* 45 (June 1964): 241–272.

1570. Nye, Frank T. "The 60th General Assembly of Iowa." *Palimpsest* 44 (Oct. 1963): 445–500.

1571. Nye, Frank T. "The 61st General Assembly of Iowa." *Palimpsest* 46 (Sept. 1965): 425–487.

1572. Nye, Frank T. "The 62d General Assembly of Iowa." *Palimpsest* 48 (Nov. 1967): 505–568.

1573. Nye, Frank T. "The 63d General Assembly of Iowa." *Palimpsest* 50 (Oct. 1969): 545–608.

1574. Nye, Frank T. "The 63d General Assembly of Iowa." *Palimpsest* 51 (July 1970): 281–320.

1575. Nye, Frank T. "The 64th General Assembly of Iowa." *Palimpsest* 52 (Sept. 1971): 433–496.

1576. Nye, Frank T. "The 64th General Assembly of Iowa." *Palimpsest* 53 (June 1972): 257–286.

1577. Patterson, Samuel C., and G. R. Boynton. *Citizens, Leaders, and Legislators: Perspectives on Support for the American Legislature.* Beverly Hills, CA: Sage, 1974.

1578. Patterson, Samuel C., Ronald D. Hedlund, and G. Robert Boynton. *Representatives and Represented: Bases of Public Support for the American Legislatures.* New York: Wiley, 1975.

1579. Poldervaart, Arie. "Legislation by Reference—A Statutory Jungle." *Iowa Law Review* 38 (Summer 1953): 705–737.

1580. Richardson, Ivan L. "Committee Structure of the Iowa General Assembly, 1949." Ph.D. dissertation, University of Iowa, 1951.

1581. Ross, Russell M. *The Government and Administration of Iowa.* New York: Crowell, 1957.

1582. Ross, Russell M. "Iowa Government in Action." *Palimpsest* 46 (Nov. 1965): 558–608.

1583. Schaffter, Dorothy. *The Bicameral System in Practice.* Iowa City: State Historical Society of Iowa, 1929.

1584. Wiggins, Charles W. "Interest Group Power Within State Legislative Systems: The Case of the Iowa Farm Bureau Federation." Ph.D. dissertation, Washington University, 1964.

1585. Wiggins, Charles W. *The Legislative Process in Iowa.* Ames: Iowa State University Press, 1972.

1586. Wiggins, Charles W. "Party Politics in the Iowa Legislature." *Midwest Journal of Political Science* 11 (Feb. 1967): 86–97.

Kansas

1587. Abernathy, Byron R. *Constitutional Limitations on the Legislature.* Lawrence: University of Kansas, Governmental Research Center, 1960.

1588. Barnard, Bernard L. "The Legislature of Kansas: An Appraisal." Ph.D. dissertation, American University, 1949.

1589. "Better Laws Through Research: Kansas Legislative Council Founded in 1933, the First of Its Kind." *National Municipal Review* 34 (Dec. 1945): 544–546.

1590. Bibb, J. W., and F. H. Guild. "Kansas Legislative School." *State Government* 34 (Winter 1961): 52–54.

1591. Boertman, C. Stewart. *Apportionment in the Kansas House of Representatives*. Emporia: Kansas State Teachers College, Graduate Division, 1952.

1592. Bonett, Herman R. "Information Processes in a State Legislative System: Kansas." Ph.D. dissertation, University of Kansas, 1976.

1593. Bonett, Herman R. "Legislative Lobbying in Kansas." *Your Government* 23 (Nov. 1967): 3–4.

1594. Brandner, Daniel C. "Kansas Legislative Council." M.A. thesis, Northwestern University, 1941.

1595. Cape, William H., and John P. Bay. *An Analysis of the Kansas Legislative Council and Its Research Department*. Lawrence: University of Kansas, Governmental Research Center, 1963.

1596. Cole, Albert M. "The Kansas Legislature and Congress—A Study in Contrasts." *Kansas Judicial Council Bulletin* 26 (Oct. 1952): 44–47.

1597. Corrick, Franklin. "General Statutes Publication in Kansas." *Journal of the Bar Association of Kansas* 15 (Feb. 1947): 248–254.

1598. Corrick, Franklin. "Legislative Developments in Kansas Since 1941." *Journal of the Bar Association of Kansas* 15 (Aug. 1946): 5–14.

1599. Corrick, Franklin. "Report on the Accomplishments of the 1945 Kansas Legislature." *Journal of the Bar Association of Kansas* 13 (May 1945): 291–327.

1600. Drury, James W., et al. *The Government of Kansas*. Lawrence: University Press of Kansas, 1961.

1601. Drury, James W., and J. E. Titus. *Legislative Apportionment in Kansas: 1960*. Lawrence: University of Kansas, Governmental Research Center, 1960.

1602. Fenton, William. *The Office of the Kansas Revisor of Statutes*. Lawrence: University of Kansas, Governmental Research Center, 1965.

1603. Flentje, Henry E. "The Legislative System: A Kansas Case." Ph.D. dissertation, University of Kansas, 1970.

1604. Grimes, Marcene. "Turnover in the Kansas Legislature, 1901–1957." *Your Government* 12 (Dec. 1956): 1–2.

1605. Guild, Frederic H. "Achievements of the Kansas Legislative Council." *American Political Science Review* 29 (Aug. 1935): 636–639.

1606. Guild, Frederic H. "The Kansas Legislative Council Considers War Legislation." *State Government* 16 (Feb. 1943): 35–37.

1607. Guild, Frederic H. *Legislative Procedure in Kansas.* Lawrence: University of Kansas, Governmental Research Center, 1956.

1608. Harder, Marvin A., and Carolyn Rampey. *The Kansas Legislature: Procedures, Personalities, and Problems.* Lawrence: University Press of Kansas, 1972.

1609. Harder, Marvin A., and Raymond Davis. *The Legislature as an Organization: A Study of the Kansas Legislature.* Lawrence: Regents Press of Kansas, 1979.

1610. Lujan, Herman D. "The Demographic Basis of Kansas Republicanism." *Rocky Mountain Social Science Journal* 6 (Oct. 1969): 82–90.

1611. McCoy, Donald R. "Alfred M. Landon, Western Governor." *Pacific Northwest Quarterly* 57 (July 1966): 120–126.

1612. McDonald, James T. *Decisions of the 1963 Kansas Legislature.* Lawrence: University of Kansas, Governmental Research Center, 1963.

1613. McDonald, James T. *Decisions of the 1964 Budget and Special Sessions of the Kansas Legislature.* Lawrence: University of Kansas, Governmental Research Center, 1964.

1614. McDonald, James T. *Decisions of the 1965 Kansas Legislature.* Lawrence: University of Kansas, Governmental Research Center, 1965.

1615. Meerse, David E. "'No Propriety in the Late Course of the Governor': The Geary-Sherrard Affair Reexamined." *Kansas Historical Quarterly* 42 (Autumn 1976): 237–262.

1616. Miller, M. C., et al. "Inherent Power of the Legislative Body to Convene Itself." *Journal of the Bar Association of Kansas* 9 (Nov. 1940): 185–191.

1617. Otis, M. "Toward a House Decree." *Kansas Judicial Council Bulletin* 27 (Apr. 1953): 4–5.

1618. Page, Thomas. "Legislative Apportionment in Kansas." Ph.D. dissertation, University of Minnesota, 1952.

1619. Parrish, William E. "The Great Kansas Legislative Imbroglio of 1893." *Journal of the West* 7 (Oct. 1968): 471–490.

1620. Smith, Rhoten A. *The Life of a Bill.* Lawrence: University of Kansas, Governmental Research Center, 1961.

1621. Smith, Stephen N. "Legislative Reapportionment in Kansas in the 1960's: A Case Study." Ph.D. dissertation, University of Kansas, 1970.

1622. Strain, Camden S. "The Kansas Legislative Council." *National Municipal Review* 22 (Sept. 1933): 462–463.

1623. Titus, James E. "Kansas Governors: A Resume of Political Leadership." *Western Political Quarterly* 17 (June 1964): 356–370.

1624. Toll, Henry W. "Aiding State Legislators." *Journal of the Bar Association of Kansas* 1 (May 1933): 296–300.

1625. Traylor, Jack W. "William Allen White's 1924 Gubernatorial Campaign." *Kansas Historical Quarterly* 42 (Summer 1976): 180–191.

1626. University of Kansas. Bureau of Government Research. *The Kansas Legislature—Its Organization and Work.* Lawrence: University of Kansas, Bureau of Government Research, 1946.

1627. University of Kansas. Bureau of Government Research. *The Kansas Legislative Council.* Lawrence: University of Kansas, Bureau of Government Research, 1947.

1628. University of Kansas. Bureau of Government Research. *Legislative Procedure in Kansas.* Lawrence: University of Kansas, Bureau of Government Research, 1930.

1629. Wilson, Don W. "Charles Robinson, First Governor of Kansas." Ph.D. dissertation, University of Cincinnati, 1972.

Kentucky

1630. Clift, G. Glenn. *Bibliography of the House and Senate Journals, Commonwealth of Kentucky, 1792–1966.* Frankfort: Kentucky Historical Society, 1967.

1631. Cox, Gary S. "The Kentucky Legislative Interim Committee System, 1968–1974." Ph.D. dissertation, University of Kentucky, 1975.

1632. Engstrom, Richard L. "Political Cartography in Kentucky: Legislative Redistricting, 1971." Ph.D. dissertation, University of Kentucky, 1971.

1633. Evans, Alvin E. "The Legislative Process." In *The Constitution of Kentucky: Suggestions for Revisions*. Lexington: University of Kentucky, Bureau of Government Research, 1948, pp. 63–76.

1634. Funk, A. E. "The Work of the General Assembly, 1940." *Kentucky Bar Association, Proceedings* 6 (1940): 46–69.

1635. Hardison, R. B. "Kentucky Legislature—What the Members Should Know." *Kentucky State Bar Journal* 13 (Sept. 1949): 144–145.

1636. Harmon, Robert B. *Government and Politics in Kentucky: An Information Source Survey*. Monticello, IL: Vance Bibliographies, 1978.

1637. Harrison, Lowell H. "Governor Magoffin and the Secession Crisis." *Register of the Kentucky Historical Society* 72 (Apr. 1974): 91–110.

1638. Ireland, Robert M. "The Place of the Justice of the Peace in the Legislature and Party System of Kentucky, 1792–1850." *American Journal of Legal History* 13 (July 1969): 202–222.

1639. Jewell, Malcolm E., and Everett W. Cunningham. *Kentucky Politics*. Lexington: University Press of Kentucky, 1968.

1640. Jones, J. Catron. "The Make-up of a State Legislature." *American Political Science Review* 25 (Feb. 1931): 116–119.

1641. Kammerer, Gladys M. "Advisory Committees in the Legislative Process." *Journal of Politics* 15 (May 1953): 171–196.

1642. Kammerer, Gladys M. "Kentucky Legislative Procedures Re-Evaluated." *Kentucky Law Journal* 45 (Spring 1957): 448–458.

1643. Kammerer, Gladys M. "Kentucky's Legislature Under the Spotlight." *Kentucky Law Journal* 39 (Nov. 1950): 45–63.

1644. Kammerer, Gladys M. "Legislative Oversight of Administration in Kentucky." *Public Administration Review* 10 (Summer 1950): 169–175.

1645. Kammerer, Gladys M. "Legislative Research and Planning in Kentucky." *Kentucky Law Journal* 36 (May 1948): 379–400.

1646. Kammerer, Gladys M. "Right About Face in Kentucky: State Creates Research Commission." *National Municipal Review* 37 (June 1948): 303–308.

1647. Kennedy, Philip W. "The Know-Nothing Movement in Kentucky." *Filson Club History Quarterly* 38 (Jan. 1964): 17–35.

1648. Kentucky Legislative Research Commission. *The Legislative Process in Kentucky.* Frankfort: Kentucky Legislative Research Commission, 1955.

1649. "Kentucky's Legislative Council Reorganized." *National Municipal Review* 29 (Feb. 1940): 124–125.

1650. Lloyd, Arthur, and James T. Fleming. "Kentucky's Grass Roots Survey of Education." *State Government* 26 (Aug. 1953): 194–197.

1651. Mathias, Frank F. "The Turbulent Years of Kentucky Politics, 1820–1850." *Register of the Kentucky Historical Society* 72 (Oct. 1974): 309–318.

1652. Myers, Rodes K. "Kentucky's Legislative Council in Action." *State Government* 13 (May 1940): 85–86.

1653. Norton, Wesley. "Reaction in the Religious Press to the Campaign for Delegates to the Kentucky Constitutional Convention in 1849." *Register of the Kentucky Historical Society* 60 (Apr. 1962): 143–152.

1654. Peters, H. Dean. "Isaac Shelby and the Gubernatorial Campaign of 1812." *Register of the Kentucky Historical Society* 73 (Oct. 1975): 340–345.

1655. Reeves, John E. "Redistricting." *Kentucky Law Journal* 41 (Nov. 1952): 60–62.

1656. Reeves, John E., and John P. De Marcus. *Kentucky Government.* 6th ed. Frankfort: Kentucky Legislative Research Commission, 1972.

1657. Stewart, R. B. "Committee System of the Kentucky House of Representatives, 1932." *Kentucky Law Journal* 22 (Jan. 1934): 298–303.

1658. Sullivan, Rodman. "Some Quantitative Aspects of Legislation in Kentucky." *Kentucky Law Journal* 34 (Jan. 1946): 118–137.

1659. University of Kentucky. Bureau of Government Research. *The Constitution of Kentucky: Suggestions for Revision.* Lexington: University of Kentucky, Bureau of Government Research, 1948.

1660. University of Kentucky. Bureau of Government Research. *Legislative and Congressional Redistricting in Kentucky.* Lexington: University of Kentucky, Bureau of Government Research, 1951.

1661. University of Kentucky. Bureau of Government Research. *The Process of Government.* Lexington: University of Kentucky, Bureau of Government Research, 1949.

1662. Vanlandingham, Kenneth E. *The Constitution and Local Government.* Frankfort: Kentucky Legislative Research Commission, 1964.

1663. Williamson, C. G. "Post-census Redistricting—A Primer for State Legislators." *Kentucky Law Journal* 59 (Winter 1971): 386–406.

Louisiana

1664. Asseff, Emmett. *Legislative Apportionment in Louisiana.* Baton Rouge: Louisiana State University, Bureau of Government Research, 1950.

1665. Badeaux, David, and Donn M. Kurtz. "Geographical Variables and Voting in the Louisiana Legislature: A Research Note." *Louisiana Studies* 10 (Winter 1971): 257–262.

1666. Barnidge, James L. "The Louisiana Constitutional Convention of 1973: The Road to Revision." *Louisiana History* 15 (Winter 1974): 35–48.

1667. Binning, F. Wayne. "Carpetbaggers' Triumph: The Louisiana State Election of 1868." *Louisiana History* 14 (Winter 1973): 21–40.

1668. Carriere, Marius. "Political Leadership of the Louisiana Know-Nothing Party." *Louisiana History* 21 (Spring 1980): 183–195.

1669. Citizens Conference on State Legislatures. *How Citizens Can Improve the Louisiana Legislature.* Kansas City: Citizens Conference on State Legislatures, 1974.

1670. Dur, Philip F., and Donn M. Kurtz. "North-South Cleavages in Louisiana Voting." *Louisiana Studies* 10 (Spring 1971): 28–44.

1671. Edwards, Edwin W. "The Role of the Governor in Louisiana Politics: An Historical Analysis." *Louisiana History* 15 (Spring 1974): 101–116.

1672. Engstrom, Richard L., and Patrick O'Conner. "Restructuring the Regime: Support for Change within the Louisiana Constitutional Convention." *Polity* 11 (Spring 1979): 440–451.

1673. Halpin, S. A. "The Anti-Gerrymander: The Impact of Section 5 of the Voting Rights Act of 1965 upon Louisiana Parish Redistricting." Ph.D. dissertation, George Washington University, 1978.

Louisiana

1674. Havard, William C. *The Government of Louisiana.* Baton Rouge: Louisiana State University, Bureau of Public Administration, 1958.

1675. Havard, William C., and Perry H. Howard. "The Louisiana Bifactional System and the Long Era: The Beginning of the End?" *Social Science Quarterly* 44 (Sept. 1963): 157–170.

1676. Hicks, Ronald G., and E. Joseph Broussard. *Legislators Rate Media Coverage of the 1979 Louisiana Legislature.* Baton Rouge: Louisiana State University, Journalism Extension Service, 1980.

1677. Hyneman, Charles S. "Political and Administrative Reform in the 1940 Legislature." *Louisiana Law Review* 3 (Nov. 1940): 1–54.

1678. Jeansonne, Glen. "De Lesseps Morrison: Why He Couldn't Become Governor of Louisiana." *Louisiana History* 14 (Summer 1973): 255–269.

1679. Jeansonne, Glen. "Racism and Longism in Louisiana: The 1959–60 Gubernatorial Elections." *Louisiana History* 11 (Summer 1970): 259–276.

1680. Jennings, Edward T. "Some Policy Consequences of the Long Revolution and Bifactional Rivalry in Louisiana." *American Journal of Political Science* 21 (May 1977): 225–246.

1681. Jones, Howard J. "Biographical Sketches of Members of the 1868 Louisiana State Senate." *Louisiana History* 19 (Winter 1978): 65–110.

1682. King, Peter J. "Huey Long: The Louisiana Kingfish." *History Today* 14 (Mar. 1964): 151–160.

1683. Lacy, Alex B., ed. *Power in American State Legislatures: Case Studies of the Arkansas, Louisiana, Mississippi, and Oklahoma Legislatures.* New Orleans: Tulane University, 1967.

1684. Loyless, Darrell M. "The Legislative Role Orientations of Louisiana State Legislators." Ph.D. dissertation, American University, 1975.

1685. Maddox, Robert J. "The 'Kingfish.'" *American History Illustrated* 5 (May 1970): 12–24.

1686. Moreau, John A. "Huey Long and His Chronicles." *Louisiana History* 6 (Spring 1965): 121–140.

1687. Owen, Kimbrough. "Research Activity Increases in Louisiana: Variety of Agencies Seek Solution to Vital Problems." *National Municipal Review* 42 (Dec. 1953): 582–583.

1688. "Political Behavior of Lawyers in the Louisiana House of Representatives." *Louisiana Law Review* 39 (Fall 1978): 43–79.

1689. Public Affairs Research Council of Louisiana. *Improving the Louisiana Legislature.* Baton Rouge: Public Affairs Research Council of Louisiana, 1965.

1690. Reed, Germaine A. "Race Legislation in Louisiana, 1864–1920." *Louisiana History* 6 (Fall 1965): 379–392.

1691. Romero, Sidney J. "The Inaugural Addresses of the Governors of the State of Louisiana: Tweedledum-and-Tweedledee—Or Contrariwise?" *Louisiana History* 14 (Summer 1973): 229–253.

1692. Vincent, Charles. "Louisiana's Black Legislators and Their Efforts to Pass a Blue Law During Reconstruction." *Journal of Black Studies* 7 (Sept. 1976): 47–56.

1693. Vincent, Charles. "Negro Leadership and Programs in the Louisiana Constitutional Convention of 1868." *Louisiana History* 10 (Fall 1969): 339–352.

1694. Wildgen, J. K. "Measuring Malapportionment in Lousiana." *Loyola Law Review* 16 (1969–1970): 383–413.

1695. Wooster, Ralph A. "The Structure of Government in Late Antebellum Louisiana." *Louisiana Studies* 14 (Winter 1975): 361–378.

Maine

1696. Dow, Edward F. "Maine's Political Chickens Come Home to Roost." *National Municipal Review* 30 (Aug. 1941): 488–493.

1697. Johnson, Reinhard O. "The Liberty Party in Maine, 1840–1848: The Politics of Antislavery Reform." *Maine Historical Society Quarterly* 19 (Winter 1980): 135–176.

1698. Palmer, Kenneth T., et al. *The Legislature Process in Maine.* Washington, D.C.: American Political Science Association, 1973.

Maryland

1699. Bain, Henry. "Five Kinds of Politics: A Historical and Comparative Study of the Making of Legislators in Five Maryland Constituencies." Ph.D. dissertation, Harvard University, 1970.

Maryland

1700. Bartlett, J. Kemp. "Limitations on Even-Year Legislative Sessions." *Maryland Law Review* 12 (Spring 1951): 124–144.

1701. Bell, George A., and Jean E. Spencer. *The Legislative Process in Maryland: A Study of the General Assembly.* 2d ed. College Park: University of Maryland, College of Business and Public Administration, Bureau of Governmental Research, 1963.

1702. Bertone, Thomas L. "Legislative Control of Executive Expenditures in Maryland State Government." D.P.A. dissertation, George Washington University, 1971.

1703. Bone, Hugh A. "A Legislative Council for Maryland." *National Municipal Review* 28 (June 1939): 428–432.

1704. Bone, Hugh A. "Maryland's Legislative Council in Action." *National Municipal Review* 31 (Mar. 1942): 146–153.

1705. Bowers, Douglas. "Ideology and Political Parties in Maryland, 1851–1856." *Maryland Historical Magazine* 64 (Fall 1969): 197–217.

1706. Bragg, Richard L. "The Maryland Black Caucus as a Racial Group in the Maryland General Assembly: Legislative Communities and Caucus Influence on Public Policy 1975–1978." Ph.D. dissertation, Howard University, 1979.

1707. Dowd, Mary Jane. "The State in the Maryland Economy, 1776–1807." *Maryland Historical Magazine* 57 (June 1962): 90–132.

1708. Everstine, Carl N. "The Establishment of Legislative Power in Maryland." *Maryland Law Review* 12 (Spring 1951): 99–121.

1709. Everstine, Carl N. *The General Assembly of Maryland, 1634–1776.* Charlottesville, VA: Michie, 1980.

1710. Everstine, Carl N. "The Legislative Process in Maryland." *Maryland Law Review* 10 (Spring 1949): 91–155.

1711. Everstine, Carl N. "Titles of Legislative Acts." *Maryland Law Review* 9 (Summer 1948): 197–245.

1712. Falb, Susan Rosenfeld. "Proxy Voting in Early Maryland Assemblies." *Maryland Historical Magazine* 73 (Sept. 1978): 217–225.

1713. Gibson, Lorenzo T. "The Role of the Governor in the Legislative Process: A Comparative Study of the Governor of Maryland and the Governor of Virginia." Ph.D. dissertation, University of Virginia, 1969.

1714. Green, Harry J. *A Study of the Legislature of the State of Maryland.* Baltimore: Johns Hopkins University Press, 1930.

1715. Hagensick, A. Clarke. "Maryland's Legislative Council in Action." Ph.D. dissertation, Johns Hopkins University, 1960.

1716. Hanson, Roger A. *Fair Representation Comes to Maryland.* New York: McGraw-Hill, 1964.

1717. Land, Aubrey C. "The Familiar Letters of Governor Horatio Sharpe." *Maryland Historical Magazine* 61 (Sept. 1966): 189–209.

1718. Land, Aubrey C. "Governor Blakiston Numbers the People: Or, Bureaucracy Confounded." *Maryland Historical Magazine* 62 (Dec. 1967): 419–421.

1719. Levin, James. "Governor Albert C. Ritchie and the Convention of 1932." *Maryland Historical Magazine* 67 (Fall 1972): 278–293.

1720. Levine, Marc V. "Standing Political Divisions and Critical Realignment: The Pattern of Maryland Politics, 1872–1948." *Journal of Politics* 38 (May 1976): 292–325.

1721. McMahon, John V. *Historical View of the Government of Maryland from Its Colonization to the Present Day.* Baltimore: Cushing and Sons, 1831.

1722. Main, Jackson T. "Political Parties in Revolutionary Maryland 1780–1787." *Maryland Historical Magazine* 62 (Mar. 1967): 1–27.

1723. Miller, Edward J. "Executive-Legislative Relations in Maryland: The Governor as Chief Legislator." Ph.D. dissertation, University of Pittsburgh, 1973.

1724. Papenfuse, Edward C., et al. *A Biographical Dictionary of the Maryland Legislature, 1635–1789.* Baltimore: Johns Hopkins University Press, 1979–.

1725. Riley, Elihu S. *A History of the General Assembly of Maryland, 1635–1904.* Port Washington, NY: Kennikat Press, 1972.

1726. Rosenthal, Alan. *Strengthening the Maryland Legislature.* New Brunswick, NJ: Rutgers University Press, 1968.

1727. Sapio, Victor. "Maryland's Federalist Revival, 1808–1812." *Maryland Historical Magazine* 64 (Spring 1969): 1–17.

1728. Wills, George S. "The Reorganization of the Maryland General Assembly, 1966–1968: A Study of the Politics of Reform." Ph.D. dissertation, Johns Hopkins University, 1969.

Massachusetts

1729. Baum, Dale. "The 'Irish Vote' and Party Politics in Massachusetts, 1860–1876." *Civil War History* 26 (June 1980): 117–141.

1730. Carroll, John J. "Legislative Party Leadership: Deference Hierarchies in the Massachusetts House." Ph.D. dissertation, Brown University, 1977.

1731. Citizens Conference on State Legislatures. *How Citizens Can Improve the Massachusetts General Court*. Kansas City: Citizens Conference on State Legislatures, 1974.

1732. Davis, Horace B. "Occupations of the Massachusetts Legislature, 1790–1950." *New England Quarterly* 24 (Mar. 1951): 89–100.

1733. Fyock, Jack W., John J. Carroll, and Rita Moniz. "The Massachusetts Silver Haired Legislature." *State Government* 54 (Fall 1981): 122–125.

1734. Goldman, Sheldon. *Roll Call Behavior in the Massachusetts House of Representatives*. Amherst, MA: University of Massachusetts, Bureau of Government Research, 1968.

1735. Goodman, Paul. *The Democratic-Republicans of Massachusetts: Politics in a Young Republic*. Cambridge, MA: Harvard University Press, 1964.

1736. Grove, Lawrence R. "Massachusetts School for Legislators." *State Government* 25 (Apr. 1952): 84–86.

1737. Haines, Wilder H. "Legislative Activity in Massachusetts, 1916." *American Political Science Review* 11 (Aug. 1917): 528–539.

1738. Lockard, Duane. *Massachusetts: The Standing Order Under Attack, and Lawmaking in Massachusetts: Traditional Pomp and Circumstance in New England State Politics*. Princeton: Princeton University Press, 1959.

1739. MacRae, Duncan. "The Relation Between Roll Call Votes and Constituencies in the Massachusetts House of Representatives." *American Political Science Review* 46 (Dec. 1952): 1046–1055.

1740. MacRae, Duncan. "The Role of the State Legislator in Massachusetts." *American Sociological Review* 19 (Apr. 1954): 185–194.

1741. Mariner, Elwyn E. *This is Your Massachusetts Government*. Arlington Heights, MA: Mariner Books, 1967.

1742. Mileur, Jerome M., and George T. Sulzner. *Campaigning for the Massachusetts Senate*. Amherst: University of Massachusetts Press, 1974.

1743. "A Movement for a Single Legislative Chamber in Massachusetts." *Massachusetts Law Quarterly* 27 (Feb. 1942): 28–30.

1744. Pesonen, Pertti. "Close and Safe Elections in Massachusetts." *American Journal of Political Science* 7 (Feb. 1963): 54–70.

1745. Plaisted, John W. *Legislative Procedure in the General Court of Massachusetts*. Boston: Commonwealth of Massachusetts Commission on Interstate Cooperation, 1948.

1746. Portnoy, Barry M. "Membership in the Club: Denizens of the Massachusetts House of Representatives." *Harvard Journal on Legislation* 6 (Jan. 1969): 199–235.

1747. Rudsten, Daniel. "City-State Conflict: A Study of the Political Relationship Between the Core City of Boston and the Massachusetts State Legislature." Ph.D. dissertation, Tufts University, 1973.

1748. Sweeney, Kevin. "Rum, Romanism, Representation, and Reform: Coalition Politics in Massachusetts, 1847–1853." *Civil War History* 22 (June 1976): 116–137.

1749. "Taxpayers in Action." *Tax Outlook* 7 (Dec. 1952): 13–16.

1750. Taylor, D. A. "Legislative Vetoes and the Massachusetts Separation of Powers Doctrine." *Suffolk University Law Review* 13 (Winter 1979): 1–13.

1751. Wood, Thomas J. "Distinctive Practices of the Massachusetts General Court." Ph.D. dissertation, Harvard University, 1947.

1752. Zemsky, Robert M. "Power, Influence, and Status: Leadership Patterns in the Massachusetts Assembly, 1740–1755." *William and Mary Quarterly* 26 (Oct. 1969): 502–520.

Michigan

1753. Becker, Robert W., Frieda Foote, Mathias Lebega, and Stephen V. Monsma. "Correlates of Legislative Voting: Michigan House of Representatives, 1954–1961." *American Journal of Political Science* 6 (Nov. 1962): 384–396.

1754. Bowlby, George M. "Some Possible Origins of Pro-Party Attitudes and Representative Role Perceptions of the Michigan

Michigan

Legislators and Their Influence on Party Conformity on Legislative Roll-Calls." Ph.D. dissertation, University of Michigan, 1967.

1755. Bromage, Arthur W. "Restrictions on Financial Powers of the Legislature in Michigan." *State Government* 20 (May 1947): 141–143.

1756. Caswell, J. T. "The State Legislature of Michigan." *Michigan History* 25 (Autumn 1941): 267–275.

1757. Chase, Fred I. *How Michigan Makes Her Laws.* Lansing: F. Pekleine Co., 1953.

1758. Chase, Fred I. "Michigan Senate." *Michigan State Bar Journal* 30 (Mar. 1951): 5–9.

1759. Curry, Richard C. "Implementing Michigan's 1963 Constitution: A Special Legislative Function." Ph.D. dissertation, University of Michigan, 1965.

1760. Deborst, James H. "State Financial Aid to Non-Public Schools in Michigan: A Case Study Analysis of Constitutionality, Interest Group Activity and Legislative Action." Ph.D. dissertation, University of Michigan, 1972.

1761. Detroit Bureau of Governmental Research. *Representative Districts.* Detroit: Detroit Bureau of Governmental Research, 1946.

1762. DeVries, Walter P. "The Michigan Lobbyist: A Study in the Bases and Perceptions of Effectiveness." Ph.D. dissertation, Michigan State University, 1960.

1763. Doolen, Richard M. "The National Greenback Party in Michigan Politics, 1876–88." *Michigan History* 47 (June 1963): 161–183.

1764. Dorr, Harold M. "A Legislative Council for Michigan." *American Political Science Review* 28 (Apr. 1934): 270–275.

1765. Durfee, Elizabeth. "Apportionment of Representation in the Legislature: A Study of State Constitutions." *Michigan Law Review* 43 (June 1945): 1091–1112.

1766. Ervin, Theodore R. *Crosscurrents of Influence in the Committee on Legislative Organization in Michigan's 1961–1962 Constitutional Convention.* East Lansing: Michigan State University, Continuing Education Service, Institute for Community Development and Services, 1964.

1767. Fennimore, Jean Joy L. "Austin Blair: Civil War Governor, 1861–1862." *Michigan History* 49 (Sept. 1965): 193–227.

1768. Fennimore, Jean Joy L. "Austin Blair: Civil War Governor, 1863–1864." *Michigan History* 49 (Dec. 1965): 344–369.

1769. Fennimore, Jean Joy L. "Austin Blair: Political Idealist, 1845–1860." *Michigan History* 48 (June 1964): 130–166.

1770. Fisher, Floyd C. *The Government of Michigan.* New York: Allyn and Bacon, 1955.

1771. Formisano, Ronald P. "A Case Study of Party Formation: Michigan, 1835." *Mid-America* 50 (Apr. 1968): 83–107.

1772. Fuller, Margaret G. *Leadership in the Michigan Legislature.* East Lansing: Michigan State University, Department of Political Science, 1957.

1773. Garfinkel, H., and L. J. Fein. *Fair Representation: A Citizen's Guide to Legislative Apportionment in Michigan.* East Lansing: Michigan State University, Bureau of Social and Political Research, 1960.

1774. Gething, Judith R. D. "Interest Groups, the Courts, and Legislative Reapportionment in Michigan." Ph.D. dissertation, University of Michigan, 1967.

1775. Grenzke, Janet M. *Influence, Change, and the Legislative Process.* Westport, CT: Greenwood, 1982.

1776. Hanawalt, Leslie. "The Doctors' War in the Michigan Legislature, 1835–1851." *Michigan History* 63 (Jan.-Feb. 1979): 29–43.

1777. Harmon, Robert B. *Government and Politics in Michigan: An Information Source Survey.* Monticello, IL: Vance Bibliographies, 1978.

1778. Herndon, James F. "Party Conflict in the Michigan Legislature." M.A. thesis, Wayne State University, 1956.

1779. Lamb, K. A., William J. Pierce, and J. P. White. *Apportionment and Representative Institutions: The Michigan Experience.* Washington, D.C.: Institute for Social Science Research, 1963.

1780. Landers, Frank M., and Howard D. Hamilton. "State Administrative Reorganization in Michigan: The Legislative Approach." *Public Administration Review* 14 (Spring 1954): 99–11.

1781. Lederle, John W., and Edmond Aherns. "Executive Bill Clearance Procedure in Michigan." *Public Administration Review* (Summer 1955): 205–209.

1782. "Legislative Action at Special Session Limited by Governor's Message." *Michigan Law Review* 33 (Mar. 1935): 816–818.

1783. Lewis, Ferris E. *State and Local Government in Michigan*. 8th ed. Hillsdale, MI: Hillsdale Educational Publishers, 1979.

1784. Lunt, Richard D. "Frank Murphy's Decision to Enter the 1936 Gubernatorial Race." *Michigan History* 47 (Dec. 1963): 327–334.

1785. McGuinness, Louis J. "Explorations into the Political-Social Background of Present and Former Michigan Legislators." M.A. thesis, Wayne State University, 1948.

1786. Michigan Bar Association. *The Legislative Structure and Procedure of Michigan: A Comprehensive Factual Survey*. Detroit: Michigan Bar Association, 1947.

1787. Michigan Public Expenditure Survey. *Making the Legislature More Important*. Detroit: Michigan Public Expenditure Survey, 1945.

1788. Michigan State University, Governmental Research Bureau. *Michigan Legislative Report, 1954: Regular and Special Sessions*. East Lansing: Michigan State University, Governmental Research Bureau, 1955.

1789. Monsma, Stephen V. "Informal Groups in the Legislative Process: A Study of the Michigan House of Representatives." Ph.D. dissertation, Michigan State University, 1965.

1790. Monsma, Stephen V. "Interpersonal Relations in the Legislative System: A Study of the 1964 Michigan House of Representatives." *American Journal of Political Science* 10 (Aug. 1966): 350–363.

1791. Orfield, Lester B. "The Unicameral Legislature in Nebraska." *Michigan Law Review* 34 (Nov. 1935): 26–36.

1792. Ortquist, Richard T. "Tax Crisis and Politics in Early Depression Michigan." *Michigan History* 59 (Spring-Summer 1975): 91–119.

1793. Ortquist, Richard T. "Unemployment and Relief: Michigan's Response to the Depression During the Hoover Years." *Michigan History* 57 (Fall 1973): 209–236.

1794. Perkins, John A. *The Role of the Governor of Michigan in the Enactment of Appropriations*. Ann Arbor: University of Michigan, Bureau of Government, 1943.

1795. Philleo, N. E. "Michigan House of Representatives." *Michigan State Bar Journal* 30 (Apr. 1951): 5–9.

1796. Pollock, James K. *The Initiative and Referendum in Michigan.* Ann Arbor: University of Michigan, Bureau of Government, 1940.

1797. Porter, Hubert O. "Legislative Expertise in Michigan." Ph.D. dissertation, University of Michigan, 1972.

1798. Rosentreter, Roger L. "Governors in Michigan." *Michigan History* 64 (Jan.-Feb. 1980): 30–45.

1799. Sayre, Josiah L. "Some Aspects of the Legislative Process in Michigan, 1925–1937." Ph.D. dissertation, University of Michigan, 1938.

1800. Scigliano, Robert G. *Michigan Legislative Report, 1954.* East Lansing: Michigan State College, Governmental Research Center, 1955.

1801. Seavoy, Ronald E. "Borrowed Laws to Speed Development: Michigan, 1835–1863." *Michigan History* 59 (Spring-Summer 1975): 39–68.

1802. Sharkoff, Eugene F. "The Michigan 'Log Jam' Rule." *State Government* 24 (Feb. 1951): 34–35.

1803. Shull, Charles W. "Legislative Council in Michigan." *National Municipal Review* 22 (Nov. 1933): 570–571.

1804. Shull, Charles W. *Legislative Reapportionment in Michigan.* Detroit: Citizens Research Council of Michigan, 1961.

1805. Shull, Charles W. "Michigan Redistricts for Its Lower House." *National Municipal Review* 42 (Sept. 1953): 402–403.

1806. Shull, Charles W. "Michigan Seeks Reapportionment Again." *National Municipal Review* 31 (June 1942): 345–347.

1807. Shull, Charles W. "Wrangling Reapportionment for Michigan." *National Municipal Review* 29 (May 1940): 305–310.

1808. Shull, Charles W., and Lewis J. McGuinness. "The Changing Pattern of Personnel in the Michigan Legislature: 1887–1947." *Michigan History* 35 (Dec. 1951): 467–478.

1809. Snow, Willis H. "Committees Compared: The Michigan Senate and Congress." Ph.D. dissertation, Ohio State University, 1978.

1810. Soule, John W. "The Influence of Political Socialization, Interpersonal Values, and Differential Recruitment Patterns on Legislative Adaptation: The Michigan House of Representatives." Ph.D. dissertation, University of Kentucky, 1967.

1811. State Bar of Michigan. *The Legislative Structure and Procedure of Michigan: A Comprehensive Factual Study.* Detroit: State Bar of Michigan, 1947.

1812. Stollman, Gerald H. "The Michigan Legislature: Some Old Hypotheses Reconsidered." Ph.D. dissertation, New York University, 1977.

1813. Stollman, Gerald H. *Michigan State Legislators and Their Work.* Washington, D.C.: University Press of America, 1979.

1814. Thomas, Norman C. "The Electorate and State Constitutional Revision: An Analysis of Four Michigan Referenda." *American Journal of Political Science* 12 (Feb. 1968): 115–129.

1815. Thomas Norman C. "Voting Machines and Voter Participation in Four Michigan Constitutional Revision Referenda." *Western Political Quarterly* 21 (Sept. 1968): 409–419.

1816. University of Michigan. Bureau of Government. *A Manual of State Administrative Organization in Michigan.* Ann Arbor: University of Michigan, Bureau of Government, 1940.

1817. Ward, Robert M., and Rhonda Katz Barnat. "Assessment of Farmland Preservation Legislation in Michigan: P.A. 116 of 1974." *Michigan Academician* 10 (Winter 1978): 307–319.

Minnesota

1818. Adrian, Charles R. "The Nonpartisan Legislature in Minnesota." Ph.D. dissertation, University of Minnesota, 1951.

1819. Adrian, Charles R. "The Origin of Minnesota's Non-Partisan Legislature." *Minnesota History* 33 (Winter 1952): 155–163.

1820. Backstrom, C., L. Robbins, and S. Eller. "Issues in Gerrymandering: An Exploratory Measure of Partisan Gerrymandering Applied to Minnesota." *Minnesota Law Review* 62 (1978): 1121–1159.

1821. Beyle, Herman C. *Identification and Analysis of Attribute—Cluster—Blocs.* New York: Johnson Reprint Corp., 1970.

1822. Bond, James A. "Legislative Reapportionment in Minnesota." Ph.D. dissertation, University of Minnesota, 1956.

1823. Brandt, Edward R. *Minnesota State Representatives: Performance and Conflict, 1977–78.* St. Paul: Carter and Lacey, 1978.

1824. Chrislock, Carl H. "A Cycle in the History of Minnesota Republicanism." *Minnesota History* 39 (Fall 1964): 93–110.

1825. Citizens Conference on State Legislatures. *How Citizens Can Improve the Minnesota Legislature.* Kansas City: Citizens Conference on State Legislatures, 1974.

1826. Cohen, Julius. "Hearing on a Bill: Legislative Folklore?" *Minnesota Law Review* 37 (Dec. 1952): 34–45.

1827. Dorweiler, Louis C. "Minnesota Farmers Rule Cities: Reapportionment of 1913 Still Stands." *National Municipal Review* 35 (Mar. 1946): 115–120.

1828. Elder, Ann H. "The Relationship Between Membership Characteristics of Interest Groups and Their Lobbying Activities Before the Minnesota State Legislature." Ph.D. dissertation, University of Minnesota, 1979.

1829. Fitzsimmons, Richard W. "The Expanding Role of History—A Legislative View." *Minnesota History* 40 (Spring 1966): 35–38.

1830. Flinn, Thomas A. "The Policy Process: The Minnesota Governor and Legislature in 1955." Ph.D. dissertation, University of Minnesota, 1957.

1831. Flom, Floyd O. "The Legislative Process: A Case Study of the Passage of the Minnesota Youth Conservation Act with Emphasis on the Role of the Individual." Ph.D. dissertation, University of Minnesota, 1957.

1832. Haugland, John C. "Alexander Ramsey and the Birth of Party Politics in Minnesota." *Minnesota History* 39 (Summer 1964): 37–48.

1833. Holbo, Paul S. "The Farmer-Labor Association: Minnesota's Party within a Party." *Minnesota History* 38 (Fall 1963): 301–309.

1834. Hunt, Leigh W. "Administrative Procedure Legislation in Minnesota." Ph.D. dissertation, University of Minnesota, 1968.

1835. Kane, Betty. "A Case Study in Lively Futility: The 1876 Legislature." *Minnesota History* 45 (Summer 1977): 223–240.

1836. Kennedy, Duncan L. *Drafting Bills for the Minnesota Legislature: Suggestions for Draftsmen in Preparing Bills for Introduction.* St. Paul: West Publishing, 1946.

1837. Kennedy, Duncan L. "The Legislative Process, with Particular Reference to Minnesota." *Minnesota Law Review* 30 (June 1946): 653–679.

Minnesota

1838. Kisa, Joseph. *Minnesota's Government.* Philadelphia: Winston, 1958.

1839. Kruschke, Merle L. *Minnesota Body Politic, 1967.* Thief River Falls: Thief River Falls Times, 1967.

1840. League of Women Voters of Minnesota. *Legislative Reorganization in Minnesota.* Minneapolis: League of Women Voters of Minnesota, 1953.

1841. League of Women Voters of Minnesota. *Ninety Days of Lawmaking in Minnesota.* Minneapolis: University of Minnesota Press, 1949.

1842. League of Women Voters of Minnesota. *Reapportionment in Minnesota: Democracy Denied.* Minneapolis: League of Women Voters of Minnesota, 1953.

1843. Levine, E. Lester. "Is Minnesota a Two-Party State Again?" *Publius* 9 (Winter 1979): 197–204.

1844. Minnesota Institute of Governmental Research. *Possible Improvements in the Operation of State Government: Ten Year Analysis of State Expenditure.* St. Paul: Minnesota Institute of Governmental Research, 1947.

1845. Moos, Malcolm. "Nonpartisan Legislative and Judicial Elections in Minnesota." M.A. thesis, University of Minnesota, 1938.

1846. Naftalin, Arthur. "The Failure of the Farmer-Labor Party to Capture Control of the Minnesota Legislature." *American Political Science Review* 38 (Feb. 1944): 71–78.

1847. Neal, Charles E. "Compliance and the State Legislature: An Empirical Analysis of Abortion and Aid to Non-Public Schools in Illinois and Minnesota." Ph.D. dissertation, University of Minnesota, 1980.

1848. Orfield, Lester B. "Improving State Legislative Procedure and Processes." *Minnesota Law Review* 31 (Jan. 1947): 161–189.

1849. Read, Horace E. "Is Referential Legislation Worth While?" *Minnesota Law Review* 25 (Feb. 1941): 261–297.

1850. Short, Lloyd M. "The Legislative Process in Minnesota." *Annals of the American Academy of Political and Social Science* 195 (Jan. 1938): 123–128.

1851. Toensing, W. F., comp. *Minnesota Congressmen, Legislators, and Other Elected Officials: An Alphabetical Check List, 1849–1971.* St. Paul: Minnesota Historical Society, 1971.

1852. Williamson, Homer E. "Legislative-Executive Relations in Minnesota." Ph.D. dissertation, University of Minnesota, 1971.

Mississippi

1853. Abney, Glenn. "Partisan Realignment in a One-Party System: The Case of Mississippi." *Journal of Politics* 31 (Nov. 1969): 1102–1106.

1854. Allen, Tip H., and Dale A. Krane. "Class Replaces Race: The Reemergence of Neopopulism in Mississippi Gubernatorial Politics." *Southern Studies* 19 (Summer 1980): 182–192.

1855. Bailey, Robert J. "The Gubernatorial Administration of George Poindexter, 1820–1822." *Journal of Mississippi History* 35 (Aug. 1973): 227–246.

1856. Bennett, William E. "From Thurmond to Wallace: Changing Electoral Patterns in Mississippi Conservatism." *Southern Quarterly* 14 (Oct. 1975): 61–69.

1857. Bigelow, Martha M. "Public Opinion and the Passage of the Mississippi Black Codes." *Negro History Bulletin* 33 (Jan. 1970): 11–16.

1858. Clark, Eric C. "Legislative Apportionment in the 1890 Constitutional Convention." *Journal of Mississippi History* 42 (Nov. 1980): 298–315.

1859. Drake, Winbourne M. "The Framing of Mississippi's First Constitution." *Journal of Mississippi History* 29 (Nov. 1967): 301–327.

1860. Ethridge, William N. *Modernizing Mississippi's Constitution.* University: University of Mississippi, Bureau of Public Administration, 1950.

1861. Fike, Claude E. "The Gubernatorial Administrations of Governor Gerard Chittocque Brandon, 1825–1832." *Journal of Mississippi History* 35 (Aug. 1973): 247–265.

1862. Fortenberry, Charles N. "Classes for Mississippi Legislators." *State Government* 25 (Apr. 1952): 85–87.

1863. Hamilton, Charles G. "The Turning Point: The Legislative Session of 1908." *Journal of Mississippi History* 25 (Apr. 1963): 93–111.

1864. Harris, William C. "The Creed of the Carpetbaggers: The Case of Mississippi." *Journal of Southern History* 40 (May 1974): 199–224.

1865. Hauberg, Robert E. "Legislative Sessions in Mississippi and the Nation." *Public Administration Survey* 15 (Nov. 1967): 1–8.

1866. Highsaw, Robert B., and Charles N. Fortenberry. *The Government and Administration of Mississippi*. New York: Crowell, 1954.

1867. Hobbs, E. H. *Legislative Apportionment in Mississippi*. University: University of Mississippi, Bureau of Public Administration, 1956.

1868. Holtz, Harold F. "Turnover in the Mississippi Legislature." *Public Administrative Survey* 5 (May 1958): 1–6.

1869. Jones, Melvin E. "Mississippi Pressure Groups and Their Influence on the State Legislature." M.A. thesis, University of Southern Mississippi, 1967.

1870. McCain, William D. "The Administrations of David Holmes, Governor of the Mississippi Territory, 1809–1817." *Journal of Mississippi History* 29 (Nov. 1967): 328–347.

1871. Mack, Ally F. "Mississippi Legislative Behavior: An Analysis of Its Nature and Implications." Ph.D. dissertation, University of Southern Mississippi, 1979.

1872. "Mississippi Holds Classes for Legislators." *National Municipal Review* 41 (May 1952): 247–248.

1873. Moss, Warner. "Governor Alexander G. McNutt (1802–1848)." *Journal of Mississippi History* 42 (Aug. 1980): 244–251.

1874. Ogle, David B. *Strengthening the Mississippi Legislature*. New Brunswick, NJ: Rutgers University Press, 1971.

1875. Rawson, Donald M. "Democratic Resurgence in Mississippi, 1852–1853." *Journal of Mississippi History* 26 (Feb. 1964): 1–27.

1876. Soapes, Thomas F. "The Governorship 'Steal' and the Republican Revival." *Bulletin of the Missouri Historical Society* 32 (Apr. 1976): 158–172.

1877. Thomas, E. T. "Work of the 1942 Session of the Mississippi Legislature." *Mississippi Law Journal* 15 (Nov. 1942): 70–76.

1878. University of Mississippi. Bureau of Public Administration. *The Legislative Process: A Handbook for Mississippi Legislators.* University: University of Mississippi, Bureau of Public Administration, 1947.

1879. Vocino, Thomas, and J. H. Morris. "Population Apportionment Principle: Its Development and Application to Mississippi's State and Local Legislative Bodies." *Mississippi Law Journal* 47 (Sept. 1976): 943–978.

1880. White, Samuel L. "Legislative and Court-Ordered Reapportionment and Minority Voting Strength: The Mississippi Experience." Ph.D. dissertation, Howard University, 1980.

1881. Wilber, L. *Reapportionment of the Mississippi Legislature: An Analysis of the Question.* Jackson: Mississippi Economic Council, 1956.

1882. Winter, William. "Governor Mike Conner and the Sales Tax, 1932." *Journal of Mississippi History* 41 (Aug. 1979): 213–230.

Missouri

1883. Brannon, Victor D. "Missouri's Apportionment Key." *National Municipal Review* 35 (Apr. 1946): 177–182.

1884. Chen, Rolet. "Voting Behavior on Proposals on the City of St. Louis in the Missouri Legislature." Ph.D. dissertation, Washington University, St. Louis, 1959.

1885. Cho, Woong-Kyu. "Representativeness of Legislators, Administrators and Judges in Michigan and Missouri." Ph.D. dissertation, University of Missouri, 1975.

1886. "Constitutional Reform in Missouri." *University of Kansas Law Review* 11 (Dec. 1942): 1–64.

1887. Derge, David R. "Metropolitan and Out-State Alignments in Illinois-Missouri Legislative Deliberations." *American Political Science Review* 52 (Dec. 1958): 1051–1065.

1888. Gosebrink, Thomas A. "Institutional Consequences of Legislative Reapportionment: The Missouri Case." Ph.D. dissertation, St. Louis University, 1979.

1889. Karsch, Robert F. *The Government of Missouri.* Columbia, MO: Lucas Brothers, 1968.

Missouri

1890. Karsch, Robert F. *The Standing Committees of the Missouri General Assembly.* Columbia: University of Missouri, Bureau of Government Research, 1959.

1891. Lang, Howard B. "They Legislate for Missouri." *Annals of the American Academy of Political and Social Science* 195 (Jan. 1938): 40–44.

1892. Leuthold, David A. *The Missouri Legislature: A Preliminary Profile.* Columbia: University of Missouri, School of Business and Public Administration, Research Center, 1967.

1893. McCandless, Carl A. *Government Politics and Administration in Missouri.* St. Louis: Education Publishers, 1949.

1894. McClintock, Roy M. "Pressure Groups in the Missouri Legislative Process." Ph.D. dissertation, University of Missouri, 1961.

1895. Missouri Public Expenditure Survey. *Shall the Length of the Sessions of Missouri's General Assembly Be Limited?* Jefferson City: Missouri Public Expenditure Survey, 1952.

1896. Napier, Milton F. *The Legislative Process in Missouri and How It Works.* St. Louis: n.p., 1950.

1897. Perry, Robert T. "The Black Legislator: A Case Study of the House of Representatives of the 75th Missouri General Assembly." Ph.D. dissertation, University of Missouri, 1972.

1898. Sharp, James R. "Governor Daniel Dunklin's Jacksonian Democracy in Missouri, 1832–1836." *Missouri Historical Review* 56 (Apr. 1962): 217–229.

1899. Shoemaker, Floyd C. "David Barton, John Rice Jones and Edward Bates: Three Missouri State and Statehood Founders." *Missouri Historical Review* 65 (July 1971): 527–544.

1900. Sparlin, Estal E. "Experts for the Lawmakers: Missouri Legislative Research Committee." *National Municipal Review* 37 (June 1948): 299–302.

1901. Van Eaton, Anson E. "The Initiative and Referendum in Missouri (1908–1953)." Ph.D. dissertation, University of Missouri, 1955.

1902. Williamson, Hugh P. "Abstracts of Bills in and Laws Enacted by the 64th General Assembly of Missouri, January to June 12, 1947." *Journal of the Missouri Bar* 3 (July 1947): 133–143.

1903. Young, George D. "The Role of Political Parties in the Missouri House of Representatives." Ph.D. dissertation, University of Missouri, 1958.

Montana

1904. The Montana-Idaho Assembly on State Legislatures. *Report and Recommendations.* Missoula: University of Montana, 1966.

1905. Neely, Gerald J. *The Montana Legislature: Its Structure and Procedure.* Billings, MT: Rocky Mountain College, Citizens' Seminar on State Government, 1969.

1906. Renne, Roland R. *The Government and Administration of Montana.* New York: Crowell, 1958.

1907. Thane, James L. "An Active Acting Governor: Thomas Francis Meagher's Administration in Montana Territory." *Journal of the West* 9 (Oct. 1970): 537–551.

1908. Vindex, Charles. "Radical Rule in Montana." *Montana: The Magazine of Western History* 18 (Jan. 1968): 2–18.

1909. Waldron, Ellis L. *Montana Legislators 1864–1979: Profiles and Biographical Directory.* Missoula: University of Montana, Bureau of Government Research, 1980.

1910. Waldron, Ellis L. "100 Years of Reapportionment in Montana." *Montana Law Review* 28 (Fall 1966): 1–24.

Nebraska

1911. Aylsworth, L. E. "Nebraska's Nonpartisan Unicameral Legislature." *National Municipal Review* 26 (Feb. 1937): 77–81.

1912. Aylsworth, L. E. "Nebraska's Unicameral Legislature Saves Money for Taxpayers. *National Municipal Review* 27 (Oct. 1938): 490–493.

1913. Breckenridge, Adam C. "Innovation in State Government: Origin and Development of the Nebraska Nonpartisan Unicameral Legislature." *Nebraska History* 59 (Spring 1978): 33–46.

1914. Breckenridge, Adam C. *One House for Two: Nebraska's Unicameral Legislature.* Washington, D.C.: Public Affairs Press, 1957.

1915. Burdette, Franklin L. "Conference Committees in the Nebraska Legislature." *American Political Science Review* 30 (Dec. 1936): 1114–1116.

1916. Burdette, Franklin L. "Legislative Conference Committees: Lessons from Nebraska's Bicameral Experience." *State Government* 11 (June 1938): 103–106.

1917. Burdette, Franklin L. "Nebraska Completes Unicameral Districting." *National Municipal Review* 24 (June 1935): 348–349.

1918. Carlyle, Adam. *One House or Two: A Study of Nebraska's Unicameral Legislature.* Washington, D.C.: Public Affairs Press, 1957.

1919. Comer, John C. "The Nebraska Nonpartisan Legislature: An Evaluation." *State and Local Government Review* 12 (Sept. 1980): 98–102.

1920. Comer, John C., and James B. Johnson, eds. *Nonpartisanship in the Legislative Process: Essays on the Nebraska Legislature.* Washington, D.C.: University Press of America, 1978.

1921. *Depth Report Number One on Nebraska's Unicameral Legislature.* Lincoln: University of Nebraska, School of Journalism, 1961.

1922. Dobbins, Harry T. "Nebraska's One House Legislature—After Six Years." *National Municipal Review* 30 (Sept. 1941): 511–514.

1923. Evans, Charles H. "Representational Behavior in the Nebraska Legislature." Ph.D. dissertation, University of Kansas, 1971.

1924. Green, Charles D. "Nebraska Launches Unicameral." *State Government* 10 (Jan. 1937): 3–5.

1925. Johnson, James B. "The Nebraska Legislative System: Legislative Roles in a Non-Partisan Setting." Ph.D. dissertation, Northwestern University, 1972.

1926. Johnson, William E. "Unicameralism Works: Nebraska's One-House Legislature." *State Government* 12 (Nov. 1939): 197–198.

1927. Kolasa, Bernard D. "Lobbying in the Nonpartisan Environment: The Case of Nebraska." *Western Political Quarterly* 24 (Mar. 1971): 65–78.

1928. Lancaster, Lane W. "Nebraska Considers a One-House Legislature." *National Municipal Review* 23 (July 1934): 373–376.

1929. Lancaster, Lane W. "Nebraska's Experience with a One-House Legislature." *University of Kansas City Law Review* 11 (Dec. 1942): 24.

1930. Lancaster, Lane W. "Nebraska's New Legislature." *Minnesota Law Review* 22 (Dec. 1937): 60–76.

1931. McCready, Eric S. "The Nebraska State Capital: Its Design, Background, and Influence." *Nebraska History* 55 (Fall 1974): 325–417.

1932. McPartland, Edward J. "A Study of Rural-Urban Conflict in the Nebraska Legislature." Ph.D. dissertation, University of Nebraska, 1970.

1933. Marvel, Richard D. "Decision-Making in the Nebraska Unicameral Legislature for the 1959, 1961, and 1963 Sessions." Ph.D. dissertation, University of Nebraska, 1966.

1934. "Nebraska's Unicameral Adjourns: The Session in Retrospect." *State Government* 10 (July 1937): 131–134.

1935. "Nebraska's Unicameral Legislature Threatened." *National Municipal Review* 42 (Dec. 1953): 563–564.

1936. Poeschl, Peg. "Housing Nebraska's Governors, 1854–1980." *Nebraska History* 61 (Fall 1980): 259–279.

1937. Riley, W. "Nonpartisan Unicameral—Benefits, Defects Reexamined." *Nebraska Law Review* 52 (1973): 377–403.

1938. Rodgers, Jack W. "One House for Twenty Years: Nebraska's Extensive Experience with Nonpartisan Unicameral Legislature." *National Municipal Review* 46 (July 1957): 338–342.

1939. Rodine, Floyd. "Legislative and Legal Struggle of the Grain Cooperatives in Nebraska, 1900–1915." *Nebraska History* 56 (Winter 1975): 457–470.

1940. Senning, John P. "Nebraska Provides for a One-House Legislature." *American Political Science Review* 29 (Feb. 1935): 69–74.

1941. Senning, John P. "Nebraska's Experience in Setting Up a One-House Legislature." *New Mexico Business Review* 6 (Jan.-Apr. 1937): 12–30.

1942. Senning, John P. "Nebraska's First Unicameral Legislative Session." *Annals of the American Academy of Political and Social Science* 195 (Jan. 1938): 159–167.

1943. Senning, John P. "Nebraska's One-House Legislature." *Southwestern Social Science Quarterly* 18 (Sept. 1937): 115–125.

1944. Senning, John P. "The One-House Legislature in Nebraska." *Nebraska Law Bulletin* (Feb. 1935): 341–350.

1945. Shumate, Roger V. "The Nebraska Unicameral Legislature." *Western Political Quarterly* 5 (Sept. 1952): 504–512.

1946. Sittig, Robert F. "Unicameralism in Nebraska." *State Government* 40 (Winter 1967): 38–41.

1947. Spencer, Richard C. "Nebraska Idea 15 Years Old." *National Municipal Review* 39 (Feb. 1950): 83–86.

1948. Summers, Harrison B., ed. *Unicameralism in Practice: The Nebraska Legislative System.* New York: H. W. Wilson, 1937.

1949. Thavenet, Dennis. "Governor William A. Richardson: Champion of Popular Sovereignty in Territorial Nebraska." *Nebraska History* 53 (Winter 1972): 463–476.

1950. Thavenet, Dennis. "The Territorial Governorship: Nebraska Territory as Example." *Nebraska History* 51 (Winter 1970): 387–409.

1951. Trask, David S. "A Natural Partnership: Nebraska's Populists and Democrats and the Development of Fusion." *Nebraska History* 56 (Fall 1975): 419–438.

1952. Wade, Harry W. "A Descriptive Analysis of Nebraska's Unicameral Legislature." Ph.D. dissertation, University of Kansas, 1969.

1953. Wesser, Robert F. "George W. Norris: The Unicameral Legislature and the Progressive Ideal." *Nebraska History* 45 (Dec. 1964): 309–322.

Nevada

1954. Glass, Mary E. "Nevada in the Fifties—A Glance at State Politics and Economics." *Nevada Historical Society Quarterly* 19 (Summer 1976): 129–138.

1955. Glass, Mary E. "Nevada Turning Points: The State Legislature of 1955." *Nevada Historical Society Quarterly* 23 (Winter 1980): 223–235.

1956. Glass, Mary E. "The Silver Governors: Immigrants in Nevada Politics, Part II." *Nevada Historical Society Quarterly* 21 (Winter 1978): 263–278.

1957. Goodwin, Victor. "Lewis Rice Bradley: Nevada Cattleman and Governor." *Nevada Historical Society Quarterly* 14 (Winter 1971): 11–22.

1958. Jack, Ronald C. "Early Utah and Nevada Electoral Politics." *Nevada Historical Society Quarterly* 17 (Winter 1974): 203–224.

1959. Jack, Ronald C. "Early Utah and Nevada Electoral Politics." *Nevada Historical Society Quarterly* 18 (Spring 1975): 3–25.

1960. Johnson, David A. "A Case of Mistaken Identity: William M. Stewart and the Rejection of Nevada's First Constitution." *Nevada Historical Society Quarterly* 22 (Fall 1979): 186–198.

1961. Moody, Eric N. "Nevada's Anti-Mormon Legislation of 1887 and Southern Idaho Annexation." *Nevada Historical Society Quarterly* 22 (Spring 1979): 21–32.

1962. Moody, Eric N. "Nevada's Bull Moose Progressives: The Formation and Function of a State Political Party in 1912." *Nevada Historical Society Quarterly* 16 (Fall 1973): 157–179.

New Hampshire

1963. Baldwin, Carolyn W. "The Dawn of the Republican Party in New Hampshire." *Historical New Hampshire* 30 (Spring 1975): 21–32.

1964. Daniell, Jere R. "Politics in New Hampshire Under Governor Benning Wentworth, 1741–1767." *William and Mary Quarterly* 23 (Jan. 1966): 76–105.

1965. Douglas, Charles G. "Judicial Review and the Separation of Powers Under the New Hampshire Consitutions of 1776 and 1784." *Historical New Hampshire* 31 (Winter 1976): 176–191.

1966. Downs, Deborah. "The New Hampshire Constitution of 1776: Weathervane of Conservatism." *Historical New Hampshire* 31 (Winter 1976): 164–175.

1967. Harvey, Lashley G. "America's Largest Legislature: An Analysis of the Bases of Representation in New Hampshire's General Court." *State Government* 15 (Mar. 1942): 65–66.

1968. Johnson, Reinhard O. "The Liberty Party in New Hampshire, 1840–1848: Antislavery Politics in the Granite State." *Historical New Hampshire* 33 (Summer 1978): 123–165.

1969. Kalijarvi, Thorsten V., and William Chamberlain. *The Government of New Hampshire.* Durham: University of New Hampshire, 1939.

1970. "Lobbying in New Hampshire." *National Municipal Review* 43 (Mar. 1954): 118–119.

1971. Morrison, Leonard S. *The Government of New Hampshire.* Concord, NH: Sugar Press, 1943.

1972. "New Hampshire Establishes Legislative Council." *National Municipal Review* 40 (Dec. 1951): 588.

1973. Taishoff, Sue. "New Hampshire State Politics and the Concept of a Party System, 1800–1840." *Historical New Hampshire* 31 (Spring-Summer 1976): 17–43.

1974. Ware, Richard A. "Legislative Apportionment in New Hampshire." *National Municipal Review* 31 (Jan. 1942): 34–36.

1975. Wiggin, J. Walker. "The General Court and the Constitution." *New Hampshire Town and City Notes* 1 (May 1948): 3–4.

New Jersey

1976. Anton, Thomas J. "The Politics of State Taxation: A Case Study of Decision-Making in the New Jersey Legislature." Ph.D. dissertation, Princeton University, 1961.

1977. Bebout, J. E. "New Jersey Citizens Direct Their 1944 Senators and Assemblymen to Undertake Revision of State's Century-Old Constitution for Submission to Voters in November: New Task for a Legislature." *National Municipal Review* 33 (Jan. 1944): 17–21.

1978. "Caucus Rule in New Jersey Senate Ends." *National Municipal Review* 43 (Jan. 1954): 40.

1979. Cole, Leonard A. *Blacks in Power: A Comparative Study of Black and White Elected Officials.* Princeton: Princeton University Press, 1976.

1980. Eagleton Institute of Politics. *The New Jersey Legislature.* New Brunswick, NJ: Rutgers University, Eagleton Institute of Politics, 1963.

1981. Eisenberg, Ralph. "Local Legislation and the Legislative Process in New Jersey." Ph.D. dissertation, Princeton University, 1961.

1982. Friedelbaum, Stanley H. "Apportionment Legislation in New Jersey." *New Jersey Historical Society Proceedings* 70 (Oct. 1952): 262–277.

1983. Friedman, Gordon D. "Issues, Partisanship and Political Subcultures: A Study of Voting in Statewide Referenda in New Jersey, 1944–1966." Ph.D. dissertation, University of North Carolina at Chapel Hill, 1971.

1984. Grant, J. A. C. "New Jersey's Popular Action in Rem to Control Legislative Procedure." *Rutger's Law Review* 3–4 (1950): 391–417.

1985. Levine, Peter D. "The Constitution of 1844: Constitutional Reform and Legislative Behavior in Nineteenth Century New Jersey." *Symposium, New Jersey Historical Commission* (1976): 63–71.

1986. Levine, Peter D. "State Legislative Parties in the Jacksonian Era: New Jersey, 1829–1844." *Journal of American History* 62 (Dec. 1975): 591–608.

1987. McGuire, Maureen. "Struggle over the Purse: Gov. Morris vs. N.J. Assembly." *New Jersey History* 82 (June 1964): 200–207.

1988. McKean, Dayton D. *Pressures on the Legislature of New Jersey.* New York: Columbia University Press, 1938.

1989. New Jersey. Law Revision and Bill Drafting Commission. *Manual for Use in Drafting Legislation for Introduction in the New Jersey Legislature.* Trenton: New Jersey, Law Revision and Bill Drafting Commission, 1948.

1990. Pierce, Arthur D. "A Governor in Skirts." *New Jersey History* 83 (Jan. 1965): 1–9.

1991. Pomper, Gerald. "New Jersey Convention Delegates of 1964." *Social Science Quarterly* 48 (June 1967): 24–33.

1992. Reock, Ernest C. *Population Inequality Among Counties in the New Jersey Legislature.* New Brunswick, NJ: Rutgers University, Bureau of Government Research, 1959.

1993. Rich, Bennett M. *The Government and Administration of New Jersey.* New York: Crowell, 1957.

1994. Rosenthal, Alan. "The New Jersey Legislature: The Contemporary Shape of an Historical Institution: Not Yet Good but Better than It Used to Be." *Symposium: New Jersey Historical Commission* (1976): 72–119.

1995. Rutgers University. Bureau of Government Research. *Legislative Apportionment in New Jersey: A Survey of Modern Methods Available.* New Brunswick, NJ: Rutgers University, Bureau of Government Research, 1952.

1996. Shank, Alan. *New Jersey Reapportionment Politics: Strategies and Tactics in the Legislative Process.* Rutherford, NJ: Fairleigh Dickenson University Press, 1969.

1997. Trafford, John E. "The New Jersey Legislative Process." *New Jersey Municipalities* 39 (Jan. 1962): 19–20.

1998. Weiss, Nathan, and Robert Laudicina. "Executive Leadership and Political Innovation in New Jersey State Politics." *Urban Education* 4 (Jan. 1970): 333–347.

New Mexico

1999. Baldwin, P. M. "The 1940 Census and Legislative Reapportionment in New Mexico." *New Mexico Quarterly Review* 11 (Feb. 1941): 37–42.

2000. Campbell, Jack M. *How a Bill Becomes a Law in the Legislature of New Mexico.* Santa Fe: Taxpayers' Association of New Mexico, 1950.

2001. Donnelly, Thomas C. *The Government of New Mexico.* Albuquerque: University of New Mexico Press, 1947.

2002. Donnelly, Thomas C. "The Legislature." In his *The Government of New Mexico.* Albuquerque: University of New Mexico Press, 1947, pp. 89–108.

2003. Donnelly, Thomas C., and Tom W. Neal. "The Proposed Split-Session Amendment." *New Mexico Business Review* 9 (Apr. 1940): 103–114.

2004. Ellis, Richard N. "Hispanic Americans and Indians in New Mexico State Politics." *New Mexico Historical Review* 53 (Oct. 1978): 361–364.

2005. Esterly, Robert E. "A Longitudinal Analysis of Legislative Roll Call Voting: Patterns of Stability and Change in the New Mexico House of Representatives, 1961–1969." Ph.D. dissertation, University of Arizona, 1971.

2006. "Expenses of the Sixteenth Legislature." *New Mexico Tax Bulletin* 22 (Aug. 1943): 113–117.

2007. Hall, John E. "The Bicameral Principle in the New Mexico Legislature." *National Municipal Review* 16 (Mar.-Apr. 1927): 185–190, 255–260.

2008. Holmes, Jack E. "New Mexico Reorganizes Its Legislative Committees." *State Government* 28 (Oct. 1955): 231–232.

2009. Holmes, Jack E. *Politics in New Mexico*. Albuquerque: University of New Mexico Press, 1967.

2010. Iron, Frederick C. "Opinion Formation Among Legislators at the Twenty-Third New Mexico Legislature." *Proceedings of the Southwestern Sociological Society* (1957): 81–90.

2011. Judah, Charles B. "New Mexico's Legislature." *New Mexico Quarterly* 27 (Winter 1957–1958): 267–275.

2012. Larson, Robert W. "Statehood for New Mexico, 1888–1912." *New Mexico Historical Review* 37 (July 1962): 161–200.

2013. "New Mexico Reapportions." *National Municipal Review* 39 (Feb. 1950): 94–95.

2014. Poldervaart, Arie. "Legislative Drafting in New Mexico." *New Mexico Tax Bulletin* 21 (Dec. 1942): 177–183.

2015. Richards, Allen R. *Legislative Services with Special Emphasis upon the Problems in New Mexico*. Albuquerque: University of New Mexico, Department of Government, Division of Research, 1953.

2016. Russell, John C. "Racial Groups in the New Mexico Legislature." *Annals of the American Academy of Political and Social Science* 195 (Jan. 1938): 62–71.

2017. Smart, Warren A. "A Survey of the Background of the New Mexico State Legislators Elected in 1948." M.A. thesis, University of New Mexico, 1950.

New York

2018. Adler, Madeline, and Jewel Bellush. "Lawyers and the Legislature: Something New in New York." *National Civic Review* 68 (May 1979): 244–246.

2019. "Apportionment of the New York State Assembly." *St. John's Law Review* 29 (May 1955): 345–356.

2020. Baaklini, Abdo I., and Charles S. Dawson. *The Politics of Legislation in New York State: How a Bill Becomes a Law*. Albany: State University of New York at Albany, Graduate School of Public Affairs, Comparative Development Studies Center, 1979.

2021. Balutis, Alan P., and James J. Heaphey. *Public Administration and the Legislative Process.* Beverly Hills, CA: Sage, 1974.

2022. Barkan, Elliott R. "The Emergence of a Whig Persuasion: Conservatism, Democratism, and the New York State Whigs." *New York History* 52 (Oct. 1971): 367–395.

2023. Benjamin, Gerald. "Patterns in New York State Politics." *Proceedings of the Academy of Political Science* 31 (May 1974): 31–44.

2024. Benson, Lee, Joel H. Silbey, and Phyllis Field. "Toward a Theory of Stability and Change in American Voting Patterns: New York State, 1792–1970." In *The History of American Electoral Behavior*, edited by Joel H. Silbey et al. Princeton: Princeton University Press, 1978, pp. 78–105.

2025. Berle, Peter A. *Does the Citizen Stand a Chance? The Politics of a State Legislature: New York.* Woodbury, NY: Barron's Educational Series, 1974.

2026. Bradley, Phillips. "Blazing New Legislature Trails." *Survey Graphic* 33 (May 1944): 234–238.

2027. Brooks, Robin. "Alexander Hamilton, Melancton Smith, and the Ratification of the Constitution in New York." *William and Mary Quarterly* 24 (July 1967): 339–358.

2028. Brydges, Earl W. "The New York Legislature Gets Its 'Impossible Dream.'" *State Government* 43 (Summer 1970): 163–165.

2029. Caldwell, Lynton K. *The Government and Administration of New York.* New York: Crowell, 1954.

2030. Chamberlain, Lawrence H. *Loyalty and Legislative Action: A Survey of Activity by the New York State Legislature, 1919–1949.* Ithaca: Cornell University Press, 1951.

2031. Champagne, Roger. "Family Politics versus Constitutional Principles: The New York Assembly Elections of 1768 and 1769." *William and Mary Quarterly* 20 (Jan. 1963): 57–79.

2032. City Club of New York. *Modernizing the Legislature.* New York: City Club of New York, 1952.

2033. Colvin, David L. "The Bicameral Principle in the New York Legislature." Ph.D. dissertation, Columbia University, 1913.

2034. Csontos, M. B. *History of Legislative Apportionment in New York State 1777–1940.* Albany: New York State Library, 1941.

2035. Dangerfield, George. "Dixon Ryan Fox's 'The Decline of Aristocracy in the Politics of New York, 1801–1840.'" *New York History* 46 (July 1965): 253–257.

2036. Delong, Dennis R. "Reapportionment: Representativeness, and Rural County Legislatures in New York State." Ph.D. dissertation, State University of New York at Albany, 1978.

2037. Field, Phyllis F. "Republicans and Black Suffrage in New York State: The Grass Roots Response." *Civil War History* 21 (June 1975): 136–147.

2038. Gunn, L. Ray. "The New York State Legislature: A Developmental Perspective, 1777–1846." *Social Science History* 4 (Summer 1980): 267–294.

2039. Hallett, George H. "An Appraisal of the 1951 Legislature." *Searchlight* 41 (May 1951): 1–6.

2040. Hevesi, Alan G. "Legislative Leadership in New York State." Ph.D. dissertation, Columbia University, 1971.

2041. Hevesi, Alan G. *Legislative Politics in New York State: A Comparative Analysis.* New York: Praeger, 1975.

2042. "How the New York State Legislature Does Its Work." *New York State Taxpayer* 12 (Jan. 1951): 6.

2043. Howe, Elizabeth A. "Intergovernmental Dependence as a Constraint on Urban Reform: New York City's Relationship with the New York State Legislature During the Second Lindsay Administration." Ph.D. dissertation, University of California, Berkeley, 1976.

2044. Lederle, John W. "New York's Legislature Under the Microscope." *American Political Science Review* 40 (June 1946): 521–527.

2045. Legislative Index Company. *The Legislative Primer: Covering Legislative Procedure from Bill to Statute in New York State.* Albany: Legislative Index Company, 1957.

2046. Lehne, R. *Legislative Reapportionment in New York.* New York: National Municipal League, 1971.

2047. Littke, George C. "The Role of the Joint Legislative Committee in the New York State Legislative System." Ph.D. dissertation, New York University, 1970.

2048. McCormick, Richard L. *From Realignment to Reform: Political Change in New York State, 1893–1910.* Ithaca: Cornell University Press, 1981.

2049. McCormick, Richard L. "Prelude to Progressivism: The Transformation of New York State Politics, 1890–1910." *New York History* 59 (July 1978): 253–276.

2050. McDonnell, Richard Heinrich. "A History of the Conservative Party of New York State, 1962–1972." Ph.D. dissertation, Pennsylvania State University, 1975.

2051. McGuire, Daniel W. "Governor Hughes and the Race Track Gambling Issue: The Special Election of 1908." *Niagara Frontier* 18 (Winter 1971): 66–72.

2052. McInnes, R. "New York Legislature Again Impedes a Progressive Governor." *National Municipal Review* 23 (July 1934): 383–388.

2053. McKnight, Gerald D. "The Perils of Reform Politics: The Abortive New York State Constitutional Reform Movement of 1915." *New York Historical Society Quarterly* 43 (July 1979): 203–227.

2054. Madaras, Lawrence H. "Theodore Roosevelt, Jr. vs. Al Smith: The New York Gubernatorial Election of 1924." *New York History* 47 (Oct. 1966): 372–390.

2055. Merchants' Association of New York. *A Unicameral Legislature Elected by Proportional Representation.* New York: Merchants' Association of New York, 1938.

2056. Milstein, Mike M., and Robert E. Jennings. *Educational Policy-Making and the State Legislature: The New York Experience.* New York: Praeger, 1973.

2057. "New York Reapportions State Senate." *National Municipal Review* 43 (Jan. 1954): 39–40.

2058. New York. Special Committee on Ethics. *The Legislature of the State of New York: Report.* Albany: Special Committee on Ethics, 1964.

2059. Nutting, Charles B. "The New York State Legislative Annals." *State Government* 26 (Dec. 1953): 291–292.

2060. Olson, James E. "The New York Assembly, the Politics of Religion, and the Origins of the American Revolution, 1768–1771." *Historical Magazine of the Protestant Episcopal Church* 43 (Mar. 1974): 21–28.

2061. Pieth, Reto A. "A Comparative Study of State Legislators' Role Cognitions in New York and Basel." Ph.D. dissertation, Syracuse University, 1972.

2062. Rochester Bureau of Municipal Research. *Reapportionment Bill Reduces Up-State Strength.* Rochester, NY: Rochester Bureau of Municipal Research, 1943.

2063. "Role of State and Federal Courts in State Legislative Reapportionment—The New York Conflict." *Minnesota Law Review* 50 (Mar. 1966): 714–736.

2064. Ruchelman, Leonard I. "Lawyers in the New York State Legislature: The Urban Factor." *American Journal of Political Science* 10 (Nov. 1966): 486–497.

2065. Ruchelman, Leonard I. "A Profile of New York Legislators 1931–1951." *Western Political Quarterly* 20 (Sept. 1967): 625–638.

2066. Sarner, Ronald. "Predicting Legislative Outcomes: An Analysis of Three Sessions of the New York State Senate." Ph.D. dissertation, State University of New York at Binghamton, 1975.

2067. Scarrow, Howard. "The Impact of Reapportionment on Party Representation in the State of New York." *Policy Studies Journal* 9 (1980–1981): 937–945.

2068. Shefter, Martin A. "City Hall and State House: State Legislative Involvement in the Politics of New York City and Boston." Ph.D. dissertation, Harvard University, 1970.

2069. Silverman, Eli B. "Legislative Budgetary Oversight in New York." *State Government* 48 (Spring 1975): 128–130.

2070. Skeen, C. Edward. "'A Political Bear-Garden . . .': Four Letters on the New York Constitutional Convention of 1821." *New York History* 59 (July 1978): 326–342.

2071. Thompson, John F. "The Legislative Process in New York State as Exemplified by the Handling of Measures Affecting Labor and Banking." Ph.D. dissertation, Harvard University, 1934.

2072. Waldman, Louis. *Albany: The Crisis in Government—The History of the Suspension, Trial and Expulsion from the New York State Legislature in 1920 of the Five Socialist Assemblymen by Their Political Opponents.* New York: Boni and Leveright, 1920.

2073. Wallace, Michael. "Changing Concepts of Party in the United States: New York, 1815–1828." *American Historical Review* 74 (Dec. 1968): 453–491.

2074. Wells, D. I. *Legislative Representation in New York State.* New York: International Ladies Garment Workers' Union, Political Department, 1963.

2075. Wesser, Robert F. "The Impeachment of a Governor: William Sulzer and the Politics of Excess." *New York History* 60 (Oct. 1979): 407–438.

2076. Wesser, Robert F. "Theodore Roosevelt: Reform and Reorganization of the Republican Party in New York, 1901–1906." *New York History* 46 (July 1965): 230–252.

2077. Witt, Stuart K. "The Legislative—Local Party Linkage in New York State." Ph.D. dissertation, Syracuse University, 1967.

2078. Zeller, Belle. "Pressure Politics in New York: A Study of Group Representation Before the Legislature." Ph.D. dissertation, Columbia University, 1937.

2079. Zimmerman, Joseph F. "Rebirth of the Item Veto in the Empire State." *State Government* 54 (Spring 1981): 51–52.

North Carolina

2080. Abrams, Douglas C. "A Progressive-Conservative Duel: The 1920 Democratic Gubernatorial Primaries in North Carolina." *North Carolina Historical Review* 55 (Oct. 1978): 421–443.

2081. Balanoff, Elizabeth. "Negro Legislators in the North Carolina General Assembly, July, 1868–February, 1872." *North Carolina Historical Review* 49 (Jan. 1972): 22–55.

2082. Counihan, Harold J. "The North Carolina Constitutional Convention of 1835: A Study in Jacksonian Democracy." *North Carolina Historical Review* 46 (Oct. 1969): 335–364.

2083. Fleer, Jack D. *North Carolina Politics.* Chapel Hill: University of North Carolina Press, 1968.

2084. Greene, Jack P. "The North Carolina Lower House and the Power to Appoint Public Treasurers, 1711–1775." *North Carolina Historical Review* 40 (Jan. 1963): 37–53.

2085. Jeffrey, Thomas E. "The Second Party System in North Carolina, 1836–1860." Ph.D. dissertation, Catholic University, 1976.

2086. Kent, Elliot N. "Personality and Legislative Activity: A Psychology of Style in the North Carolina House of Representatives." Ph.D. dissertation, University of North Carolina, 1978.

2087. Lewis, Henry W. *The General Assembly of North Carolina Guidebook of Organization and Procedure.* Chapel Hill: University of North Carolina, Institute of Government, 1951.

2088. Lewis, Henry W. *Legislative Committees in North Carolina.* Chapel Hill: University of North Carolina, Institute of Government, 1952.

2089. Moore, John R. "The Shaping of a Political Leader: Josiah W. Bailey and the Gubernatorial Campaign of 1924." *North Carolina Historical Review* 41 (Apr. 1964): 190–213.

2090. Morgan, Thomas S. "A 'Folly... Manifest to Everyone': The Movement to Enact Unemployment Insurance Legislation in North Carolina, 1935–1936." *North Carolina Historical Review* 52 (July 1975): 283–302.

2091. North Carolina. Legislative Research Commission. *Administrative Rules: Report to the 1981 General Assembly of North Carolina.* Raleigh, NC: North Carolina, Legislative Research Commission, 1980.

2092. Rankin, Robert S. *The Government and Administration of North Carolina.* New York: Crowell, 1955.

2093. Roller, David C. "Republican Factionalism in North Carolina, 1904–1906." *North Carolina Historical Review* 41 (Jan. 1964): 62–73.

2094. Sprengel, Donald P. "Legislative Perceptions of Gubernatorial Power in North Carolina." Ph.D. dissertation, University of North Carolina, 1966.

2095. "State Senatorial Rotation." *Popular Government* 18 (May 1952): 1–2.

2096. Steelman, Joseph F. "Edward J. Justice: Profile of a Progressive Legislator, 1899–1913." *North Carolina Historical Review* 48 (Apr. 1971): 148–161.

2097. Steelman, Joseph F. "Jonathan Elwood Cox and North Carolina's Gubernatorial Campaign of 1908." *North Carolina Historical Review* 41 (Oct. 1964): 436–447.

2098. Steelman, Joseph F. "Origins of the Campaign for Constitutional Reform in North Carolina, 1912–1913." *North Carolina Historical Review* 56 (Oct. 1979): 396–418.

2099. Steelman, Joseph F. "The Progressive Democratic Convention of 1914 in North Carolina." *North Carolina Historical Review* 46 (Apr. 1969): 83–104.

2100. Steelman, Joseph F. "Republican Party Strategists and the Issue of Fusion with Populists in North Carolina, 1893–1894." *North Carolina Historical Review* 47 (July 1970): 244–269.

2101. Steelman, Joseph F. "Republicanism in North Carolina: John Motley Morehead's Campaign to Revive a Moribund Party, 1908–1910." *North Carolina Historical Review* 42 (Apr. 1965): 153–168.

2102. Steelman, Joseph F. "The Trials of a Republican State Chairman: John Motley Morehead and North Carolina Politics, 1910–1912." *North Carolina Historical Review* 43 (Jan. 1966): 31–42.

2103. Stewart, Debra W. "Public Policy and Decision Processes: The Impact of Women's Policy Issues on Decision-Making in the North Carolina Legislature." Ph.D. dissertation, University of North Carolina, 1975.

2104. Trelease, Allen W. "Republican Reconstruction in North Carolina: A Roll-Call Analysis of the State House of Representatives, 1868–1870. *Journal of Southern History* 42 (Aug. 1976): 319–344.

2105. University of North Carolina. Institute for Research in Social Science. *Technical Aids to North Carolina Officials: An Analysis.* Chapel Hill: University of North Carolina, Institute for Research in Social Science, 1948.

2106. Wager, Paul W. *North Carolina: The State and Its Government.* New York: Oxford Book Co., 1947.

2107. Watterson, John S. "The Ordeal of Governor Burke." *North Carolina Historical Review* 48 (Apr. 1971): 95–117.

2108. Williams, Max R. "The Foundations of the Whig Party in North Carolina." *North Carolina Historical Review* 47 (Apr. 1970): 115–129.

2109. Williams, Max R. "William A. Graham and the Election of 1844: A Study in North Carolina Politics." *North Carolina Historical Review* 45 (Jan. 1968): 23–46.

North Dakota

2110. Baum, Dale. "The New Day in North Dakota: The Nonpartisan League and the Politics of Negative Revolution." *North Dakota History* 40 (Spring 1973): 5–19.

2111. Grau, Craig H., and Dale W. Olsen. *Voting in Unicameral Referenda in North Dakota and Montana.* Grand Forks: University of North Dakota, Bureau of Governmental Affairs, 1976.

2112. Hunter, William C. "John Miller, First Governor of North Dakota." *North Dakota History* 34 (Winter 1967): 30–45.

2113. Martens, Sharon W. *Turnover in the North Dakota State Legislative Assembly, 1965 –1971.* Grand Forks: University of North Dakota, Bureau of Governmental Affairs, 1972.

2114. Strinden, Earl S. "The North Dakota Legislative Research Committee." M.A. thesis, University of North Dakota, 1958.

Ohio

2115. Aumann, Francis R., and Harvey Walker. *The Government and Administration of Ohio.* New York: Crowell, 1956.

2116. Aumann, Francis R. "'Rotten Borough' Representation in Ohio." *National Municipal Review* 20 (Feb. 1931): 82 –86.

2117. Baker, Roscoe. "The Reference Committee of the Ohio House of Representatives." *American Political Science Review* 34 (Apr. 1940): 306 –310.

2118. Brito, Patricia. "Protective Legislation in Ohio: The Inter-War Years." *Ohio History* 88 (Spring 1979): 173 –197.

2119. Campbell, Willard D. "Code Revision in Ohio." *State Government* 20 (July 1947): 195 –196.

2120. Campbell, Willard D. "Continuous Code Revision in Ohio." *Ohio State Law Journal* 11 (Autumn 1950): 533 –550.

2121. Chance, Charles W. "Analysis of Legislative Agreements: The Case of Ohio." Ph.D. dissertation, Ohio State University, 1970.

2122. Chance, Charles W., and Higdon C. Roberts. "Staffing Legislative Standing Committees: The Ohio Experience." *State Government* 43 (Winter 1970): 31 –38.

2123. Citizens Conference on State Legislatures. *How Citizens Can Improve the Ohio General Assembly.* Kansas City: Citizens Conference on State Legislatures, 1974.

2124. Citizens League of Greater Cleveland. *Ohio's Apportionment and Subdistricting.* Cleveland: Citizens League of Greater Cleveland, 1963.

2125. Colston, Freddie C. "The Influence of the Black Legislators in the Ohio House of Representatives." Ph.D. dissertation, Ohio State University, 1972.

2126. Craft, Ralph H. "The Effects of Institutional Changes on Legislative Processes and Performances: The Case of Ohio, 1959 to 1974." Ph.D. dissertation, Rutgers University, 1977.

2127. Erickson, Leonard. "Politics and Repeal of Ohio's Black Laws, 1837–1849." *Ohio History* 82 (Summer-Autumn 1973): 154–175.

2128. Fletcher, Mona. "Bicameralism as Illustrated by the Nineteenth General Assembly of Ohio." *American Political Science Review* 32 (Feb. 1938): 80–85.

2129. Fletcher, Mona. "A Decade of Bicameralism in Ohio with Special References to the 1930's." Ph.D. dissertation, Ohio State University, 1949.

2130. Flinn, Thomas A. "Continuity and Change in Ohio Politics." *Journal of Politics* 24 (Aug. 1962): 521–544.

2131. Flinn, Thomas A. "The Ohio General Assembly: A Developmental Analysis." In *State Legislative Innovation: Case Studies of Washington, Ohio, Florida, Illinois, Wisconsin, and California*, edited by James A. Robinson. New York: Praeger, 1973, pp. 236–278.

2132. Flinn, Thomas A. "An Outline of Ohio Politics." *Western Political Quarterly* 13 (Sept. 1960): 702–723.

2133. Glosser, Lauren A. "Ohio Legislators Get Help . . . Program Commission." *National Municipal Review* 40 (Oct. 1951): 468–472.

2134. Glosser, Lauren A. "The Ohio Program Commission: A New Approach to Legislative Studies." *State Government* 24 (Feb. 1951): 35, 44.

2135. Green, Alexander. *Ohio Government*. Englewood Cliffs, NJ: Prentice-Hall, 1961.

2136. Griswold, Thelma I. *Bicameralism in Ohio*. Cleveland: Western Reserve University Book Store, 1937.

2137. Harmon, Robert B. *Government and Politics in Ohio: An Information Source Survey*. Monticello, IL: Vance Bibliographies, 1979.

2138. Horne, William E. Van. "Lewis D. Campbell and the Know-Nothing Party in Ohio." *Ohio History* 76 (Autumn 1967): 202–221.

2139. Johnston, David A. "Politics and Policy in Ohio: A Study of Equal Rights, Pollution Control, and Unemployment Compensation Legislation." Ph.D. dissertation, Ohio State University, 1972.

2140. Kremm, Thomas W. "The Old Order Trembles: The Formation of the Republican Party in Ohio." *Cincinnati Historical Society Bulletin* 36 (Fall 1978): 193–215.

2141. Lowry, Robert E. *A Statistical Study of the 88th and 89th Sessions of the Ohio General Assembly.* Columbus: Ohio State University, Department of Political Science, 1932.

2142. Mallison, W. T. "General versus Special Statutes in Ohio." *Ohio State Law Journal* 11 (Autumn 1950): 462–494.

2143. Marshall, George B. "Life History of a Bill in the Ohio Legislature." *Ohio State Law Journal* 11 (Autumn 1950): 447–455.

2144. Metzenbaum, Howard M. "Judicial Interpretation of Constitutional Limitations on Legislative Procedure in Ohio." *Ohio State Law Journal* 11 (Autumn 1950): 456–461.

2145. Nowlin, William F. "Legislative Investigating Committees in Ohio, 1925–1945." Ph.D. dissertation, Ohio State University, 1950.

2146. Pollack, Ervin H., and Charles F. O'Brien. "The History of Legislative Publications in Ohio." *Ohio State Law Journal* 13 (Summer 1952): 307–349.

2147. Porter, Daniel R. "Governor Rutherford B. Hayes." *Ohio History* 77 (Winter-Spring-Summer 1968): 58–75.

2148. Ratcliffe, Donald J. "The Role of Voters and Issues in Party Formation: Ohio, 1824." *Journal of American History* 59 (Mar. 1973): 847–870.

2149. Reilly, Archer. "New Legislative Service Commission Gets Under Way." *Ohio Bar* 26 (Oct. 1953): 666–670.

2150. Rose, Albert H. *Ohio Government: State and Local.* 4th ed. Dubuque, IA: Kendall/Hunt, 1974.

2151. Schwartz, Arthur A. "Ohio Legislative Reference Bureau and Its Place in the Legislative Process." *Ohio State Law Journal* 11 (Autumn 1950): 436–446.

2152. Sidlow, Edward I. "Professionalism in a State Legislature: The Case of Ohio." Ph.D. dissertation, Ohio State University, 1979.

2153. Sponholtz, Lloyd. "The 1912 Constitutional Convention in Ohio: The Call-Up and Nonpartisan Selection of Delegates." *Ohio History* 79 (Summer-Autumn 1970): 209–218.

2154. "A Unicameral Legislature for Ohio: Four Proposals." *Toledo City Journal* 12 (March 6, 1937): 109–110.

2155. Waksmundski, John. "Governor McKinley and the Workingman." *Historian* 38 (Aug. 1976): 629–647.

Oklahoma

2156. *The Apportionment Problem in Oklahoma.* Norman: University of Oklahoma, Bureau of Government Research, 1959.

2157. Bernick, E. Lee. *Legislative Decision-Making and the Politics of Tax Reform: The Oklahoma Senate.* Norman: University of Oklahoma, Bureau of Government Research, 1975.

2158. Bernick, Emil L. *Legislative Voting Patterns and Partisan Cohesion in a One-Party Dominant Legislature.* Norman: University of Oklahoma, Bureau of Government Research, 1973.

2159. Bingham, R. D. *Reapportionment of the Oklahoma House of Representatives: Politics and Process.* Norman: University of Oklahoma, Bureau of Government Research, 1972.

2160. Bowen, Don L. "They All Get into the Show." *National Municipal Review* 39 (Oct. 1950): 450–454.

2161. Ellinger, Charles W. "The Drive for Statehood in Oklahoma, 1889–1906." *Chronicles of Oklahoma* 41 (Spring 1963): 15–37.

2162. Ellinger, Charles W. "Political Obstacles Barring Oklahoma's Admission to Statehood 1890–1906." *Great Plains Journal* 3 (Spring 1964): 60–83.

2163. Gill, Jerry L. "Thompson Benton Ferguson: Governor of Oklahoma Territory, 1901–1906." *Chronicles of Oklahoma* 53 (Spring 1975): 109–127.

2164. Hanson, Bertil L. "Oklahoma's Experience with Direct Legislation." *Social Science Quarterly* 47 (Dec. 1966): 263–273.

2165. Harkey, Paul. "Televising the Legislature in Oklahoma." *State Government* 24 (Oct. 1951): 249–251.

2166. Harmon, Robert B. *Government and Politics in Oklahoma: An Information Source Survey.* Monticello, IL: Vance Bibliographies, 1979.

2167. Johnson, B. H. "Reports of the Governors of Oklahoma Territory 1891 to 1899." *Chronicles of Oklahoma* 44 (Winter 1966–1967): 365–379.

2168. Jones, Stephen. "Captain Frank Frantz, the Rough Rider Governor of Oklahoma Territory." *Chronicles of Oklahoma* 43 (Winter 1965–1966): 374–393.

2169. Kirkpatrick, Samuel A. *The Legislative Process in Oklahoma: Policy Making, People, and Politics.* Norman: University of Oklahoma Press, 1978.

2170. *Legislative Apportionment in Oklahoma.* Norman: University of Oklahoma, Bureau of Government Research, 1956.

2171. *Legislative Attitudes Toward State Constitutional Revision—The Oklahoma Case.* Norman: University of Oklahoma, Bureau of Government Research, 1971.

2172. Lien, A. J. "Convening the Special Session, Oklahoma's Predicament." *National Municipal Review* 17 (Mar. 1928): 139–141.

2173. McCarty, J. D. *Notes on the Oklahoma Legislative Council.* Houston: Southern Conference of the Council of State Government, 1966.

2174. McDonald, Jean G. *Legislators and Patronage in Oklahoma.* Norman: University of Oklahoma, Bureau of Government Research, 1975.

2175. McLemore, Lelan E. *Behavioral Orientations Toward Party Leadership and System Norms: An Exploratory Analysis.* Norman: University of Oklahoma, Bureau of Government Research, 1975.

2176. McLemore, Lelan E. *Task-Related Norms in a State Legislature: The Case of Oklahoma.* Norman: University of Oklahoma, Bureau of Government Research, 1973.

2177. Mauer, George J. "Political Equality and Legislative Apportionment in Oklahoma, 1907–1964." Ph.D. dissertation, University of Oklahoma, 1964.

2178. Murphy, L. V. "Legislative Apportionment in Oklahoma." *Southwestern Social Science Quarterly* 13 (Sept. 1932): 161–168.

2179. Neuringer, Sheldon. "Governor Walton's War on the Ku Klux Klan: An Episode in Oklahoma History 1923–1924." *Chronicles of Oklahoma* 45 (Summer 1967): 153–179.

2180. Patterson, Samuel C. "The Role of the Lobbyist: The Case of Oklahoma." *Journal of Politics* 25 (Feb. 1963): 72–92.

2181. Thornton, H. V. "Oklahoma Cities Weakened." *National Municipal Review* 35 (June 1946): 295–298.

2182. Thornton, H. V., and Gene Aldrich. *The Government of Oklahoma.* Oklahoma City: Harlow, 1960.

2183. Walker, Larry. *State Legislative Control of Federal Aid Funds: The Case of Oklahoma.* Norman: University of Oklahoma, Bureau of Government Research, 1978.

2184. Wright, James R. "The Assiduous Wedge: Woman Suffrage and the Oklahoma Constitutional Convention." *Chronicles of Oklahoma* 51 (Winter 1973–1974): 421–443.

Oregon

2185. Balmer, Donald G. *Financing State Senate Campaigns: Multnomah County, Oregon, 1964.* Princeton, NJ: Citizens Research Foundation, 1966.

2186. Balmer, Donald G. "The Role of Political Leadership in the Passage of Oregon's Migratory Labor Legislation." *Western Political Quarterly* 15 (Mar. 1962): 146–156.

2187. Balmer, Donald G. *State Election Services in Oregon.* Princeton, NJ: Citizens Research Foundation, 1972.

2188. Belton, Howard C. *Under Eleven Governors.* Portland, OR: Binford and Mort, 1977.

2189. Campbell, Ernest H. *The State Legislatures of Alaska, Oregon and Washington.* Seattle: University of Washington and the Northwest Regional American Assembly, 1966.

2190. Childs, Charles. *The Oregon Legislature.* Portland, OR: Metropolitan Press, 1937.

2191. Cullen, Robert K. "Revision of the Oregon Statutes." *Oregon Law Review* 28 (Feb. 1949): 120–137.

2192. French, G. L. "One State Senator for Each County." *Oregon Voter* 35 (Dec. 3, 1949): 1291–1294.

2193. Hendrickson, James E. "The Rupture of the Democratic Party in Oregon, 1858." *Pacific Northwest Quarterly* 58 (Apr. 1967): 65–73.

2194. Lamb, B. S. "Emergency Board: Oregon's System of Interim Fiscal Adjustment." *Oregon Law Review* 55 (1976): 197–225.

2195. Laws, Frank D. "Political Sponsors and the Recruitment of Legislative Candidates in Oregon." Ph.D. dissertation, University of Oregon, 1970.

2196. "Legislators' Compensation Constitutional Amendment." *Portland City Club Bulletin* 23 (Oct. 2, 1942): 60–61.

2197. Linde, H. A., and D. Frohnmayer. "Prescription for the Citizen Legislature: Cutting the Gordian Knot." *Oregon Law Review* 56 (1977): 3–29.

2198. Miller, Warren E. "A Study of Some Statistical Techniques for Investigating Legislative Voting Behavior, Including an Exploratory Analysis of a Legislative Body, the 1947 Oregon State Senate." M.A. thesis, University of Oregon, 1950.

2199. "More than One-Third of Oregon Legislators Are Present or Former City Officials." *Western City* 15 (Jan. 1939): 24.

2200. Neuberger, Richard L. *Adventures in Politics: We Go to the Legislature.* New York: Oxford University Press, 1954.

2201. Neuberger, Richard L. "Confessions of a State Senator." *Tomorrow* 10 (Apr. 1951): 18–23.

2202. Neuberger, Richard L. "I Go to the Legislature." *Survey Graphic* 30 (July 1941): 373–376.

2203. Probert, Walter. "The Constitutional Restriction on Titles of Acts in Oregon." *Oregon Law Review* 31 (Feb. 1952): 111–161.

2204. "Procedure in Oregon State Legislature." *Oregon Voter* 36 (Jan. 7, 1950): 3–4.

2205. "Reapportionment: County Figures for Computers." *Oregon Voter* 36 (Jan. 28, 1950): 79–81.

2206. "Reapportionment." *Oregon Voter* 35 (Nov. 19, 1949): 1241–1248.

2207. "Report on Amendment Creating Legislative Assembly Emergency Committee." *Portland City Club Bulletin* 33 (Oct. 17, 1952): 81–82.

2208. "Report on Constitutional Amendment for Legislative Representation Reapportionment." *Portland City Club Bulletin* 31 (Oct. 27, 1950): 121–130.

2209. Reuling, J. A. "Apportionment in Oregon." *Willamette Law Journal* 5 (Winter 1969): 203–227.

2210. Schumacher, Waldo. "Reapportionment in Oregon." *Western Political Quarterly* 3 (Sept. 1950): 428–434.

2211. Seligman, Lester G. "Political Change: Legislative Elites and Parties in Oregon." *Western Political Quarterly* 17 (June 1964): 177–187.

2212. Smith, Barbara L. "Oregon Legislative Politics: The Case of Education." Ph.D. dissertation, University of Oregon, 1970.

2213. Treadgold, Alva G. "Constitutional Provisions Regulating the Mechanics of Statutory Enactment in Oregon—Effect of Enrollment." *Oregon Law Review* 27 (Dec. 1947): 46–74.

2214. Valleau, John F. *Press Coverage of the Oregon Legislature*. Eugene: University of Oregon School of Journalism, 1952.

2215. Valleau, John F. "Oregon Legislative Reporting." *Journalism Quarterly* 29 (Spring 1952): 158–170.

2216. Wilson, Darrell C. "A Study of Role Conflict in the Oregon Legislature." Ph.D. dissertation, University of Oregon, 1965.

Pennsylvania

2217. Beers, Paul B. *Pennsylvania Politics Today and Yesterday: The Tolerable Accommodation*. University Park: Pennsylvania State University Press, 1980.

2218. "The Biography of a Bill." *Currents* 2 (Spring 1951): 16–17.

2219. Braham, W. Walter. "Reform of Pennsylvania's Legislative Procedure." *Temple Law Quarterly* 25 (Apr. 1952): 420–427.

2220. Burnham, Walter Dean, and John Sprague. "Additive and Multiplicative Models of the Voting Universe: The Case of Pennsylvania, 1960–1968." *American Political Science Review* 64 (June 1970): 471–490.

2221. Butera, Robert J. "Open Committees in Pennsylvania: Lessons for the Leadership." *State Government* 47 (Summer 1974): 162–164.

2222. Farmerie, Samuel A. "Pennsylvania Legislators, 1901–1963." *Pennsylvania History* 34 (Jan. 1967): 31–43.

2223. Fisher, Philip, W. Kelley, and T. Timoney. "Limitations on the Legislature: Pennsylvania Constitution Article III." *University of Pennsylvania Law Review* 100 (June 1952): 1217–1236.

2224. Foner, Philip S., ed. "A Pennsylvania State Senator on Women's Rights in 1868." *Pennsylvania History* 41 (Oct. 1974): 423–426.

2225. Fox, William T. R. "Legislative Personnel in Pennsylvania." *Annals of the American Academy of Political and Social Science* 195 (Jan. 1938): 32–39.

2226. Gerrity, Frank. "The Masons, the Antimasons, and the Pennsylvania Legislature, 1834–1836." *Pennsylvania Magazine of History and Biography* 99 (Apr. 1975): 180–206.

2227. Harrison, Robert. "The Hornets' Nest at Harrisburg: A Study of the Pennsylvania Legislature in the Late 1870's." *Pennsylvania Magazine of History and Biography* 103 (July 1979): 334–355.

2228. Healy, Robert L. "Interparty Competition in Pennsylvania, 1954–68: A Historical and Political Perspective." *Pennsylvania History* 37 (Oct. 1970): 352–380.

2229. Hutton, A. J. W. "Pennsylvania General Assembly of 1931." *Dickinson Law Review* 36 (Jan. 1932): 15–33, 86–98.

2230. Ireland, Owen. "Partisanship and the Constitution: Pennsylvania 1787." *Pennsylvania History* 45 (Oct. 1978): 315–332.

2231. Keefe, William J. "Parties, Partisanship, and Public Policy in the Pennsylvania Legislature." *American Political Science Review* 48 (June 1954): 450–464.

2232. Korask, Tadeus Z., and Richard Di Salle. "Legislative Apportionment in Pennsylvania." *University of Pittsburgh Law Review* 12 (Winter 1951): 215–243.

2233. Lyons, William E. "Populism in Pennsylvania, 1892–1901." *Pennsylvania History* 32 (Jan. 1965): 49–65.

2234. Palmer, Kenneth T. "The Legislative Committee System in Pennsylvania." Ph.D. dissertation, Pennsylvania State University, 1964.

2235. Pennsylvania Regional American Assembly on State Legislatures in American Politics. *The Pennsylvania Assembly on State Legislatures in American Politics.* Pittsburgh: Pennsylvania Regional American Assembly on State Legislatures in American Politics, 1968.

2236. Rabin, Walter W. "Referential Legislation in Pennsylvania." *Temple Law Quarterly* 25 (July 1951): 59–63.

2237. Smith, William F. "Legislative Patterns of Adaptation: A Study of the Pennsylvania House of Representatives." Ph.D. dissertation, University of Pittsburgh, 1978.

2238. Sorauf, Frank J. *Party and Representation: Legislative Politics in Pennsylvania.* New York: Atherton Press, 1963.

2239. Sterling, Philip. "Some Practical Aspects of Legislation." *Pennsylvania Bar Association* 38 (1932): 381–420.

2240. Stevens, R. Michael. *Occupation Legislator: An Exploration of Political Culture in the Pennsylvania General Assembly.* Philadelphia: Temple University, Center for the Study of Federalism, 1971.

2241. Tanger, Jacob, Harold Aldefer, and M. McGeary. *Pennsylvania Government: State and Local.* State College, PA: Penns Valley Publishers, 1950.

2242. Tully, Alan. "Constituent-Representative Relationships in Early America: The Case of Pre-Revolutionary Pennsylvania." *Canadian Journal of History* 11 (Aug. 1976): 139–154.

2243. Watts, Irma A. "Why Pennsylvania Abandoned Unicameralism." *State Government* 9 (Mar. 1936): 54–55.

2244. Wendel, Thomas. "The Speaker of the House, Pennsylvania, 1701–1776." *Pennsylvania Magazine of History and Biography* 97 (Jan. 1973): 3–21.

2245. Young, Chester R. "The Evolution of the Pennsylvania Assembly, 1682–1748." *Pennsylvania History* 35 (Apr. 1968): 147–168.

Rhode Island

2246. Eagleton Institute of Politics. *The Rhode Island Legislature.* New Brunswick, NJ: Rutgers University, Eagleton Institute of Politics, 1967.

2247. Foster, H. *Apportionment and Metropolitan Planning in Rhode Island.* Kingston: University of Rhode Island, Bureau of Government Research, 1967.

2248. Goodman, Jay S. *The Democrats and Labor in Rhode Island, 1952–62: Changes in the Old Alliance.* Providence: Brown University Press, 1967.

2249. Goodman, Jay S. "A Note on Legislative Research: Labor Representation in Rhode Island." *American Political Science Review* 61 (June 1967): 468–473.

2250. Grant, Philip A. "Party Chaos Embroils Rhode Island." *Rhode Island History* 26 (Oct. 1967): 113–125.

2251. Marsis, James L. "Agrarian Politics in Rhode Island, 1800–1860." *Rhode Island History* 34 (Feb. 1975): 12–21.

2252. Polishook, Irvin H. "Peter Edes's Report of the Proceedings of the Rhode Island General Assembly, 1787–1790." *Rhode Island History* 25 (Apr. 1966): 33–42.

2253. Prisley, Alexander V. "Rhode Island Legislative Politics: A Study of the 1961–1962 General Assembly." Ph.D. dissertation, Brown University, 1966.

2254. Rand, Larry A. "The Know-Nothing Party in Rhode Island." *Rhode Island History* 23 (Oct. 1964): 102–116.

2255. Ray, John M. "Anti-Catholicism and Know-Nothingism in Rhode Island." *American Ecclesiastical Review* 148 (Jan. 1963): 27–36.

2256. Smith, Matthew J. "Rhode Island Politics 1956–1964: Party Realignment." *Rhode Island History* 35 (May 1976): 49–61.

2257. Tantillo, Charles. *Strengthening the Rhode Island Legislature: An Eagleton Institute Study and Report.* New Brunswick, NJ: Rutgers University Press, 1968.

South Carolina

2258. Bryant, Lawrence C., ed. *Negro Lawmakers in the South Carolina Legislature, 1869–1902.* Orangeburg: South Carolina State College, School of Graduate Studies, 1968.

2259. Bryant, Lawrence C., ed. *Negro Senators and Representatives in the South Carolina Legislature, 1868–1902.* Orangeburg: South Carolina State College, School of Graduate Studies, 1968.

2260. Cauthen, John K. *Speaker Blatt: His Challenges Were Greater.* Columbia: University of South Carolina Press, 1978.

2261. Eisenberg, Ralph. "The Logroll, South Carolina Style." In *Cases in State and Local Government*, edited by Richard P. Frost. Englewood Cliffs, NJ: Prentice-Hall, 1961, pp. 155–163.

2262. Larsen, Christian L., and Miles Ryan. *Aids for State Legislators.* Columbia: University of South Carolina, Bureau of Public Adminstration, 1947.

2263. Lee, Charles E., and Ruth S. Green. "A Guide to South Carolina Council Journals, 1671–1775." *South Carolina Historical Magazine* 68 (Jan. 1967): 1–13.

South Dakota 173

2264. Lee, Charles E., and Ruth S. Green. "A Guide to the Commons House Journals of the South Carolina General Assembly, 1692–1721." *South Carolina Historical Magazine* 68 (July 1967): 165–183.

2265. Lee, Charles E., and Ruth S. Green. "A Guide to the Upper House Journals of the South Carolina General Assembly, 1721–1775." *South Carolina Historical Magazine* 67 (Oct. 1966): 187–202.

2266. McConaughy, John B. "Certain Personality Factors of State Legislators in South Carolina." *American Political Science Review* 44 (Dec. 1950): 897–903.

2267. Matthews, Linda M. "Keeping Down Jim Crow: The Railroads and the Separate Coach Bills in South Carolina." *South Atlantic Quarterly* 73 (Winter 1974): 117–129.

2268. Palmer, J. David. "Revitalizing State Legislatures." *University of South Carolina Governmental Review* (Nov. 1966): 1–4.

2269. "South Carolina House Asks Biennial Sessions." *National Municipal Review* 41 (May 1952): 247.

2270. Stone, Richard G. "The Privy Council of South Carolina, 1776–1790: A Study in Shared Executive Power." Ph.D. dissertation, University of Tennessee, 1973.

2271. Way, Almon L. "The Role of the Governor in the State Legislative Process: A Case Study of South Carolina." Ph.D. dissertation, University of South Carolina, 1974.

South Dakota

2272. Clem, Alan L. *Prairie State Politics: Popular Democracy in South Dakota.* Washington, D.C.: Public Affairs Press, 1967.

2273. Clem, Alan L. "Roll Call Voting Behavior in the South Dakota Legislature." *Public Affairs* (May 1966): 1–8.

2274. Elliott, Sheldon P. "The Role of Legislatures in the Development of Law." *South Dakota Law Review* 1 (Spring 1956): 26–55.

2275. Farber, W. O., et al. *Government of South Dakota.* Sioux Falls: Midwest-Beach, 1962.

2276. Gates, Janet, and Charles O. Jones. *Legislative Turnover.* Vermillion: State University of South Dakota, Governmental Research Bureau, 1957.

2277. Geary, T. C. *Law Making in South Dakota.* Vermillion: State University of South Dakota, Governmental Research Bureau, 1958.

2278. Grant, H. Roger. "Origins of a Progressive Reform: The Initiative and Referendum Movement in South Dakota." *South Dakota History* 3 (Fall 1973): 390–407.

2279. Hendrickson, Kenneth E. "Some Political Aspects of the Populist Movement in South Dakota." *North Dakota History* 34 (Winter 1967): 77–92.

2280. "Inevitable Clash of Power? Determining the Proper Role of the Legislature in the Administration of Justice." *South Dakota Law Review* 22 (Spring 1977): 387–406.

2281. Jones, Charles O. *Legislative Turnover.* Vermillion: University of South Dakota, Governmental Research Bureau, 1952.

2282. *Law Making in South Dakota.* Vermillion: University of South Dakota, Governmental Research Bureau, 1959.

2283. Lord, Alan. *Work Load of the South Dakota Legislature.* Vermillion: State University of South Dakota, Governmental Research Bureau, 1952.

2284. Schell, James S. *A Study of the Need for Reorganizing the System of Standing Committees in the South Dakota Legislature.* Vermillion: University of South Dakota, Governmental Research Bureau, 1952.

2285. Schenk, Willis J. *Occupational Profile of the South Dakota Legislature, 1900–1949.* Vermillion: University of South Dakota, 1950.

2286. Sturm, Albert L. "State Governmental Modernization and South Dakota." *Public Affairs* (Aug. 1968): 1–5.

2287. University of South Dakota. Governmental Research Bureau. *An Analysis of the Constitutional Provisions Pertaining to Legislative Organization in South Dakota.* Vermillion: University of South Dakota, Governmental Research Bureau, 1952.

Tennessee

2288. Adams, J. W. "Governor Gordon Browning, Campaigner Extraordinary." *West Tennessee Historical Society Papers* 30 (1976): 5–23.

2289. Bergeron, Paul H. "Politics and Patronage in Tennessee During the Adams and Jackson Years." *Prologue* 2 (Spring 1970): 19–24.

2290. Binning, F. Wayne. "The Tennessee Republicans in Decline, 1869–1876." *Tennessee Historical Quarterly* 39 (Winter 1980): 471–484.

2291. Cartwright, Joseph H. "Black Legislators in Tennessee in the 1880's: A Case Study in Black Political Leadership." *Tennessee Historical Quarterly* 32 (Fall 1973): 265–284.

2292. Coomer, James C. "The Impact of Reapportionment on the Tennessee Legislative Process: An Analysis of the Tennessee General Assembly, 84th and 85th Sessions." Ph.D. dissertation, University of Tennessee, 1975.

2293. Dykeman, Wilma. "Too Much Talent in Tennessee?" *Harper's* 210 (Mar. 1953): 48–53.

2294. Hudson, Irby R. "The Compensation of Legislators." In *Papers on Constitutional Revision*. Knoxville: University of Tennessee: Bureau of Public Administration, 1947, vol. 2, pp. 57–63.

2295. Hudson, Irby R. "Constitutional Provisions Governing Terms of the Legislature." In *Papers on Constitutional Revision*. Knoxville: University of Tennessee, Bureau of Public Administration, 1947, vol. 2, pp. 18–21.

2296. Hudson, Irby R. "Legislative Sessions." In *Papers on Constitutional Revision*. Knoxville: University of Tennessee: Bureau of Public Administration, 1947, vol. 2, pp. 22–31.

2297. Hudson, Irby R. "The Unicameral vs. the Bicameral Legislature." In *Papers on Constitutional Revision*. Knoxville: University of Tennessee, Bureau of Public Administration, 1947, vol. 2, pp. 1–3.

2298. Isaac, Paul E. "The Problems of a Republican Governor in a Southern State: Ben Hooper of Tennessee." *Tennessee Historical Quarterly* 27 (Fall 1968): 229–248.

2299. Iverson, Evan A., and Lee S. Greene. "The Apportionment of Legislative Seats." In *Papers on Constitutional Revision*. Knoxville: University of Tennessee, Bureau of Public Administration, 1947, vol. 2, pp. 4–17.

2300. Kousser, J. Morgan. "Post-Reconstruction Suffrage Restrictions in Tennessee: A New Look at the V. O. Key Thesis." *Political Science Quarterly* 88 (Dec. 1973): 655–683.

2301. Lee, David D. "The Attempt to Impeach Governor Horton." *Tennessee Historical Quarterly* 34 (Summer 1975): 188–201.

2302. Lee, David D. "The Triumph of Boss Crump: The Tennessee Gubernatorial Election of 1932." *Tennessee Historical Quarterly* 35 (Winter 1976): 393–413.

2303. MacPherson, Joseph T. "Democratic Progressivism in Tennessee: The Administration of Governor Austin Peay, 1923–1927." *East Tennessee Historical Society's Publications* 40 (1968): 50–61.

2304. Mallard, Carl B. "The Governor as Legislative Leader in Tennessee." Ph.D. dissertation, University of Tennessee, 1979.

2305. Miller, Harold V. "Tennessee's New Legislative Reference Bureau." *Tennessee Government* 8 (Oct.-Nov. 1949): 2.

2306. Parks, Norman L. "Tennessee Politics Since Kefauver and Reece: A 'Generalist' View." *Journal of Politics* 28 (Feb. 1966): 141–168.

2307. Prescott, Frank W. "Constitutional Provisions on Legislative Procedure." In *Papers on Constitutional Revision*. Knoxville: University of Tennessee, Bureau of Public Administration, 1947, vol. 2, pp. 32–56.

2308. Reichard, Gary W. "The Defeat of Governor Roberts." *Tennessee Historical Quarterly* 30 (Spring 1971): 94–109.

2309. Reiners, Fred G. "Help for Legislators." *Tennessee Planner* 9 (Oct.-Dec. 1948): 45–49.

2310. Robison, Dan M. "Little Men and Big Events: A Passing Look at Some Tennessee Legislators." *East Tennessee Historical Society's Publications* 41 (1969): 3–16.

2311. Shahan, J. M. "The Rhetoric of Reform: The 1906 Gubernatorial Race in Tennessee." *Tennessee Historical Quarterly* 35 (Spring 1976): 65–82.

2312. Tilley, Betty. "Portrait of Legislators." *Tennessee Planner* 15 (Dec. 1954): 92–96.

2313. Williams, Henry N. "Constitutional Provisions Regulating the Mechanics of Enactment in Tennessee." *Vanderbilt Law Review* 5 (Apr. 1952): 614–621.

2314. Williams, Henry N. "Legislative Apportionment in Tennessee." *Tennessee Law Review* 20 (Apr. 1948): 235–245.

2315. Williams, Henry N. "The Legislative Process in Tennessee with Special Reference to Gubernatorial Control." Ph.D. dissertation, University of Chicago, 1952.

Texas

2316. Benton, Wilbourn. *Texas: Its Government and Politics.* Englewood Cliffs, NJ: Prentice-Hall, 1961.

2317. Brauer, Kinley J. "The Massachusetts State Texas Committee: A Last Stand Against the Annexation of Texas." *Journal of American History* 51 (Sept. 1964): 214–231.

2318. Brewer, Thomas B. "State Anti-Labor Legislation: Texas—A Case Study." *Labor History* 11 (Winter 1970): 58–76.

2319. Casdorph, Paul D. "Norris Wright Cuney and Texas Republican Politics, 1883–1896." *Southwestern Historical Quarterly* 68 (Apr. 1965): 455–464.

2320. Chumlea, Wesley S. "The Politics of Legislative Apportionment in Texas—1921–1957." Ph.D. dissertation, University of Texas, 1959.

2321. Claunch, J. M., ed. *Legislative Redistricting in Texas.* Dallas: Arnold Foundation, 1965.

2322. Davis, Clarice M. *Legislative Malapportionment and Roll-Call Voting in Texas, 1961–1963.* Austin: University of Texas, Institute of Public Affairs, 1965.

2323. Ericson, J. E., and James H. McCrocklin. "From Religion to Commerce: The Evolution and Enforcement of Blue Laws in Texas." *Social Science Quarterly* 45 (June 1964): 50–58.

2324. Gould, Lewis L. "Progressives and Prohibitionists: Texas Democratic Politics, 1911–1921." *Southwestern Historical Quarterly* 75 (July 1971): 5–18.

2325. Griffin, Roger A. "Intrastate Sectionalism in the Texas Governor's Race of 1853." *Southwestern Historical Quarterly* 76 (Oct. 1972): 142–160.

2326. Hicks, Jimmie. "Texas and Separate Independence, 1860–61." *East Texas Historical Journal* 4 (Oct. 1966): 85–106.

2327. Hinckley, Katherine A. "The Opportunity Structure of Legislative Leadership: The Case of Texas from a Comparative Perspective." Ph.D. dissertation, Stanford University, 1971.

2328. Holcombe, John W. "The Legislative Perceptions of Texas State Representatives: The Sixty-Second Legislature." Ph.D. dissertation, Claremont Graduate School, 1972.

2329. Huey, Mary Evelyn. *Texas Constitutional Revision: The Legislative Branch.* Dallas: Southern Methodist University, Arnold Foundation, 1962.

2330. Jensen, J. R. *Legislative Apportionment in Texas.* Houston: University of Houston, Public Affairs Research Center, 1964.

2331. Jones, Bryan D. "Responsiveness and Policy: Models of Representation in the Texas Legislature." Ph.D. dissertation, University of Texas, 1970.

2332. Keith, Gary A. "Legislative Leadership and Opposition in an Anti-Party Era: The Texas and Massachusetts Houses of Representatives in the 1970s." Ph.D. dissertation, Brandeis University, 1980.

2333. Lindsey, Jim T. "The Texas Legislative Council." *Baylor Law Review* 2 (Spring 1950): 303–317.

2334. Lutz, Donald S., and Richard W. Murray. "Coalition Formation in the Texas Legislature: Issues, Payoffs, and Winning Coalition Size." *Western Political Quarterly* 28 (June 1975): 296–315.

2335. McCleske, Clifton. *The Government and Politics of Texas.* 2d ed. Boston: Little, Brown, 1966.

2336. MacCorkle, Stuart A. "Texas Apportionment Problem." *National Municipal Review* 34 (Dec. 1945): 540–543.

2337. MacCorkle, Stuart A., and Dick Smith. *Texas Government.* 4th ed. New York: McGraw-Hill, 1960.

2338. Meiners, Fredericka A. "The Texas Governorship, 1861–1865: Biography of an Office." Ph.D. dissertation, Rice University, 1975.

2339. Miller, Lawrence W. "Legislative Turnover and Political Careers: A Study of Texas Legislators, 1969–1975." Ph.D. dissertation, Texas Tech University, 1977.

2340. Moon, John S., and Nancy Saunders. "The Ideological Characteristics of Party Leaders: A Case of Texas." *Western Political Quarterly* 32 (June 1979): 209–214.

2341. Moore, Robert E. "Legislative Resolutions—Their Function and Effect." *Texas Law Review* 31 (Apr. 1953): 417–429.

2342. Morris, Willie. "Legislating in Texas." *Commentary* 38 (Nov. 1964): 40–46.

2343. Nichols, R. V. "Expose of the Constitutional Amendment Proposing Annual Legislative Sessions." *Texas Bar Journal* 12 (Sept. 1949): 402–403.

2344. Nokes, George O. "Constitution and Legislature in Texas." *State Government* 21 (July 1948): 149–153.

2345. Nyitray, Joseph P. "Amateur and Professional Democrats at the 1972 Texas State Convention." *Western Political Quarterly* 28 (Dec. 1975): 685–699.

2346. Oden, William E. "Some Characteristics of Recent Texas Legislators." *Rocky Mountain Social Science Journal* 4 (Oct. 1967): 110–119.

2347. Oden, William E. "Tenure and Turnover in Recent Texas Legislatures." *Social Science Quarterly* 45 (Mar. 1965): 371–374.

2348. Olson, David M. *Legislative Primary Elections in Austin, Texas, 1962.* Austin: University of Texas, Institute of Public Affairs, 1963.

2349. Patterson, Caleb P., Sam McAlister, and George Hester. *State and Local Government in Texas.* New York: MacMillan, 1948.

2350. Pope, J., and S. McConnico. "Texas Civil Procedure Rule Making." *Baylor Law Review* 30 (Winter 1978): 5–22.

2351. Ray, Joseph M. "Procedural Limitations on the Texas Legislature." *Southwestern Social Science Quarterly* 19 (Sept. 1938): 152–160.

2352. Ray, Joseph M. "Some Texas Constitutional Limitations on Legislative Action." Ph.D. dissertation, University of Texas, 1937.

2353. Samuels, S. "Legislature Is King." *Texas Law Review* (Oct. 1932): 221–226.

2354. Schmelzer, Janet. "Thomas M. Campbell: Progressive Governor of Texas." *Red River Valley Historical Review* 3 (Fall 1978): 52–63.

2355. Skinner, A. E. "Footnotes to Texas History: General Sheridan, the Buffalo and the Texas Legislature." *Texana* 11 (1973): 275–280.

2356. Sneed, Edgar P. "Historiography of Reconstruction in Texas: Some Myths and Problems." *Southwestern Historical Quarterly* 72 (Apr. 1969): 435–448.

2357. Southern Methodist University. Arnold School of Government. *Government Reform in Texas*. Dallas: Southern Methodist University, Arnold School of Government, 1936.

2358. Still, Rae F. *The Gilmer-Aikin Bills: A Study in the Legislative Process*. Austin: Steck, 1950.

2359. Texas Legislative Council. *Compensation of Legislators and Frequency of Legislative Sessions*. Austin: Texas Legislative Council, 1956.

2360. Texas Legislative Council. *Legislator's Guide to the Texas Legislative Council*. Austin: Texas Legislative Council, 1980.

2361. University of Texas. Bureau of Municipal Research. *How Bills Become Law in Texas*. Austin: University of Texas, Bureau of Municipal Research, 1945.

2362. University of Texas. Institute of Public Affairs. *The Fifty-Third Texas Legislature: A Review of Its Work*. Austin: University of Texas, Institute of Public Affairs, 1953.

2363. Weeks, O. Douglas. "The Texas Legislature—A Problem for Constitutional Revision." *Texas Law Review* 21 (May 1943): 490–499.

2364. Weeks, O. Douglas. "Towards a More Effective Legislature." *Texas Law Review* 35 (Oct. 1957): 907–918.

2365. Weeks, O. Douglas. *Two Legislative Houses or One*. Dallas: Southern Methodist University, Arnold Foundation, 1938.

2366. Woodward, Earl F. "Internal Improvements in Texas Under Governor Peter Hansborough Bell's Administration, 1849–1853." *Southwestern Historical Quarterly* 76 (Oct. 1972): 161–182.

2367. Woodward, Walter. "Legislative Procedure." *Texas Bar Journal* 1 (Mar. 1938): 65–68.

2368. Wooster, Ralph A. "An Analysis of the Texas Know Nothings." *Southwestern Historical Quarterly* 70 (Jan. 1967): 414–423.

2369. Wooster, Ralph A. "Ben H. Epperson: East Texas Lawyer, Legislator, and Civic Leader." *East Texas Historical Journal* 5 (Mar. 1967): 29–42.

2370. Wooster, Ralph A. "Early Texas Politics: The Henderson Administration." *Southwestern Historical Quarterly* 73 (Oct. 1969): 176–192.

2371. Wooster, Ralph A. "Early Texas Politics: The Wood Administration." *Texana* 8 (1970): 181–199.

2372. Wooster, Ralph A. "Membership in Early Texas Legislatures, 1850–1860." *Southwestern Historical Quarterly* 69 (Oct. 1965): 163–173.

Utah

2373. Alexander, Thomas G. "An Experiment in Progressive Legislation: The Granting of Woman Suffrage in Utah in 1870." *Utah Historical Quarterly* 38 (Winter 1970): 20–30.

2374. Durham, G. Homer. *Prescribing for the Body Politic: Suggestions for Legislative-Administrative Adjustments in the Government of Utah.* Salt Lake City: University of Utah, Extension Division, 1951.

2375. Ellsworth, S. George. "Utah's Struggle for Statehood." *Utah Historical Quarterly* 31 (Winter 1963): 60–69.

2376. Emenhiser, De John, ed. *The Dragon on the Hill: Utah's 38th Legislature—Analysis and Comment.* Salt Lake City: University of Utah Press, 1970.

2377. Griffiths, David B. "Far Western Populism: The Case of Utah, 1893–1900." *Utah Historical Quarterly* 37 (Fall 1969): 396–407.

2378. Grow, Stewart L. "The Utah Legislature and the Income Tax Amendment." *Utah Historical Quarterly* 36 (Summer 1968): 222–232.

2379. Jack, Ronald C. "Early Utah and Nevada Electoral Politics." *Nevada Historical Society Quarterly* 17 (Fall 1974): 131–143.

2380. Lamar, Howard R. "Statehood for Utah: A Different Path." *Utah Historical Quarterly* 39 (Fall 1971): 307–327.

2381. Poll, Richard D. "A State Is Born." *Utah Historical Quarterly* 32 (Winter 1964): 9–31.

2382. Shipps, Jan. "Utah Comes of Age Politically: A Study of the State's Politics in the Early Years of the Twentieth Century." *Utah Historical Quarterly* 35 (Spring 1967): 91–111.

2383. Utah Foundation. *State and Local Government in Utah.* Salt Lake City: Utah Foundation, 1954.

2384. Weaver, Ellsworth E. "The Evolution of Political Institutions in Utah." Ph.D. dissertation, New York University, 1953.

2385. Weaver, Ellsworth E. *Legislative Reapportionment in Utah.* Salt Lake City: University of Utah, Institute of Government, 1950.

2386. White, Jean B. "Gentle Persuaders: Utah's First Women Legislators." *Utah Historical Quarterly* 38 (Winter 1970): 31–49.

2387. Wolfinger, Henry J. "A Reexamination of the Woodruff Manifesto in the Light of Utah Constitutional History." *Utah Historical Quarterly* 39 (Fall 1971): 328–349.

Vermont

2388. Bassett, T. D. Seymour. "Vermont Politics and the Press in the 1840's." *Vermont History* 47 (Summer 1979): 196–213.

2389. Bryan, Frank M. "Reducing the Time-Lock in the Vermont Constitution: An Analysis of the 1974 Referendum." *Vermont History* 44 (Winter 1976): 38–47.

2390. Bryan, Frank M. "Who Is Legislating? No Drastic Changes Are Seen as a Result of Vermont's Reapportionment." *National Civic Review* 56 (Dec. 1967): 627–633.

2391. Bryan, Frank M. *Yankee Politics in Rural Vermont.* Hanover, NH: University Press of New England, 1974.

2392. Carroll, Daniel B. "The Unicameral Legislature of Vermont." Ph.D. dissertation, University of Wisconsin, 1930.

2393. Hand, Samuel B., and D. Gregory Sanford. "Carrying Water on Both Shoulders: George D. Aiken's 1936 Gubernatorial Campaign in Vermont." *Vermont History* 43 (Fall 1975): 292–306.

2394. Morse, Sidney G. "The Representation Issue in Vermont a Century Ago." *Vermont Quarterly* 21 (Apr. 1953): 83–100.

2395. Neuenschwander, John A. "An Engineer for Governor: James Hartness in 1920." *Vermont History* 38 (Spring 1970): 139–149.

2396. Nuquist, Andrew E., and Edith W. Nuquist. *Vermont State Government and Administration.* Burlington: University of Vermont, Government Research Center, 1966.

2397. Smallwood, Frank. *Free and Independent.* Brattleboro, VT: Greene Press, 1976.

2398. Smith, Elsie B. "William J. Anderson: Shoreham's Negro Legislator in the Vermont House of Representatives." *Vermont History* 44 (Fall 1976): 203–213.

Virginia

2399. Billings, Warren M. "The Growth of Political Institutions in Virginia, 1634 to 1676." *William and Mary Quarterly* 31 (Apr. 1974): 225–242.

2400. Chichester, Cassius M. "Interim Activities in Aid of Legislation: Legislative Function Supplemented by New Process." *State Government* 16 (Apr. 1943): 87–89.

2401. Chitwood, W. R. "Governor John Floyd, Physician." *Virginia Cavalcade* 26 (Autumn 1976): 86–95.

2402. Crater, Flora, Carolyn Brickey, and Meg Williams. *The Almanac of Virginia Politics, 1977: The State Senators and Delegates, Their Records and Districts.* Falls Church, VA: Woman Activist, 1977.

2403. Detweiler, Robert. "Political Factionalism and the Geographic Distribution of Standing Committee Assignments in the Virginia House of Burgesses, 1730–1776." *Virginia Magazine of History and Biography* 80 (July 1972): 267–285.

2404. Dorman, John Frederick. "Governor Samuel Mathews, Jr." *Virginia Magazine of History and Biography* 74 (Oct. 1966): 429–432.

2405. Fogarty, Andrew B. "Legislative Attitudes Toward Reform of the Budgetary Process: A Comparative Study of Virginia and Florida." Ph.D. dissertation, Florida State University, 1979.

2406. Gibson, Tucker L. "The Governor of Virginia as Legislative Leader." *University of Virginia Newsletter* 45 (Jan. 1969): 17–20.

2407. Greene, Jack P. "The Attempt to Separate the Offices of Speaker and Treasurer in Virginia, 1758–1766." *Virginia Magazine of History and Biography* 71 (Jan. 1963): 11–18.

2408. Hall, Alvin L. "Virginia Back in the Fold: The Gubernatorial Campaign and Election of 1929." *Virginia Magazine of History and Biography* 73 (July 1965): 280–302.

2409. Heinemann, Ronald L. *Depression and New Deal in Virginia: The Enduring Dominion*. Charlottesville: University Press of Virginia, 1983.

2410. Hemphill, William E., Marvin W. Schlegel, and Sadie E. Engelberg. *Cavalier Commonwealth: History and Government of Virginia*. New York: McGraw, 1957.

2411. Hodges, Wiley E. "Pro-Governmentalism in Virginia, 1789–1836: A Pragmatic Liberal Pattern in the Political Heritage." *Journal of Politics* 25 (May 1963): 333–360.

2412. Holt, Wythe W. "The Virginia Constitutional Convention of 1901–1902: A Reform Movement Which Lacked Substance." *Virginia Magazine of History and Biography* 76 (Jan. 1968): 67–103.

2413. Hounshell, Charles D. "The Legislative Function of the Virginia General Assembly." Ph.D. dissertation, University of Virginia, 1950.

2414. Hounshell, Charles D. *The Legislative Process in Virginia*. Charlottesville: University of Virginia, Extension Division, 1951.

2415. Hume, Richard L. "The Membership of the Virginia Constitutional Convention of 1867–1868: A Study of the Beginnings of Congressional Reconstruction in the Upper South." *Virginia Magazine of History and Biography* 86 (Oct. 1978): 461–484.

2416. "The Inequality of Representation in the General Assembly of Virginia: Memorial to the Legislature of the Commonwealth of Virginia, Adopted at Full Meeting of the Citizens of Kanawha." *West Virginia History* 25 (July 1964): 283–298.

2417. Kirby, Jack T. "Alcohol and Irony: The Campaign of Westmoreland Davis for Governor, 1909–1917." *Virginia Magazine of History and Biography* 73 (July 1965): 259–279.

2418. Lingley, Charles R. *The Transition in Virginia from Colony to Commonwealth*. New York: Longmans, Green, 1910.

2419. Lowe, Richard G. "The Republican Party in Antebellum Virginia, 1856–1860." *Virginia Magazine of History and Biography* 81 (July 1973): 259–279.

2420. McBain, Howard L. *Government and Politics in Virginia*. Richmond: Bell, Book, and Stationery Co., 1922.

2421. Martin, P. L. "County Reapportionment in Virginia." *Virginia Law Review* 55 (Oct. 1969): 1167–1181.

2422. Pate, James E. "The Legislature of Virginia: Its Organization and Procedure." Ph.D. dissertation, Johns Hopkins University, 1925.

2423. Pate, James E. *State Government in Virginia*. Richmond: Appeals Press, 1932.

2424. Risjord, Norman K. "The Virginia Federalists." *Journal of Southern History* 33 (Nov. 1967): 486–517.

2425. Singleton, Marvin K. "New Light in the Chancery Side of Virginia's Evolution to Statehood." *Journal of American Studies* 2 (Oct. 1968): 149–160.

2426. Stanley, Robert H. "Party Conflict and the Secessionist Alternative: The Virginia House of Delegates as a Test Case, 1855–1860." *Essays in History* 24 (1980): 5–28.

2427. Wells, Thomas L. "The Legislative Consequences of Urban Growth: The Case of Virginia, 1966." Ph.D. dissertation, University of Virginia, 1968.

2428. Williams, Murat W. "Virginia Politics: Winds of Change." *Virginia Quarterly Review* 42 (Spring 1966): 177–188.

2429. Wynes, Charles E. "The Evolution of Jim Crow Laws in Twentieth Century Virginia." *Phylon* 28 (Winter 1967): 416–425.

Washington

2430. Avery, Mary W. *Government of Washington State*. Rev. ed. Seattle: University of Washington Press, 1973.

2431. Baker, Gordon E. "Legislative Power to Amend Initiatives in Washington State." *Pacific Northwest Quarterly* 55 (Jan. 1964): 28–34.

2432. Baker, Gordon E. *The Politics of Reapportionment in Washington State*. New York: McGraw-Hill, 1960.

2433. Beckett, Paul L. *From Wilderness to Enabling Act: The Evolution of a State of Washington*. Pullman: Washington State University Press, 1968.

2434. Best, James J. "The Impact of Reapportionment on the Washington House of Representatives." In *State Legislative Innovation*, edited by James A. Robinson. New York: Praeger, 1973, pp. 136–183.

2435. Bone, Hugh A., and Robert C. Benedict. "Perspectives on Direct Legislation: Washington State's Experience, 1914–1973." *Western Political Quarterly* 28 (June 1975): 330–351.

2436. Chapin, Richard U. "Washington: The Legislative Climate." *State Government* 46 (Summer 1973): 180–182.

2437. *The Citizen and the Legislature: Proceedings of the Twenty-Eighth Annual Summer Institute of Government, 1963.* Seattle: University of Washington, Bureau of Governmental Research and Services, 1963.

2438. Countryman, Vern. *Un-American Activities in the State of Washington: The Work of the Canwell Committee.* Ithaca: Cornell University Press, 1951.

2439. Cravens, Hamilton. "The Emergence of the Farmer-Labor Party in Washington Politics, 1919–1920." *Pacific Northwest Quarterly* 57 (Oct. 1966): 148–157.

2440. Deutsch, Herman J. *History and Government of the State of Washington.* Pullman: State College of Washington, 1941.

2441. Howard, Helen A. "Isaac Ingalls Stevens: First Governor of Washington Territory." *Journal of the West* 2 (July 1963): 336–346.

2442. Kerr, William T. "The Progressives of Washington, 1910–12." *Pacific Northwest Quarterly* 55 (Jan. 1964): 16–27.

2443. McDermott, W. B. "Judicial Sanctions and Legislative Redistricting in Washington State." *Washington Law Review* 45 (1970): 681–724.

2444. Moitoret, Anthony F. "Business and the 1953 Washington State Legislature." *Pacific Northwest Industry* 12 (May 1953): 148–154.

2445. Oliphant, J. Orin. "Congressional and Legislative Redistricting in Washington." *National Municipal Review* 21 (May 1932): 340.

2446. Rader, Melvin. *False Witness.* Seattle: University of Washington Press, 1969.

2447. "Restructuring the Legislature: A Proposal for Unicameralism in Washington." *Washington Law Review* 51 (Oct. 1976): 901–952.

2448. Sheldon, Charles H., and Frank P. Weaver. *Politicians, Judges, and the People: A Study in Citizen's Participation.* Westport, CT: Greenwood Press, 1980.

2449. Simmons, Robert H. "The Transition of the Washington Executive from Territory to Statehood." *Pacific Northwest Quarterly* 55 (Apr. 1964): 76–86.

2450. Tripp, Joseph F. "Toward an Efficient and Moral Society: Washington State Minimum-Wage Law, 1913–1925." *Pacific Northwest Quarterly* 67 (July 1976): 97–112.

2451. University of Washington. Bureau of Governmental Research and Services. *Bill Drafting in Washington.* Seattle: University of Washington, Bureau of Governmental Research and Services, 1950.

2452. University of Washington. Bureau of Governmental Research and Services. *The Legislature and the Legislative Process in the State of Washington.* Seattle: University of Washington Press, 1966.

2453. "Washington Legislative Council Held Legal." *National Municipal Review* 37 (Feb. 1948): 91–92.

West Virginia

2454. Bullard, Todd H. "The West Virginia Labor Federation and the West Virginia Legislature, 1957–1961." Ph.D. dissertation, University of Pittsburgh, 1964.

2455. Burckel, Nicholas C. "Governor Albert B. White and the Beginning of Progressive Reform, 1901–1905." *West Virginia History* 40 (Fall 1978): 1–12.

2456. "The Clock but Not the Law Was Stopped." *National Municipal Review* 41 (June 1952): 305.

2457. Coghill, Kenneth L. *The Lawmaking Process in West Virginia: A Study in Legislative Ethics.* Parsons, WV: McClain Printing Co., 1970.

2458. Curry, Richard O. "A Reappraisal of Statehood Politics in West Virginia." *Journal of Southern History* 28 (Nov. 1962): 403–421.

2459. Davis, Claude J. *West Virginia State and Local Government.* Morgantown: West Virginia University, Bureau for Government Research, 1963.

2460. Faust, Martin L. "Results of the Split-Session System of the West Virginia Legislature." *American Political Science Review* 22 (Feb. 1928): 109–121.

2461. Fisher, Lucy Lee. "John J. Cornwell, Governor of West Virginia, 1917–1921." *West Virginia History* 24 (Apr. 1963): 258–288.

2462. Flanner, William E. "Legislative Tape Recording—West Virginia." *State Government* 24 (Sept. 1951): 238–239.

2463. Frasure, Carl M. *Some Reflections on the Legislative Process in West Virginia.* Morgantown: West Virginia University, Bureau for Government Research, 1967.

2463A. Ham, P. Gerald. "The Mind of a Copperhead: Letters of John J. Davis on the Secession Crisis and Statehood Politics in Western Virginia, 1860–1862." *West Virginia History* 24 (Jan. 1963): 93–109.

2464. Horack, Frank E. "Constitutional Limitations on Legislative Procedure in West Virginia." *West Virginia Law Quarterly* 39 (June 1933): 294–322.

2465. Jackameit, William P. "The Sims Higher Education Cases of West Virginia: A Study of Conflict Between a State Elected Official and the Governing Boards of Public Higher Education, 1949–1957." *West Virginia History* 37 (Oct. 1975): 1–10.

2466. Lambert, Oscar D. *West Virginia and Its Government.* Boston: D. C. Heath, 1951.

2466A. Lewis, Virgil A. *History and Government of West Virginia.* New York: American Book Co., 1922.

2467. Lutz, Paul F. "The 1952 West Virginia Gubernatorial Election." *West Virginia History* 39 (Jan.-Apr. 1978): 210–235.

2468. McManus, Lewis N. "The West Virginia Legislature's Public Information Program." *State Government* 45 (Summer 1972): 161–164.

2469. Massay, Glenn F. "Legislators, Lobbyists, and Loopholes: Coal Mining Legislation in West Viginia 1875–1901." *West Virginia History* 32 (Apr. 1971): 135–170.

2470. Oxendale, James R. "An Exchange Model of Voluntary Legislative Withdrawal: A Case of the West Virginia House of Delegates." Ph.D. dissertation, West Virginia University, 1974.

2471. Ross, W. R. *House of Delegates Apportionment in West Virginia.* Morgantown: West Virginia University, Bureau for Government Research, 1961.

2472. Squires, J. Duane. "Lincoln and West Virginia Statehood." *West Virginia History* 24 (July 1963): 325–331.

2473. Talbott, Forrest. "Some Legislative and Legal Aspects of the Negro Question in West Virginia During the Civil War and Reconstruction." *West Virginia History* 24 (Oct. 1962): 1–31.

2474. West Virginia University. Bureau for Government Research. *The Legislative Process in West Virginia*. Morgantown: West Virginia University, Bureau for Government Research, 1953.

2475. Williams, John A. "The New Dominion and the Old: Antebellum and Statehood Politics as the Background of West Virginia's 'Bourbon Democracy.'" *West Virginia History* 33 (July 1972): 317–407.

2476. Winston, Sheldon. "Statehood for West Virginia—An Illegal Act?" *West Virginia History* 30 (Apr. 1969): 530–534.

Wisconsin

2477. Acrea, Kenneth. "The Wisconsin Reform Coalition, 1892 to 1900: La Follette's Rise to Power." *Wisconsin Magazine of History* 52 (Winter 1968–1969): 132–157.

2478. Asher, Robert. "The 1911 Wisconsin Workmen's Compensation Law: A Study in Conservative Labor Reform." *Wisconsin Magazine of History* 57 (Winter 1973–1974): 123–140.

2479. Baggaley, Andrew R. "Religious Influence on Wisconsin Voting, 1928–1960." *American Political Science Review* 56 (Mar. 1962): 66–70.

2480. Bartell, A. B. "Wisconsin Legislature: Some Notes and Anecdotes on 140 Years of the People's Business." *Wisconsin Bar Bulletin* 49 (Apr. 1976): 16–19.

2481. Buholz, Gordon A. "Improving Government through Legislative Research." *Governmental News* 3 (Apr. 1952): 7–9.

2482. Bunn, G. "Legislative Committee Review of Administrative Rules in Wisconsin." *Wisconsin Law Review* (1977): 935–988.

2483. Campbell, Ballard C. "Ethnicity and the 1893 Wisconsin Assembly." *Journal of American History* 62 (June 1975): 74–94.

2484. Chaffey, Douglas C. "Legislative Party Leaders: A Comparative Analysis." Ph.D. dissertation, University of Wisconsin, 1967.

2485. Chartock, Alan S., and Max Berking. *Strengthening the Wisconsin Legislature*. New Brunswick, NJ: Rutgers University Press, 1970.

2486. Cosmos, Graham A. "The Democracy in Search of Issues: The Wisconsin Reform Party, 1873–1877." *Wisconsin Magazine of History* 46 (Winter 1962–1963): 93–108.

2487. Crane, Wilder. "The Legislative Struggle in Wisconsin: Decision Making in the 1957 Wisconsin Assembly." Ph.D. dissertation, University of Wisconsin, 1959.

2488. Craven, Eugene C. "Discriminating Factors Among Legislator Voting Groups Within the Wisconsin State Legislature, 1945–1967." Ph.D. dissertation, University of Wisconsin, 1969.

2489. Current, Richard N. "The Politics of Reconstruction in Wisconsin, 1865–1873." *Wisconsin Magazine of History* 60 (Winter 1976–1977): 83–108.

2490. "An Executive Council Established in Wisconsin." *National Municipal Review* 20 (Aug. 1931): 479–480.

2491. Friedman, M., and Michael J. Spector. "Tenement House Legislation in Wisconsin: Reform and Reaction." *American Journal of Legal History* 9 (Jan. 1965): 41–63.

2492. Gaus, John M. "The Wisconsin Executive Council." *American Political Science Review* 26 (Oct. 1932): 914–920.

2493. Hamm, Keith E. "The Effects of Organized Demand Patterns on State Legislative Policy-Making: The Case of Wisconsin." Ph.D. dissertation, University of Wisconsin at Milwaukee, 1977.

2494. Hartmark, Leif S. "The Effects of Rationalistic Budgeting and Legislative Staff upon University Policy-Making Independence: The Wisconsin Experience." Ph.D. dissertation, State University of New York at Albany, 1978.

2495. Hass, Paul H. "Sin in Wisconsin: The Teasdale Vice Committee of 1913." *Wisconsin Magazine of History* 49 (Winter 1965–1966): 138–151.

2496. Hedlund, Ronald D., and Keith E. Hamm. "Institutional Development and Legislative Effectiveness: Rules Changes in the Wisconsin Assembly." In *Comparative Legislative Reforms and Innovations,* edited by Abdul S. Backleme and Jane J. Hefe. Albany: State University of New York at Albany, 1977, pp. 173–213.

2497. Heim, Joseph P. "Decision-Making in the Wisconsin Legislature: A Case Study of the Merger of the University of Wisconsin and the Wisconsin State University Systems." Ph.D. dissertation, University of Wisconsin at Milwaukee, 1976.

2498. Hesse, Michael B. "A Coorientation Study of Wisconsin State Senators and Their Constituencies." *Journalism Quarterly* 53 (Winter 1976): 626–633.

Wisconsin

2499. Kirsch, Mary M. "The Wisconsin Legislative Reference Library." *Special Libraries* 21 (Jan. 1930): 7–15.

2500. Lamb, F. "Work of the Wisconsin Legislature for the 1933 Session." *Wisconsin Law Review* 9 (Feb. 1934): 117–140.

2501. "Legislative Council: Eleven Committees Submitting Recommendations for Approval." *Wisconsin Taxpayer* 20 (Nov. 1952): 82–88.

2502. "Legislative Reapportionment: 1955 Legislature to Have Unusual Senate Districts—Four Counties Without Senators." *Wisconsin Taxpayer* 22 (Feb. 1954): 3–5.

2503. "The Legislative Reference Library." *Wisconsin Library Bulletin* 48 (Mar.-Apr. 1952): 61–63.

2504. Moore, William G. "Legislative Apportionment." *Wisconsin Law Review* (July 1949): 761–784.

2505. Ohm, Howard F. "Legislative Reference in Wisconsin." *State Government* 21 (Dec. 1948): 240–243.

2506. Olson, David J. "Citizens Grievance Letters as a Gubernatorial Control Device in Wisconsin." *Journal of Politics* 31 (Aug. 1969): 741–755.

2507. Patterson, Samuel C. "Patterns of Interpersonal Relations in a State Legislative Group: The Wisconsin Assembly." *Public Opinion Quarterly* 23 (Spring 1959): 101–109.

2508. Patterson, Samuel C. "The Role of the Deviant in the State Legislative System: The Wisconsin Assembly." *Western Political Quarterly* 14 (June 1961): 460–472.

2509. "Reapportionment Referendum: Questions and Answers to Help Voters Decide on April 7 Referendum." *Wisconsin Taxpayer* 21 (Apr. 1953): 2–3.

2510. "Recent Development in the Legislative Redistricting Struggle in Wisconsin." *Wisconsin Law Review* (Jan. 1955): 125–139.

2511. Renner, August N. "Legislative Reapportionment in Wisconsin." M.A. thesis, University of Wisconsin, 1948.

2512. Roherty, James M. "The Legislative Council as Legislative Institution: A Study of the Wisconsin Joint Legislative Council." Ph.D. dissertation, University of Wisconsin, 1957.

2513. Sharp, Walter R. "The Chief Executive and Auxiliary Agencies in the State of Wisconsin." *Revue Internationale des Sciences Administratives* 9 (Oct.-Dec. 1936): 563–598.

2514. Stampen, Jacob O. "Voting Behavior in the Wisconsin State Legislature, 1945–1967." Ph.D. dissertation, University of Wisconsin, 1969.

2515. Sullivan, Sheila. "Wisconsin Anti-Secrecy Law." *Neiman Reports* 16 (Mar. 1963): 25–28.

2516. Theobald, H. Rupert. "Equal Representation in Wisconsin: A Study of Legislative and Congressional Apportionment." Ph.D. dissertation, University of Wisconsin, 1972.

2517. Toepel, M. G. "The Legislative Reference Library: Serving Wisconsin." *Wisconsin Law Review* (Jan. 1951): 114–124.

2518. Van Meter, Donald S. "The Policy Implications of State Legislative Reapportionment: A Longitudinal Analysis." Ph.D. dissertation, University of Wisconsin, 1972.

2519. Weibull, Jörgen. "The Wisconsin Progressives, 1900–1914." *Mid-America* 47 (July 1965): 191–221.

2520. "Wisconsin Redistricting Referendum Challenged." *National Municipal Review* 41 (Mar. 1952): 149–150.

2521. "Wisconsin's 'Areacrats' Blocked by Court." *National Municipal Review* 42 (Dec. 1953): 564.

2522. Witte, Edwin E. "A Law-Making Laboratory." *State Government* 3 (Apr. 1930): 3–10.

2523. Woody, Carroll H. "The Legislature: Watchdog or Doghouse." *State Government* 4 (June 1931): 12–13.

2524. Wyman, Roger E. "Agrarian or Working-Class Radicalism? The Electoral Basis of Populism in Wisconsin." *Political Science Quarterly* 89 (Winter 1974–1975): 825–847.

Wyoming

2525. Frome, Ted C. "Stopping the Clock in the Wyoming Legislature." *Wyoming Law Journal* 10 (Spring 1956): 203–207.

2526. Gould, Lewis L. "Joseph M. Carey and Wyoming Statehood." *Annals of Wyoming* 37 (Oct. 1965): 157–170.

Wyoming

2527. Griffiths, David B. "Populism in Wyoming." *Annals of Wyoming* 40 (Apr. 1968): 57–72.

2528. Hajjar, S., and J. K. Anderson. *Reapportionment and Its Impact on Education Bills in Wyoming.* Laramie: University of Wyoming, Government Research Bureau, 1972.

2529. Holsinger, M. Paul. "Willis Van Devanter: Wyoming Leader, 1884–1897." *Annals of Wyoming* 37 (Oct. 1965): 171–206.

2530. Larson, T. A. "Wyoming Statehood." *Annals of Wyoming* 37 (Apr. 1965): 5–30.

2531. Olson, Frederick I. "The Self-Made Man in Wyoming: An Autobiographical Fragment from Governor Deforest Richards." *Annals of Wyoming* 37 (Oct. 1965): 207–209.

2532. Trachsel, Herman H., and Ralph M. Wade. *The Government and Administration of Wyoming.* New York: Crowell, 1953.

Author Index

Abernathy, Byron R., 1587
Abney, Glenn, 287, 736, 755, 1853
Abrams, A. J., 737
Abrams, Burton A., 635
Abrams, Douglas C., 2080
Acrea, Kenneth, 2477
Adams, Bruce, 180, 706
Adams, J. W., 2288
Adams, William C., 288
Adelman, Lynn, 1013
Adickes, R., 1112
Adler, Madeline, 2018
Adrian, Charles R., 1, 738, 881, 1818–1819
Aherns, Edmond, 1781
Aldefer, Harold, 2241
Aldrich, Gene, 2182
Alexander, Henry M., 1099
Alexander, Thomas G., 2373
Allen, Russ, 782
Allen, Tip H., 1854
Aly, Bower, 132
American Assembly, 2
American Historical Association, 898
American Legislators' Association, 841
American Political Science Association, Committee on American Legislatures, 3
Anderson, C. David, 1403
Anderson, J. K., 2528
Anderson, Lee F., 636
Anderson, Robert M., 1100
Anderson, William, 5
Andrews, James H., 1439
Antognini, Richard, 1113
Anton, Thomas J., 970, 1440, 1976
Arizona Legislative Council, 1085

Arrington, W. Russell, 971
Arseneau, Robert, 111
Asch, S. H., 440
Asher, Herbert B., 503
Asher, Robert, 2478
Askew, J. Thomas, 1414
Asseff, Emmett, 1664
Atkins, Leah, 1047
Atwood, Evangeline, 1082
Aumann, Francis R., 2115–2116
Austermann, Winnie, 665
Avery, Mary W., 2430
Aylsworth, L. E., 1911–1912

Baaklini, Abdo I., 842, 2020
Bachrach, Peter, 562
Backstrom, C., 1820
Badeaux, David, 1665
Baer, Michael A., 783, 812–813, 996
Baggaley, Andrew R., 2479
Bailey, Robert J., 1855
Bain, Henry, 1699
Baird, Lawrence M., 1114
Baker, Earl M., 289
Baker, Gordon E., 182–183, 290, 2431–2432
Baker, Kendall L., 815
Baker, M. L., 1342
Baker, Roscoe, 2117
Bakken, Gordon M., 1278
Balanoff, Elizabeth, 2081
Baldwin, Carolyn W., 1963
Baldwin, P. M., 1999
Balmer, Donald G., 2185–2187
Balutis, Alan P., 666, 739, 843, 899, 930, 1489, 2021
Baratz, Morton S., 562

Barber, James D., 331, 504, 590
Barclay, Thomas S., 1115–1118
Barkan, Elliott R., 2022
Barker, Twiley W., 462
Barnard, Bernard L., 1588
Barnard, William D., 1048
Barnat, Rhonda Katz, 1817
Barnidge, James L., 1666
Barrett, Edward L., 1119
Barrow, Timothy A., 931
Bartell, A. B., 2480
Bartlett, J. Kemp, 1700
Bartley, David M., 463
Bartley, Ernest R., 1343
Basehart, Hubert H., 505
Bassett, T. D. Seymour, 2388
Battle, Haron J., 972
Baum, Dale, 1729, 2110
Bay, John P., 1595
Beardsley, J. E., 1528
Beardsley, Janet, 591–592, 667, 1344
Beasley, James R., 1303
Bebout, John E., 256, 1977
Becker, Robert W., 1753
Beckett, Paul L., 2433
Beek, Joseph A., 1120
Beers, Paul B., 2217
Beiser, Edward N., 768
Belknap, George M., 506
Bell, Charles G., 1121–1122, 1235
Bell, George A., 1701
Bellush, Jewel, 2018
Belsky, M. H., 184
Belton, Howard C., 2188
Bemis, George W., 1123
Benedict, Robert C., 2435
Benjamin, Gerald, 2023
Bennett, William E., 1856
Benson, Lee, 2024
Benton, Wilbourn, 2316
Bergeron, Paul H., 2289
Berking, Max, 2485
Berle, Peter A., 2025
Bernardini, C. R., 1442
Bernick, Emil Lee, 560, 563, 637, 740, 2157–2158
Bertone, Thomas L., 1702
Berwanger, Eugene H., 1124
Best, James J., 2434
Best, Wallace H., 1125
Beth, Loren P., 1345, 1364

BeVier, Michael J., 1126
Beyle, Herman C., 1821
Beyle, Thad L., 564–566, 603
Bibb, J. W., 1590
Bibby, John F., 258
Bicker, William E., 1519
Bickerstaff, S., 185
Bigelow, Martha M., 1857
Billings, Warren M., 2399
Binford, Robert K., 1127
Bingham, R. D., 2159
Binning, F. Wayne, 1667, 2290
Black, Merle, 6
Blackford, Mansel G., 1128
Blair, Diane K., 507
Blair, George S., 133, 1129, 1443–1445
Blank, Robert H., 134
Blankenbeckler, George M., 668–669
Blitz, L. Franklin, 1075
Boertman, C. Stewart, 1591
Bogert, G. T., 1446
Bollens, John C., 1151
Bond, James A., 1822
Bone, Hugh A., 1703–1704, 2435
Bonett, Herman R., 1592–1593
Borit, G. S., 1447
Bortnick, Jane, 962
Bosworth, Carl A., 617
Bowen, Don L., 2160
Bower, Robert K., 1557
Bowers, Douglas, 1705
Bowlby, George M., 1754
Bowles, Brinton D., 1130–1131
Boyd, W. J. D., 186
Boynton, G. R., 291, 357, 816, 1577–1578
Brademas, John, 135
Bradley, Phillips, 7, 900, 2026
Bradley, Robert B., 901
Brady, D. W., 187
Bragg, Richard L., 1706
Braham, W. Walter, 2219
Brake, Hale D., 844
Brandner, Daniel C., 1594
Brandsma, Richard W., 1259–1260
Brandt, Edward R., 1823
Brannon, Victor D., 1883
Brauer, Kinley J., 2317
Breckenridge, Adam C., 22, 53, 1913–1914

Author Index

Bremmer, John A., 1520
Bresnick, David, 973
Brewer, J. H., 1070
Brewer, Thomas B., 2318
Brickey, Carolyn, 2402
Bridge, Franklin M., 1521
Brigman, William E., 9
Brinegar, David F., 1087
Brito, Patricia, 2118
Brittain, Joseph M., 1049
Broach, Glen T., 188, 638
Brockbank, W. Hughes, 741
Brodbeck, Arthur J., 1540
Broh, C. Anthony, 259
Bromage, Arthur W., 1755
Brooks, Robin, 2027
Broussard, E. Joseph, 1676
Broussard, James H., 380
Brown, Charles A., 1050–1053
Brown, Richard E., 707–710, 733
Brown, Seyom, 1190
Bruner, Charles H., 292
Bryan, Frank M., 136, 2389–2391
Bryant, Lawrence C., 2258–2259
Brydges, Earl W., 2028
Buchanan, William, 97, 293, 1133
Buck, A. E., 845
Buckley, William E., 1304
Buechner, John C., 8
Buehler, Ezra C., 137
Buell, Erwin C., 9
Buenker, John D., 1448
Buholz, Gordon A., 2481
Bullard, Todd H., 2454
Bunn, G., 2482
Burckel, Nicholas C., 2455
Burdette, Franklin L., 1915–1917
Burdick, Eugene, 1540
Bureau of Municipal Research, (Philadelphia), 189
Burk, Robert E., 1134
Burke, Norris J., 1135
Burnham, Walter Dean, 2220
Bushman, Donald O., 190
Bushnell, E., 191
Butera, Robert J., 2221
Butler, Daron K., 666, 1489
Butler, F., 464
Byrne, Paul L., 1136

Caldeira, Gregory A., 260
Caldwell, Kenneth S., 974
Caldwell, Lynton K., 846, 2029
Caldwell, Mary Ellen, 902
Calhoun, Charles W., 1522
California State Chamber of Commerce, 1137–1138
Calkins, S., 697
Calvert, Jerry, 332
Campbell, Alan K., 670
Campbell, Ballard, 10, 2483
Campbell, Ernest H., 1083, 2189
Campbell, Jack M., 2000
Campbell, Willard D., 2119–2120
Cantwell, Frank V., 817
Cape, William H., 1595
Capell, Elizabeth A., 1138
Carlson, Eric H., 663
Carlson, Richard J., 1468–1469
Carlson, Richard W., 1468
Carlson, Theodore L., 1449
Carlyle, Adam, 1918
Carmines, Edward G., 381
Carpentier, Charles F., 1450
Carriere, Marius, 1668
Carroll, Daniel B., 2392
Carroll, John J., 108, 1730, 1733
Carter, Edward F., 1346
Cartwright, Joseph H., 2291
Carver, Joan S., 1347
Casdorph, Paul D., 2319
Case, Karl E., 671
Casjens, Robert S., 1139
Cassidy, John Thomas, 1451
Caswell, J. T., 1756
Catterson, Lorace E., 1348
Cauthen, John K., 2260
Cave, Floyd A., 1272
Caver, Manning J., 1349
Chadwin, Mark L., 711
Chaffey, Douglas C., 138, 593, 2484
Chamberlain, Joseph P., 465
Chamberlain, Lawrence H., 2030
Chamberlain, William, 1969
Chamberlayne, Donald W., 304
Champagne, Roger, 2031
Chance, Charles W., 2121–2122
Chapin, Richard U., 2436
Chartock, Alan S., 2485
Chartrand, Robert L., 962
Chase, Fred I., 1757–1758
Chen, Rolet, 1884

Chester, Edward W., 975
Chichester, Cassius M., 2400
Childs, Charles, 2190
Chitwood, W. R., 2401
Cho, Woong-Kyu, 1885
Cho, Yong Hyo, 192, 208
Chrislock, Carl H., 1824
Christensen, Asher N., 466
Chumlea, Wesley S., 2320
Citizens' Committee for Equal Representation in the California State Senate, 1140
Citizens Conference on State Legislatures, 11, 105, 139, 818, 847–850, 1669, 1731, 1825, 2123
Citizens Constitution Committee of Florida, 1350
Citizens League of Greater Cleveland, 2124
City Club of New York, 2032
Civic Federation of Chicago, 1452–1453
Clark, Calvin W., 333–334, 346, 467, 903
Clark, D. H., 1556
Clark, Eric C., 1858
Clark, I. G., 976
Clark, Jill, 782
Clark, Robert B., 382
Clarke, Harold D., 335, 399
Clarke, Mary Patterson, 12
Claunch, J. M., 2321
Clausen, Aage, 294
Clayton, Dorothy H., 140
Cleary, Robert E., 594–595
Clem, Alan L., 193–194, 2272–2273
Clift, G. Glenn, 1630
Cloner, Alexander, 1141–1142
Coates, C. C., 1528
Coghill, Kenneth L., 2457
Cohen, Jeffrey E., 260A
Cohen, Julius, 904, 1826
Coigne, Armand B., 905
Colburn, David R., 1351
Cole, Albert M., 1596
Cole, Leonard A., 1979
Collings, R. A., 1143
Colston, Freddie C., 2125
Colvin, David L., 2033
Comer, John C., 1919–1920

Committee for Economic Development, 851
Commonwealth Club of Californa, 1144–1146
Conard, Alfred F., 907
Conklin, Patrick J., 508
Connecticut Citizens Conference on the General Assembly, 1306
Connecticut Public Expenditures Council, 1307–1310
Conolly, John H., 742
Constantini, Edmond, 1147–1148, 1228
Conway, Mary M., 1523
Coomer, James C., 2292
Cornelius, William G., 1398
Cornell, J. A., 1311
Cornwell, Elmer E., Jr., 111, 344, 615, 662, 797
Corrick, Franklin, 441, 1597–1599
Cosman, Bernard, 262
Cosmas, Graham A., 2486
Cottrell, Edwin A., 1149
Coulter, E. Merton, 1399–1400
Council of State Governments, 14–15, 141–143, 197, 295, 336, 415–416, 442, 468–469, 596, 672–673, 712, 852, 908–915
  Midwest Regional Conference, 417
  National Conference on Comparative Statistics, 618
  National Legislative Conference, 16, 470, 917
  National Legislative Conference, Committee on Legislative Rules, 713
  and Public Administration Service, 916
Counihan, Harold J., 2082
Countryman, Vern, 2438
Cowart, Andrew T., 263
Cox, Gary S., 1631
Craft, Ralph, 464, 709, 714–715, 1101, 2126
Craik, K. H., 1148
Crain, W. M., 471, 597, 639
Crane, Edgar G., 13, 502, 716, 1454, 1483
Crane, Stephen C., 717
Crane, Wilder, 144, 296, 640, 784, 2487

Author Index

Crater, Flora, 2402
Craven, Eugene C., 2488
Cravens, Hamilton, 2439
Crawford, Charles W., 1102
Creamer, William H., 1371
Crew, Robert E., 17, 210
Crittenden, John, 853
Crouch, Winston W., 1150–1151
Csontos, M. B., 2034
Cullen, Robert K., 2191
Culver, Dorothy C., 145
Culver, John H., 1152
Culver, Margaret S., 854
Cunningham, Everett W., 1639
Current, Richard N., 2489
Curry, Richard C., 1759
Curry, Richard O., 2458

D'Alemberte, Talbot, 855
Daley, Dennis M., 743
Dalton, Robert, 565
Dangerfield, George, 2035
Daniell, Jere R., 1964
Daniels, Bruce C., 1312
Danziger, James N., 1153
Danziger, Robert, 350
Dauer, Manning J., 1352
Davey, Harold W., 443
David, Paul T., 297
Davies, Race D., 1154
Davis, Clarice M., 2322
Davis, Claude J., 2459
Davis, Horace B., 1732
Davis, I. Ridgway, 1313
Davis, Raymond G., 1155, 1609
Dawson, Charles S., 2020
Dawson, Richard E., 977
Day, William L., 18, 918
Daynes, Byron W., 1542
DeAngelis, Eugene P., 1156
DeArmond, Robert N., 1082
Deborst, James H., 1760
DeClercq, Eugene R., 146–147
Deleon, Richard E., 674
Delong, Dennis R., 2036
Delorme, Roland L., 1279
DeMarcus, John P., 1656
Dengler, Louise W., 1088
Derfner, Armand, 198
Derge, David R., 619, 1455, 1524, 1887

Detroit Bureau of Governmental Research, 1761
Detweiler, Robert, 2403
Deutsch, Herman J., 2440
DeVries, Walter P., 1762
DeWitt, Paul B., 1558
Diamond, Irene, 337–338
Dickerson, Reed, 472
Dillard, Tom, 1103
Dillehay, Ronald C., 531
Dines, A., 199
Di Salle, Richard, 2232
Dishman, Robert B., 19
Dittenhofer, Mortimer A., 718
Dixon, K. H., 1353
Dixon, Robert G., 200, 298
Dobbins, Charles G., 1054
Dobbins, Harry T., 1922
Dodd, Sue Hutchinson, 1456
Dodd, Walter F., 107, 1456
Dodds, Harold W., 473
Dolan, Paul, 1339
Dometrius, Nelson C., 567
Donaho, John A., 687
Donnelly, Thomas C., 2001–2003
Doolen, Richard M., 1763
Dorman, John Frederick, 2404
Dorr, Harold M., 1764
Dorweiler, Louis C., Jr., 1827
Doubleday, D. Jay, 1157
Douglas, Charles G., 1965
Dovell, J. E., 1354
Dow, Edward F., 1696
Dowd, Mary Jane, 1707
Downs, Deborah, 1966
Doyle, Wilson K., 1355
Drake, Winbourne M., 1859
Dreyer, Edward C., 383
Driscoll, James D., 1158
Driscoll, Jean C., 299
Drury, James W., 1600–1601
Dubeck, Paula J., 264
Duke University, Law School, Department of Legislative Research and Drafting, 919
Duncan, Michael P., 1457
Dunn, Charles W., 785
Dunn, Delmer D., 819
Dunn, Richard E., 971
Dur, Philip F., 1670
Durfee, Elizabeth, 1765
Durham, G. Homer, 2374

Dvorin, Eugene P., 1159
Dye, Thomas R., 20–21, 201, 300, 568, 675, 978
Dyer, J. A., 641
Dykeman, Wilma, 2293
Dykstra, Robert R., 1559

Eagleton Institute of Politics, 1980, 2246
Echols, Margaret T., 1356
Edmar, F. Robert, 744
Edmonds, D., 187
Edsall, Preston W., 301
Edwards, Edwin W., 1671
Eisenberg, Ralph, 297, 1981, 2261
Elazar, Daniel J., 745, 1458
Elder, Ann H., 1828
Elkins, F. Clark, 786
Elkins, James S., 920
Eller, S., 1820
Elling, Richard C., 315, 384, 509, 719
Ellinger, Charles W., 2161–2162
Elliott, Sheldon P., 2274
Ellis, Richard N., 2004
Ellsworth, S. George, 2375
Elson, Alex, 1459
Elson, Charles Myer, 1401
Emenhiser, De John, 2376
Emery, D. R., 1170
Engelberg, Sadie E., 2410
Engelbert, Ernest A., 746, 1160
Engle, R. H., 302
English, Arthur, 108, 549
Engstrom, Richard L., 856, 1632, 1672
Entman, Robert M., 510
Erickson, Leonard, 2127
Ericson, J. E., 2323
Erikson, Robert S., 203, 303, 385, 820
Ershkowitz, Herbert, 511
Ervin, Theodore R., 1766
Esterly, Robert E., 2005
Ethridge, Marcus E., 418, 719A
Ethridge, William N., 1860
Eulau, Heinz, 97, 204, 322, 339–341, 512, 539, 554, 569, 607
Evans, Alvin E., 444, 598, 1633
Evans, Charles H., 1923

Everstine, Carl N., 1708–1711
Ezer, Mitchell J., 1271

Faber, W., 193
Fahrnkopf, Nancy, 1460
Fairlie, John A., 205, 419, 747
Falb, Susan Rosenfeld, 1712
Farabee, D. H., 979
Farber, Stephan B., 570
Farber, W. O., 676, 2275
Farmer, Hallie, 1056–1057
Farmerie, Samuel A., 2222
Faust, Martin L., 2460
Feder, Edward L., 1233
Feibelman, Herbert U., 1357
Feig, D. G., 677
Fein, L. J., 1773
Feller, Irwin, 921–922, 980
Fellman, David, 22
Fennimore, Jean Joy L., 1767–1769
Fenton, John H., 304
Fenton, William, 1602
Ferber, Paul H., 288
Ferguson, LeRoy C., 97, 643
Fesler, James W., 23
Ficklin, L. R., 748
Field, Phyllis F., 2024, 2037
Fiellin, Alan, 787
Fike, Claude E., 1861
Findley, James C., 1161
Firestine, R. E., 206
Fishburne, Charles, 855
Fisher, Floyd C., 1770
Fisher, Lucy Lee, 2461
Fisher, Mary L., 923
Fisher, Philip, 2223
Fitzsimons, Richard W., 1829
Flanner, William E., 2462
Fleer, Jack D., 2083
Fleming, James T., 1650
Flentje, Henry E., 1603
Fletcher, Mona, 513, 924, 2128–2129
Flinn, Thomas A., 386, 1830, 2130–2132
Flom, Floyd O., 1831
Florida Institute of Government, 1358
Flory, Claude R., 1359
Flournoy, Houston I., 1129
Flynt, Wayne, 1058, 1360

Fogarty, Andrew B., 720, 2405
Foner, Philip S., 2224
Foote, Frieda, 1753
Fordham, Jefferson B., 24, 109, 149
Formisano, Ronald P., 1771
Fortenberry, Charles N., 1862, 1866
Forth, Rod, 81, 491
Foster, H., 2247
Fountain, M. R., 420
Fox, Kel M., 1089
Fox, William T. R., 2225
Francis, Wayne L., 25, 387, 514, 571, 788, 981, 1525
Franklin, William E., 1162
Frasure, Carl M., 2463
Frederickson, H. George, 192, 208
Freeman, Patricia K., 621, 727A
Freitas, Carol Ann, 1163
French, G. L., 2192
Friedelbaum, Stanley H., 1982
Friedman, Gordon D., 1983
Friedman, M., 2491
Friedman, Robert S., 110
Friesema, H. Paul, 308
Frohnmayer, David, 769, 2197
Froman, Lewis A., 789
Frome, Ted C., 2525
Frost, Richard T., 26, 265
Fuhrman, Susan, 609
Fuller, Margaret G., 1772
Funk, A. E., 1634
Furniss, Susan W., 1280–1281
Fyock, Jack W., 749, 1733

Gable, Richard W., 1142, 1254
Galiette, R. T., 1337
Gallagher, Hubert R., 445, 572
Gallagher, J. F., 1164–1165
Gallup, Christopher M., 421
Garceau, Oliver, 790
Garcia, Thomas V., 388
Garfinkel, H., 1773
Garland, Michael, 27
Garnett, James L., 857
Garoury, William J., 1429
Garvey, Neil F., 1461
Gary, Lawrence E., 982
Gates, Janet, 2276
Gatewood, Willard G., Jr., 1104
Gatlin, Douglas S., 389
Gaus, John M., 2492

Geary, T. C., 2277
Gerrity, Frank, 2226
Gething, Judith R. D., 1774
Gibbs, Clayton R., 791
Gibson, Lorenzo T., Jr., 1713
Gibson, Tucker L., 2406
Gilbert, Charles E., 750
Gill, Jerry L., 2163
Ginger, Laura, 1542
Githens, Marianne, 342
Glass, Mary E., 1954–1956
Glosser, Lauren A., 2133–2134
Gold, David, 343, 1560
Goldberg, Delphis C., 751
Goldman, Sheldon, 1734
Gomez, Rudolph, 1282, 1296
Goodman, Jay S., 111, 344, 615, 662, 797, 2248–2249
Goodman, Paul, 1735
Goodwin, George, 19
Goodwin, Victor, 1957
Gordon, Dudley, 1166
Gormley, William T., 821–822
Gosebrink, Thomas A., 1888
Gosnell, Cullen B., 28, 1402–1403
Gould, Lewis L., 2324, 2526
Gove, Samuel K., 752, 1462–1470, 1507, 1509
Grant, Daniel R., 29
Grant, Edward D., 112
Grant, H. Roger, 2278
Grant, J. A. C., 474, 1167–1168, 1984
Grant, Philip A., 2250
Grau, Craig H., 266, 2111
Graves, W. Brooke, 30, 113, 345
Gray, Virginia, 678, 983–985
Green, Alexander, 2135
Green, Charles D., 1924
Green, Harry J., 1714
Green, Ruth S., 2263–2265
Greenberg, David, 1169
Greene, Evarts, 1471
Greene, Jack P., 150, 2084, 2407
Greene, Lee S., 2299
Greenfield, Arnold L., 644
Greenfield, M., 1170
Greenhouse, Linda, 792
Greenstein, Fred I., 645
Gregson, Ronald E., 1283
Grenzke, Janet M., 1775
Griffin, Roger A., 2325

Griffiths, David B., 2377, 2527
Grimes, Marcene, 1604
Griswold, Thelma I., 2136
Grobman, Hulda, 1361
Grody, Harvey P., 1171
Gross, Bertram M., 573
Grove, Lawrence R., 1736
Grow, Stewart L., 2378
Grumm, John G., 151–154, 346, 515, 574, 793
Grupp, Fred W., 823
Guhde, Robert, 680
Guild, Frederic H., 446–449, 925, 1590, 1605–1607
Gunn, L. Ray, 2038
Gupton, Kevin, 475
Guzzo, Peter P., 926

Hadley, David J., 1526–1527
Hagensick, A. Clarke, 1715
Hahn, Harlan, 646, 1561
Hain, Paul L., 305, 347
Haines, Charles G., 114
Haines, Wilder H., 1737
Hajjar, S., 2528
Hall, Alvin L., 2408
Hall, Frances P., 1315
Hall, John E., 2007
Hall, Kristin, 927
Hall, William K., 267, 1472
Hallett, George H., 2039
Halpin, S. A., 1673
Ham, P. Gerald, 2463A
Hamilton, Charles G., 1863
Hamilton, H. D., 306, 1528, 1780
Hamilton, T. H., 824
Hamm, Keith E., 209, 422–423, 518, 647, 721–722, 2493, 2496
Hanawalt, Leslie, 1776
Hand, Samuel B., 2393
Hansell, Stafford, 986
Hanson, Bertil L., 2164
Hanson, Roger A., 210, 1716
Hanson, Russell, 390
Harder, Marvin A., 1608–1609
Hardin, Charles M., 211
Hardison, R. B., 1635
Hardy, John L., 753–754
Hardy, Leroy C., 1172–1173, 1219
Harick, John, 279
Harkey, Paul, 2165

Harlow, Ralph Volney, 476
Harmon, Robert B., 1059, 1090, 1105, 1174, 1284, 1316, 1404, 1473, 1636, 1777, 2137, 2166
Harrington, Joseph D., 986A
Harris, Joseph P., 858–859, 928, 1175
Harris, William C., 1864
Harrison, Lowell H., 1637
Harrison, Robert, 2227
Harrold, Frances, 31
Hart, Henry C., 987
Hart, James, 477
Hartmann, George W., 825
Hartmark, Leif S., 2494
Harvey, Lashley G., 307, 1967
Harvey, Richard B., 1176–1177
Hass, Paul H., 2495
Hastings, Fred W., 212
Hatch, Richard A., 1474
Hatry, Harry P., 681
Hattery, Lowell H., 826
Hauberg, Robert E., 1865
Haugherty, James H., 1317
Haugland, John C., 1832
Havard, William C., 516, 1345, 1362–1364, 1674–1675
Havens, Murray C., 1060
Hawkins, B. W., 1404
Hayden, Richard D., 1178
Hazard, William R., 988
Healy, Robert L., 2228
Heaphey, James J., 842, 899, 929–930, 2021
Heard, Alexander, 32, 177, 393
Hebert, F. Ted, 517
Hedlund, Ronald D., 291, 308, 518, 620–621, 647, 722, 1475, 1562, 1578, 2496
Heim, Joseph P., 2497
Heinemann, Ronald L., 2409
Hemphill, William E., 2410
Henderson, Thomas, 287, 736, 755
Hendrick, Irving G., 1179
Hendrickson, James E., 2193
Hendrickson, Kenneth E., 2279
Henhoe, Kenneth W., 1285
Hennings, Robert E., 1180
Henry, Ann R., 507
Henry, C. T., 794
Henry, Hubert D., 1286–1287
Herndon, James F., 1778

Author Index

Herring, Pendleton, 756
Herwitz, Oren C., 723
Herzberg, Donald G., 155
Hesse, Michael B., 2498
Hester, George, 2349
Hester, Lewis A., 1365
Hevesi, Alan G., 2040–2041
Hichborn, Franklin, 1181–1184
Hicks, Jimmie, 2326
Hicks, Ronald G., 1676
Highsaw, Robert B., 1866
Hightower, Nikki R. Van, 348
Hill, A. Spencer, 213
Hill, David B., 519
Hill, Gladwin, 1185
Hinckley, Katherine A., 2327
Hjelm, Victor S., 1288–1289
Hobbs, E. H., 1867
Hodes, Richard S., 724
Hodges, Wiley E., 2411
Hofferbert, Richard I., 33, 599, 989, 1026
Hofstetter, C. Richard, 1529
Holbo, Paul S., 1833
Holcombe, John W., 2328
Holland, Lynwood, 28
Holloway, William V., 34, 303
Holmes, Jack E., 2008–2009
Holsinger, M. Paul, 2529
Holt, Wythe W., 2412
Holtz, Harold F., 1868
Hool, James N., 1078
Hoopes, David C., 1186
Hopkins, Anne H., 284, 827, 990
Hopper, Stanley, 1187
Horack, Frank E., 860, 1563, 2464
Hornbein, Marjorie, 1290
Horne, William E. Van, 2138
Horowitz, Sol D., 1366
Hotard, Ken, 795
Hounshell, Charles D., 2413–2414
House, Albert V., 1530
Howard, Alan J., 725
Howard, Helen A., 2441
Howard, Perry H., 1675
Howard, Victor B., 1476–1477
Howe, C. B., 520
Howe, Elizabeth A., 2043
Howorth, L. S., 35
Hoy, Suellen M., 1531
Hrebenar, R. J., 682
Huckshorn, Robert J., 622, 1430

Hudson, Irby R., 2294–2297
Huey, Mary Evelyn, 2329
Huff, Lawrence, 1405
Hume, Richard L., 1367, 2415
Humphrey, E. F., 1318
Humphrey, Hubert H., 861
Humphrey, Thomas F., 991
Hunt, Leigh W., 1834
Hunter, William C., 2112
Hurst, James W., 36
Hushaw, Charles W., 1188
Hutchinson, W. H., 1189
Hutton, A. J. W., 2229
Huwa, Randy, 424, 992
Hyink, Bernard L., 1190
Hyneman, Charles S., 37, 521, 1478, 1532–1534, 1564, 1677

Illinois Commission on the Organization of the General Assembly, 1479
Illinois General Assembly, Efficiency and Economy Committee, 1481
Indiana Legislative Council, 1535
Indiana University, Institute of Politics, 1536
Ingram, Denny L., 38
Ingram, Helen M., 309–310, 993
Iowa State College, Advisory Council for Iowa Economic Studies, 1565
Ippolito, Dennis S., 391
Ireland, Owen, 2230
Ireland, Robert M., 1638
Iron, Frederick C., 2010
Irwin, Frank, 425
Isaac, Paul E., 2298
Isakoff, Jack, 1507
Iverson, Evan A., 2299

Jack, Ronald C., 1958–1959, 2379
Jackameit, William P., 2465
Jackson, Alton, 645
Jackson, Edwin L., 725, 1407
Jackson, John, III, 547
Jacob, Herbert, 39, 349, 393, 575
Jacobs, Clyde E., 1192
Jacobs, David, 994–995
Jacquin, William C., 931

Janda, Kenneth F., 522
Jaros, D., 996
Jeansonne, Glen, 1678–1679
Jeffrey, Thomas E., 2085
Jennings, Edward T., 997, 1680
Jennings, M. Kent, 40, 394
Jennings, Robert E., 2056
Jensen, J. R., 2330
Jensen, James E., 1193
Jensen, Richard, 1484
Jewell, Malcolm E., 41–43, 268–269, 311–313, 395, 593, 648, 770, 873, 932, 1639
Joffee, J. M., 44
Johnson, Alvin W., 156–157
Johnson, B. H., 2167
Johnson, Claudius O., 45
Johnson, David A., 1960
Johnson, Dozier, 1368
Johnson, James B., 1920, 1925
Johnson, Kenneth M., 1194
Johnson, Marc A., 998
Johnson, Reinhard O., 1697, 1968
Johnson, Roy H., 450
Johnson, William C., 1195
Johnson, William E., 1926
Johnston, David A., 2139
Johnston, Heather W., 999
Jones, Allen W., 1061
Jones, Bryan D., 396, 2331
Jones, Charles O., 270, 1000, 2276, 2281
Jones, E. B., 1001
Jones, Harry W., 933
Jones, Howard J., 1681
Jones, J. Catron, 1640
Jones, Lloyd P., 576
Jones, Melvin E., 1869
Jones, Philippe, 1030
Jones, Stephen, 2168
Judah, Charles B., 2011
Juergensmeyer, J. E., 1485
Jung, Peter M., 115
Junkins, Lowell L., 1566

Kaff, David, 341
Kahle, Richard F., 1424
Kahn, Melvin A., 1537
Kaiser, Henry F., 214–215
Kalijarvi, Thorsten V., 1969
Kamins, Robert, 1426

Kammerer, Gladys M., 934, 1352, 1641–1646
Kampelman, Max, 623, 750
Kane, Betty, 1835
Kane, Thomas J., 523
Karnig, Albert, 806, 862
Karsch, Robert F., 1889–1890
Kassel, Charles, 863
Katsky, David, 162
Keating, Edward, 1291
Keefe, William J., 158, 397, 600, 864, 1486–1487, 2231
Keegan, Myrtle, 494
Keith, Gary A., 46, 2332
Kelleher, Sean A., 549, 797
Kelley, W., 2223
Kelly, F., 683
Kemp, K. A., 757
Kendell, Willmoore, 47
Kennedy, Duncan L., 1836–1837
Kennedy, Leo F., 935
Kennedy, Patrick J., 601
Kennedy, Philip W., 1647
Kenney, David, 1488, 1513
Kenny, R. W., 1196
Kent, Elliot N., 2086
Kent, James P., 1489
Kenton, Carolyn L., 216, 936
Kentucky Legislative Research Commission, 1648
Kerle, Donald F., 48
Kerr, William T., 2442
Kessler, James B., 1538–1539
Key, V. O., 49–50, 217, 271, 828, 1540
Keynes, Edward, 350, 370
Killpatrick, E. W., 798
King, Michael, 967
King, Peter J., 1682
Kinney, Richard S., 1431
Kirby, Jack T., 2417
Kirby, James C., 116
Kirk, Frank A., 1002
Kirkpatrick, Samuel A., 524, 2169
Kirsch, Mary M., 2499
Kirst, Michael W., 1003
Kirwin, Alice, 1197
Kisa, Joseph, 1838
Klain, Maurice, 314
Klass, Gary M., 1004
Klay, William E., 624
Klein, Bernard W., 398, 643

Author Index

Kleps, Ralph N., 1198
Kneier, Charles M., 1490
Knight, Barbara B., 218
Kolasa, Bernard D., 1927
Kopel, Gerald H., 726
Korask, Tadeus Z., 2232
Kornberg, Allan, 335, 399, 525, 550
Kousser, J. Morgan, 2300
Krane, Dale A., 1854
Kremm, Thomas W., 2140
Kruschke, Merle L., 1839
Kuklinski, James H., 272, 315–316, 1491
Kurfess, Charles F., 51
Kurtz, Donn M., 1665, 1670
Kurtz, Karl T., 52

Lacy, Alex B., 1683
Laird, Angus, 1355
Lamar, Howard R., 2380
Lamb, B. S., 2194
Lamb, F., 2500
Lamb, K. A., 1779
Lambert, Oscar D., 2466
Lancaster, Lane W., 22, 53, 1928–1930
Land, Aubrey C., 1717–1718
Landers, Frank M., 1780
Lane, Edgar, 799
Laney, Nancy K., 310
Lang, Howard B., 1891
Larsen, Christian L., 1199, 2262
Larson, J. E., 1062
Larson, Robert W., 2012
Larson, T. A., 2530
Lau, K. K., 1425
Laudicina, Robert, 1998
Laws, Frank D., 2195
Lawton, Frederick J., 684
Lay, H., 1534
League of Women Voters of California, 1200
League of Women Voters of Illinois, 1492–1493
League of Women Voters of Minnesota, 1840–1842
Lebega, Mathias, 1753
Le Blanc, Hugh L., 649
Ledbetter, Cal L., 54, 1005, 1106

Lederle, John W., 865, 937, 1781, 2044
Lee, Charles E., 2263–2265
Lee, David D., 2301–2302
Lee, Eugene C., 1201–1202
Lee, McDowell, 1063
Lee, Robert D., 685, 1029
Leek, John H., 938–940
Lees, John D., 426
Legislative Index Company (Albany), 2045
Lehne, R., 2046
Leiden, Carl, 1568
Leister, D. R., 1206
Leiter, William M., 1207
LeLoup, Lance T., 577, 650
LeMay, Michael, 686
Lennertz, James E., 1006
Lentz, Gilbert G., 867
Leonard, James M., 220
Lepawsky, Albert, 55
Leroy, David J., 1370
Lester, J. P., 478
Leuthold, David A., 1208, 1892
Levin, James, 1719
Levine, E. Lester, 1371, 1843
Levine, Marc V., 1720
Levine, Peter D., 1985–1986
Levit, Victor B., 1209–1210
Lewis, C., 727
Lewis, Ferris E., 1783
Lewis, Henry W., 2087–2088
Lewis, Virgil A., 2466A
Lewis, William O., 1432
Lien, A. J., 2172
Light, A., 705
Lijphart, Arend, 273
Limbaugh, Ronald H., 1433
Lincoln, L. H., 1211
Linde, H. A., 2197
Lindsey, Jim T., 452, 2333
Lingley, Charles R., 2418
Lipsky, Michael, 575
Lipson, Albert J., 1169, 1212
Littell, Noble K., 1541
Littke, George C., 2047
Littlewood, Thomas B., 1494
Lloyd, Arthur, 1650
Lloyd, William J., 772
Lockard, Duane, 56–58, 352, 1319–1322, 1738
Loewenberg, Gerhard, 932

Logan, John W., 687
Long, J. J., 749
Long, Russell B., 688
Longley, Lawrence D., 800–801
Lorch, Robert S., 1292
Lord, Alan, 2283
Lovrich, Nicholas P., 321, 1542
Lowe, Richard G., 2419
Lowi, Theodore J., 59
Lowrie, S. G., 526
Lowry, Robert E., 2141
Loyless, Darrell M., 1684
Luce, Robert, 480, 625
Lujan, Herman D., 1434, 1610
Lunt, Richard D., 1784
Luttbeg, Norman R., 60, 303
Lutz, Donald S., 118, 228, 651, 2334
Lutz, Paul F., 2467
Lyle, Mary L., 1372
Lyons, William E., 222, 2233
Lyons, William V., 578, 727A–729

MacCorkle, Stuart A., 2336–2337
MacDonald, Austin F., 62–63
Mack, Ally F., 1871
Mackey, E. S., 868
MacNeil, Douglas H., 317
MacPherson, Joseph T., 2303
MacRae, Duncan, 653–656, 1503, 1739–1740
MacRae, E., 656
Madaras, Lawrence H., 2054
Maddox, Robert J., 1685
Maguire, Amelia Rea, 1374–1375
Main, Jackson T., 64–65, 353, 1722
Mallard, Carl B., 2304
Mallison, W. T., 2142
Malone, Michael J., 1435
Mann, Dean E., 1091, 1217
Mann, Thomas, 886
Marcantonio, Edward J., 119
Margolis, Larry, 869
Mariner, Elwyn E., 1741
Mars, David, 1323
Marshall, George B., 2143
Marsis, James L., 2251
Martens, Sharon W., 2113
Martin, Curtis, 1296–1297
Martin, David L., 1064
Martin, John B., 318

Martin, P. L., 2421
Martin, Roscoe C., 1065
Marvel, Richard D., 730, 1933
Marvick, Dwaine, 354
Mason, John B., 355
Mason, Paul, 483, 945
Mason, R. P., 690
Massay, Glenn F., 2469
Masters, Nicholas A., 1007
Mather, W. W., 160
Mathias, Frank F., 1651
Matthews, Donald C., 356
Matthews, Linda M., 2267
Mauer, George J., 2177
Mazur, Gilbert G., 484
McAlister, Sam, 2349
McBain, Howard L., 2420
McCain, John R., 310
McCain, William D., 1870
McCally, Sarah P., 602
McCandless, Carl A., 1893
McCarthy, G. Michael, 1293–1295
McCarty, J. D., 2173
McClain, Robert H., 223
McCleske, Clifton, 2335
McClintock, Roy M., 1894
McConaughy, John B., 2266
McConnico, S., 2350
McCormick, Richard L., 2048–2049
McCormick, Robert E., 527
McCoy, Donald R., 1611
McCready, Eric S., 1931
McCrocklin, James H., 2323
McCrone, Donald J., 316
McCurdy, Kathleen B., 61
McDaniel, Ruth Currie, 1408
McDermott, W. B., 2443
McDonald, James T., 1612–1614
McDonald, Jean G., 2174
McDonell, Victoria H., 1373
McDonnell, Richard Heinrich, 2049
McDowell, James L., 1495, 1543–1544
McDuffie, James M., 1409
McGeary, M. Nelson, 481, 2241
McGee, Vernon A., 689
McGriggs, Lee Augustus, 1496
McGuinness, Louis J., 1785, 1808
McGuire, Daniel W., 2050
McGuire, Maureen, 1987
McHenry, Dean E., 159, 1213–1216

Author Index

McInnes, R., 2051
McKay, Fred J., 944
McKay, Robert B., 224
McKean, Dayton D., 1988
McKenna, William J., 482
McKnight, Gerald D., 2053
McLemore, Lelan E., 517, 524, 528, 2175–2176
McMahon, John V., 1721
McManus, Lewis N., 2468
McMurray, Carl D., 652, 829, 1380
McNickle, R. K., 225
McNitt, Andrew D., 274
McPartland, Edward J., 1932
McPherson, Edwin B., 1545
Mead, Lawrence M., 66
Meerse, David E., 1615
Meiners, Fredericka A., 2338
Melcher, Daniel P., 1218
Meller, Norman, 529–530, 946, 1426
Meltz, David B., 400
Menard, Albert R., 947
Merchants' Association of New York, 2055
Mervin, David, 275
Metzenbaum, Howard M., 2144
Mezey, Michael, 284
Michael, Jerry B., 531
Michaelson, Ronald D., 579
Michel, J. B., 626
Michelson, S., 870
Michigan Bar Association, 1786
Michigan Public Expenditure Survey, 1787
Michigan State University, Governmental Research Bureau, 1788
Mid-America Assembly on State Legislatures in American Politics, 67
Mikesell, J. L., 691
Mileur, Jerome M., 1742
Miller, Edward J., 580, 1723
Miller, Harold V., 2305
Miller, James N., 871
Miller, Lawrence W., 2339
Miller, M. C., 1616
Miller, Warren E., 2198
Milstein, Mike M., 2056
Minnesota Institute of Governmental Research, 1844
Misner, Arthur J., 1159

Missouri Public Expenditure Survey, 1895
Mitau, G. T., 68
Moffat, Abbot L., 485
Moffett, Anthony J., 1324
Moflitt, H. L., 486
Moitoret, Anthony F., 2444
Moncrief, Gary, 423, 692, 872–873
Moniz, Rita, 1733
Monsma, Stephen V., 401, 1753, 1789–1790
Montague, R. L., 226
Montana-Idaho Asssembly on State Legislatures, 1436, 1904
Moody, Eric N., 1961–1962
Moon, John S., 2340
Moore, Blaine F., 1497
Moore, Dan K., 758
Moore, David W., 1546
Moore, John R., 2089
Moore, Robert E., 2341
Moore, William G., 2504
Moos, Malcolm, 1845
Moran, T. F., 161
Moreau, John A., 1686
Morehouse, Sarah M., 402–403, 627
Morgan, Thomas S., 2090
Morlan, Robert L., 1219
Morrill, Richard L., 227
Morris, Allen, 1374–1375
Morris, J. H., 1879
Morris, John R., 1298
Morris, Willie, 2342
Morrison, Leonard S., 1971
Morrison, Peter A., 1008
Morse, Sidney G., 2394
Moschos, Demitrios M., 162
Moss, Warner, 1873
Mott, Rodney L., 948
Moyers, David, 1107
Muchmore, Lynn, 603, 693
Mueller, John E., 1220
Mulligan, William G., 723
Munger, Frank J., 284, 1540
Murphy, Jerome T., 874
Murphy, L. V., 2178
Murray, Keith, 69
Murray, Mary, 1325
Murray, Richard M., 1410
Murray, Richard W., 228, 281, 2334
Mushkin, S. J., 1009
Mustafa, Husain, 680

Myers, Rodes K., 1652
Myers, Thomas R., 404

Nadworny, Milton J., 1010
Naftalin, Arthur, 1846
Napier, Milton F., 1896
Nash, Gerald D., 1221
Nathan, Harriet, 1222
National Conference of State Legislatures, 875
National Legislative Conference, 487
  Committee on Legislative Process and Procedures, 70
  Committee on Legislative Rules, 163, 427
  Committee on Organization of Legislative Services, 488
National Municipal League, 120–121, 949
  Committee on State Government, 122
Naylor, M. A., 1326
Neal, Charles E., 1847
Neal, Tom W., 2003
Neely, Gerald J., 1905
Neuberger, Maurine, 532
Neuberger, Richard L., 71, 229, 276, 2200–2202
Neuenschwander, John A., 2395
Neuman, Dale A., 319
Neuringer, Sheldon, 2179
Newell, C., 230
New Jersey, Law Revision and Bill Drafting Commission, 1989
Newkirk, Glenn, 830–831, 950
Newton, Martha R., 1223
New York, Special Committee on Ethics, 2058
Nichols, George A., 1498
Nichols, R. V., 2343
Nickell, Ralph L., 630
Nightingale, Bernard, 1411
Nimmo, Dan P., 328
Nixon, H. Clarence, 29, 72
Noell, J., 1011
Nokes, George O., 2344
Nolan, Val, 1547
Norris, George W., 73–74
North Carolina, Legislative Research Commission, 2091

Northwest Regional American Assembly on State Legislatures in American Politics, 876
Norton, Wesley, 1653
Nortrup, Jack, 123
Nowlin, William, 538, 2145
Nunn, Walter, 334, 467
Nuquist, Andrew E., 2396
Nuquist, Edith W., 2396
Nutting, Charles B., 2059
Nye, Frank T., 1569–1576
Nyitray, Joseph P., 2345

O'Brien, Charles F., 2146
O'Conner, Patrick F., 856, 1108, 1672
O'Connor, Robert, 967
Oden, William E., 2346–2347
Ogle, David B., 1327–1328, 1874
Ogul, Morris S., 158
Ohio Regional American Assembly on State Legislatures in American Politics (Indiana-Michigan-Ohio), 877
Ohm, Howard F., 2505
Ohnimus, Arthur A., 1224–1225
Okaji, Dick H., 1427
Oldfield, Jennifer D., 1012
Oliphant, J. Orin, 2445
O'Loughlin, John, 320
Olsen, Dale W., 2111
Olsen, Raymond T., 581
Olson, David J., 2506
Olson, David M., 164, 277, 395, 2348
Olson, Edward, 1229
Olson, Frederick I., 2531
Olson, James E., 2060
Orfield, Lester B., 1791, 1848
O'Rourke, Lawrence W., 951
O'Rourke, Timothy G., 231–232
Ortquist, Richard T., 1792–1793
Oshita, Edward J., 1226
Otis, M., 1617
Overstreet, Jack, 1397
Owen, Kimbrough, 1687
Owens, John R., 1227–1229
Oxendale, James R., 428, 533, 2470

Author Index

Padilla, Fernando V., 1230
Padover, Saul K., 1499
Page, Thomas, 1618
Palmer, J. David, 2268
Palmer, Kenneth T., 1698, 2234
Papenfuse, Edward C., 1724
Parker, Graham, 1013
Parks, Norman L., 2306
Parrish, William E., 1619
Parsons, Malcolm B., 829, 1377
Parsons, Robert S., 730
Pate, James E., 2422-2423
Patterson, Caleb P., 2349
Patterson, Samuel C., 43, 75, 260, 291, 357, 406, 534-537, 604-605, 628, 629, 657-658, 1577-1578, 2180, 2507-2508
Paulsen, Monrad, 1013
Peel, Roy V., 233
Peltier, David P., 1340
Penning, James M., 278
Pennsylvania General Assembly's Commission for Legislative Modernization, 878
Pennsylvania Regional American Assembly on State Legislatures in American Politics, 2235
Pepper, H. C., 1412
Perkins, John A., 76, 165, 1794
Pernacciaro, Samuel J., 1513
Perry, Charles E., 1304
Perry, Robert T., 1897
Pesonen, Pertti, 1744
Peters, H. Dean, 1654
Peters, John G., 557-559, 731-732, 879, 1016, 1463
Petersen, Eric F., 1231-1232
Peterson, C. Petrus, 832
Pethtel, Ray D., 710, 733
Petty, Janice, 1515
Philleo, N. E., 1795
Pickerell, Albert G., 1233
Pierce, Arthur D., 1990
Pierce, John C., 321
Pierce, Melvin, 1548
Pierce, William J., 1779
Pieth, Reto A., 2061
Pilcher, Dan, 234-235, 406A, 833
Pindur, Wolfgang, 358
Pisciotte, Joseph P., 1289, 1299
Pitstick, W. J., 802

Plaisted, John W., 1745
Plosila, Walter H., 759
Poeschl, Peg, 1936
Poldervaart, Arie, 1579, 2014
Polinard, Jerry L., 1092
Polishook, Irvin H., 2252
Poll, Richard D., 2381
Pollack, Ervin H., 2146
Pollock, James K., 1796
Pomper, Gerald, 1991
Pope, J., 2350
Porter, Daniel R., 2147
Porter, H. Owen, 834-835, 1797
Portney, Kent E., 694
Portnoy, Barry M., 1746
Poschman, Gene S., 77
Pound, Merritt B., 1413-1414
Pow, Alex S., 1066-1067
Powell, Paul, 1500
Prendergast, William B., 78
Prescott, Frank W., 582-583, 2307
Press, Charles, 880-881
Press, L., 979
Prestage, Jewel, 342
Prewitt, Kenneth, 322, 538-539, 606
Price, Charles M., 1014, 1121-1122, 1234-1235
Price, Douglas, 952
Prisley, Alexander V., 2253
Probert, Walter, 2203
Proffer, Lanny, 123A, 773
Public Affairs Research Council of Louisiana, 1689
Pulsipher, Allan G., 236
Putnam, Jackson K., 1236-1237
Putney, Bryant, 166, 453
Pye, Lucian W., 760

Rabin, Walter W., 2236
Rackleff, Robert B., 1378
Rader, Melvin, 2446
Radin, Max, 1238
Ragsdale, Lyn, 607
Rainey, Robert L., 774
Rakoff, Stuart H., 630, 659
Rampey, Carolyn, 1608
Rand, Larry A., 2254
Rankin, Robert S., 2092
Ranney, Austin, 1356, 1501
Ransom, David F., 1329

Ransone, Coleman B., 584, 608
Ratchford, William R., 695
Ratcliffe, Donald J., 2148
Rawson, Donald M., 1875
Ray, David H., 279, 359–360, 541
Ray, John M., 2255
Ray, Joseph M., 2351–2352
Ray, Robert F., 429
Read, Horace E., 1849
Reed, Germaine A., 1690
Reenstra-Bryant, Robin, 953
Reeves, John E., 1655–1656
Regens, J. L., 1015
Rehfuss, John A., 323
Reichard, Gary W., 2308
Reilly, Archer, 2149
Reiners, Fred G., 2309
Renne, Roland R., 1906
Renner, August N., 2511
Reock, Ernest C., 237, 1992
Reuling, J. A., 2209
Rhode, William E., 430
Rhodes, Jack A., 454–455
Rhodes, Robert M., 742
Rice, Ross R., 1093
Rice, Tom W., 601
Rich, Bennett M., 1993
Rich, William P., 1239
Richards, Alan, 823
Richards, Allen R., 2015
Richards, Barbara, 836
Richardson, Ivan L., 1580
Richardson, Joe, 1379
Ricketts, Edmond F., 1564
Riege, John H., 1330
Riggs, Robert E., 1094
Riker, William H., 660
Riley, Dennis D., 407
Riley, Elihu S., 1725
Riley, W., 1937
Ringold, May S., 79
Risjord, Norman K., 2424
Ritt, Leonard B., 882, 1016
Roady, Elston, 1380
Robbins, L., 1820
Robeck, Bruce W., 324, 1240–1242
Roberts, Albert B., 954
Roberts, Derrell C., 1381, 1415
Roberts, George B., 1545
Roberts, Higdon C., 2122
Robertson, Roby D., 721
Robey, John S., 804

Robinson, James A., 977, 1017, 1275, 1465
Robison, Dan M., 2310
Rochester Bureau of Municipal Research, 2062
Rodabaugh, Karl, 1068
Rodgers, Jack W., 1938
Rodine, Floyd, 1939
Rodnick, David, 1331
Roeder, Philip W., 883
Roessner, J. D., 1018
Rogers, V., 671
Rogers, W. H., 1382
Rogers, William W., 1069
Rogin, Michael W., 1243–1244
Roherty, James M., 2512
Roll, Charles W., 124
Roller, David C., 2093
Romero, Sidney J., 1691
Roper, Donald M., 585
Roper, Robert T., 778
Rose, Albert H., 2150
Rose, Douglas D., 1019
Rosebaugh, D. L., 696
Rosen, Corey M., 542, 586
Rosenbaum, Walter A., 1245
Rosenthal, Alan, 80–81, 360A, 424, 431–432, 489–491, 543–544, 609, 734, 884–886, 992, 1726, 1994
Rosentreter, Roger L., 1798
Ross, G. Robert, 1005
Ross, John P., 697
Ross, Michael J., 1246
Ross, Russell M., 1559, 1581–1582
Ross, W. R., 2471
Rossell, Beatrice S., 82
Rossotti, J. E., 238
Rostker, Bernard, 1169
Rousse, Thomas A., 887
Routt, Garland C., 610
Rowell, David T., 631
Ruchelman, Leonard I., 361, 2064–2065
Rudsten, Daniel, 1747
Rule, Wilma, 362
Rusco, Elmer R., 1095
Russell, John C., 2016
Rutgers University Bureau of Government Research, 1995
Ryan, Miles, 2262

Author Index

Sabatier, Paul A., 1020, 1247
Saffell, David C., 83, 239
Salamon, Lester M., 611
Salisbury, Robert H., 1007
Saltiel, Edward P., 1502
Salzman, Ed, 1248
Samish, Arthur H., 1249
Samuels, S., 2353
Sanders, J. L., 240
Sanders, Ruby H., 1096
Sanderson, Winn, 730
Sands, C. Dallas, 492, 1070
Sanford, Gregory D., 2393
Sanford, Terry, 84
Sanstead, W. G., 955
Sapio, Victor, 1727
Sarner, Ronald, 630, 659, 2066
Satter, Robert, 775, 1332
Saunders, Nancy, 2340
Savage, R. L., 1021
Sawyer, Jack, 1503
Saye, Albert B., 1416–1417
Sayre, Josiah L., 1799
Scarrow, Howard, 2067
Schaffter, Dorothy, 1583
Schapiro, Beth S., 363
Schell, James S., 2284
Schenk, Willis J., 2285
Scher, Richard K., 1351
Scher, Seymour, 587
Schlegel, Marvin W., 2410
Schlesinger, Joseph A., 545
Schmelzer, Janet, 2354
Schmidhauser, John, 1560
Schmidt, Karl M., 85
Schnader, William A., 125
Schneider, Mark, 325, 1022
Scholten, Pat C., 1549
Schramm, Sarah S., 546
Schriftgiesser, Karl, 805
Schuck, Victoria, 1250, 1383
Schuiteman, John G., 837
Schulman, Mark A., 326
Schumacher, Waldo, 364, 2210
Schwartz, Arthur A., 2151
Schwartz, Sally, 1341
Scigliano, Robert G., 1800
Scobie, Ingrid W., 1251
Scott, Robert W., 612
Scott, Stanley, 1151, 1252
Seavoy, Ronald E., 1801
Segal, Morley, 1253

Seligman, Lester G., 365, 2211
Senning, John P., 167–168, 493, 1940–1944
Sessums, T. Terrell, 1023
Shade, William G., 511
Shaeffer, John N., 1418
Shaffer, William R., 408, 1024, 1040
Shahan, J. M., 2311
Shank, Alan, 1996
Shankman, Arnold, 1504
Shapley, Lloyd S., 660
Shapley, T. S., 433
Sharkansky, Ira, 698–702, 1025–1026, 1419
Sharkoff, Eugene F., 1802
Sharp, James R., 1898
Sharp, Walter R., 2513
Shattuck, H. L., 776
Shaw, Malcolm, 426
Shefter, Martin A., 2068
Sheldon, Addison E., 494
Sheldon, Charles H., 2448
Shepherd, Rececca A., 1550
Sherman, Betsy, 706
Sherman, Sharon, 408A
Sherwood, Frank P., 1254
Shin, Kwang, 547
Shipps, Jan, 2382
Shoemaker, Floyd C., 1899
Shofner, Jerrell H., 1384–1386
Short, Lloyd M., 1850
Shover, John L., 1255
Shubik, Martin, 433
Shull, Charles W., 169–170, 241–243, 280, 888, 1803–1808
Shumate, Roger V., 1945
Sidlow, Edward I., 2152
Siffin, William J., 456
Sigale, Merwin K., 1505
Sigelman, Lee, 806, 862
Sikes, Pressly S., 1551–1552
Silbey, Joel H., 661, 2024
Silliman, J. W., 889
Silva, Ruth C., 244
Silverman, Corinne, 495, 790
Silverman, Eli B., 2069
Simmons, Robert H., 703, 761, 2449
Simon, Lucinda, 956–958
Simon, Paul, 1506
Simons, Janet, 245

Singer, W. S., 1446
Singleton, Marvin K., 2425
Sittig, Robert F., 1946
Skeen, C. Edward, 2070
Skelton, Lynda W., 1420
Skinner, A. E., 2355
Skok, James E., 762
Smallwood, Frank, 2397
Smart, Warren A., 2017
Smidt, Corwin E., 278
Smith, Barbara L., 2212
Smith, C. Lynwood, 1387
Smith, David W., 457
Smith, Dick, 2337
Smith, Edwin O., 1333
Smith, Elsie B., 2398
Smith, F. Leslie, 1370
Smith, George B., 246–247
Smith, Harold T., 1109
Smith, Joel, 399
Smith, Matthew J., 2256
Smith, Morgan, 496
Smith, Peter W., 807
Smith, Rhoten A., 1620
Smith, Russell L., 578, 890
Smith, Stephen N., 1621
Smith, Thomas V., 86–87
Smith, William F., 2237
Smylie, Robert E., 838, 1437
Sneed, Edgar P., 2356
Snider, Clyde F., 88
Snow, Willis H., 1809
Soapes, Thomas F., 1876
Sohner, Charles P., 1173, 1256
Sokolow, Alvin D., 1192, 1257–1260
Solomon, Samuel R., 497, 613
Sorauf, Frank J., 2238
Sorenson, Robert C., 839
Soule, John W., 1810
Southern Assembly, 89
Southern Methodist University, Arnold School of Government, 2357
Spadaro, R., 840
Sparlin, Estal E., 1900
Spector, Michael J., 2491
Spencer, Charles F., 891
Spencer, Jean E., 1701
Spencer, Richard C., 171, 1507, 1947
Spicer, Erik J., 172

Spiesman, Guy D., 931
Spitz, Allan, 1428
Sponholtz, Lloyd, 2153
Sprague, John, 340, 409, 2220
Sprengel, Donald P., 2094
Squires, J. Duane, 2472
Staffeldt, Raymond, 685
Stampen, Jacob O., 2514
Staniford, Edward F., 1262
Stanley, Harold W., 1071
Stanley, Robert H., 2426
Stanley, William R., 190, 248
State Bar of Michigan, 1811
Staub, Stephen A., 366
Stavisky, Leonard, 1027
Stealey, Wallace, 1297
Steck, E., 1264
Steelman, Joseph F., 2096–2102
Steinbach, Carol, 90A
Steindl, Frank G., 1028
Steiner, Gilbert Y., 1470, 1508–1509
Sterk, H. E., 1063
Sterling, Philip, 2239
Stevens, Arthur R., 548
Stevens, J. M., 1029
Stevens, R. Michael, 2240
Stever, James A., 90
Stewart, Debra W., 2103
Stewart, R. B., 1657
Stewart, William H., 1072
Stigler, G. J., 173
Still, Rae F., 2358
Stoiber, Susanne A., 91
Stokes, S. L., 110
Stollman, Gerald H., 1812–1813
Stone, Richard G., 2270
Stowe, Noel J., 1265
Strahan, Frank, 1366
Strain, Camden S., 1622
Strange, M. L., 367
Strinden, Earl S., 2114
Strouse, James C., 1030–1031
Sturm, Albert L., 126–127, 2286
Sullivan, Rodman, 1658
Sullivan, Sheila, 2515
Sulzner, George T., 1742
Summers, Harrison B., 174, 1948
Sumner, Bruce W., 1266
Swanson, Wayne R., 111, 344, 549, 615, 662
Swap, C. Ralph, 1084

Author Index

Sweeney, Kevin, 1748
Swinton, David, 1022
Syer, John C., 1152

Taeuber, Cynthia M., 1032
Taeuber, Richard C., 1032
Taishoff, Sue, 1973
Talbott, Floyd C., 960
Talbott, Forrest, 2473
Tanger, Jacob, 2241
Tantillo, Charles, 2257
Taylor, D. A., 1750
Taylor, James S., 1073
Tedin, Kent L., 281
Teitelbaum, Fred, 1033
Teune, Henry J., 808, 1553
Texas Legislative Council, 2359–2360
Texas Pre-Session Legislative Conference, 92
Thacker, Ernest W., 1190
Thane, James L., 1907
Thavenet, Dennis, 1949–1950
Theobald, H. Rupert, 2516
Thomas, Bob, 1249
Thomas, E. T., 1877
Thomas, James D., 1074–1075
Thomas, Larry W., 728–729
Thomas, Norman C., 257, 394, 550, 1814–1815
Thomas, Robert D., 777, 1034
Thomason, Hugh M., 1421
Thomason, William R., 1510
Thompson, Fred, 632
Thompson, Joel A., 692, 778
Thompson, John F., 2071
Thompson, K., 1041
Thompson, William N., 128
Thornton, H. V., 2181–2182
Thurber, James A., 368, 763
Tilden, Richard A., 1035
Tilley, Betty, 2312
Tilson, J. Q., 1335
Timoney, T., 2223
Titus, James E., 1601, 1623
Tobin, Richard J., 129, 282, 350, 369, 370
Todd, John R., 1388
Toensing, W. F., 1851
Toepel, M. G., 93, 2517

Toll, Henry W., 94, 371, 551, 961, 1624
Tollison, R. D., 471, 527, 597, 639
Toussaint, George W., 1511
Trachsel, Herman H., 2532
Trafford, John E., 1997
Trask, David S., 1951
Traylor, Jack W., 1625
Treadgold, Alva G., 2213
Trelease, Allen W., 2104
Treon, John A., 1110
Tripp, Joseph F., 2450
Trippett, Frank, 95
Tubbesing, Carl D., 175
Tucker, Harvey J., 249A, 410
Tucker, Joseph P., 1512
Tucker, W. P., 372
Tully, Alan, 2242
Turett, J. Stephen, 616
Turk, William L., 412
Turnbull, Augustus B., 720, 1389
Turner, Henry A., 1267
Tyler, G., 779

United States, Library of Congress, Science Policy Research Division, 962
United States Advisory Commission on Intergovernmental Relations, 764
University of Alabama, Bureau of Public Administration, 1076–1077
University of California
  Institute of Governmental Studies, 1268
  School of Law, 893
University of Chicago, Law School, 250
University of Colorado, Bureau of Governmental Research and Service, 1300
University of Connecticut, Institute of Public Service, 1336
University of Florida, Public Administration Clearing Service, 1390–1391
University of Georgia, Institute of Government, 1422

University of Kansas, Bureau of Government Research, 1626–1628
University of Kentucky, Bureau of Government Research, 176, 1659–1661
University of Michigan, Bureau of Government, 1816
University of Mississippi, Bureau of Public Administration, 1878
University of North Carolina
  Institute of Government, 499
  Institute for Research in Social Science, 2105
University of South Dakota, Governmental Research Bureau, 2287
University of Texas
  Bureau of Municipal Research, 2361
  Institute of Public Affairs, 2362
University of Washington
  Bureau of Governmental Research and Services, 2451–2452
  Bureau of Public Administration, 963
Unruh, Jesse M., 96, 155, 633, 894, 1269
Uslaner, Eric M., 327, 552, 588, 634, 1036–1037
Utah Foundation, 2383

Valenti, J. J., 1337
Valleau, John F., 2214–2215
Van Alstyne, Arvo, 1271
Van der Slik, Jack R., 1513
Van der Vries, Bernice T., 375, 964
Van Eaton, Anson E., 1901
Vanlandingham, Kenneth E., 1662
Van Meter, Donald S., 2518
Van Petten, Donald, 1097
Vickrey, William, 251
Vieg, John A., 1267
Vincent, Charles, 1692–1693
Vindex, Charles, 1908
Vines, Kenneth N., 39
Vocino, Thomas, 1078, 1879

Wade, Harry W., 1952
Wade, Ralph M., 2532
Wager, Paul W., 2106
Wagner, Marvin H., 1038
Wagy, Thomas R., 1392–1393
Wahlke, John C., 97, 177, 553–556, 809
Waksmundski, John, 2155
Waldman, Louis, 2072
Waldron, Ellis L., 1909–1910
Walker, Dennis L., 411
Walker, Harvey, 98–99, 460, 895, 2115
Walker, Jack L., 1039
Walker, Larry, 2183
Walker, Robert A., 1272
Wallace, L. J., 1554
Wallace, Michael, 2073
Waller, Robert A., 1514
Walter, B. Oliver, 815
Walter, David O., 252–254
Walton, Brian G., 1423
Wanat, S. W., 216
Ward, Robert M., 1817
Ware, Alan, 1301
Ware, Richard A., 1974
Wathen, Richard B., 1555
Watson, George H., 780
Watterson, John S., 2107
Watts, Irma A., 2243
Watts, Meredith W., 144, 636
Way, Almon L., 2271
Weatherby, James L., Jr., 236
Weaver, Ellsworth E., 2384–2385
Weaver, Frank P., 2448
Webb, Robert, 965
Weber, Ronald E., 283–284, 327, 552, 588, 634, 890, 981, 990, 1024, 1037, 1040
Webster, Donald H., 285
Weeks, O. Douglas, 100, 178, 810, 2363–2365
Weibull, Jörgen, 2519
Weilder, Edward, 5
Weinberg, A. A., 376
Weinstein, Jack B., 130
Weiss, Nathan, 1998
Weiss, S. S., 1355, 1394
Weissert, Carol S., 735
Welch, Susan, 377, 557–559, 663, 731–732, 879, 1016, 1041, 1463
Welch, William P., 704

Author Index

Wellman, Charles, 434
Wells, D. I., 2074
Wells, Thomas L., 255, 2427
Wendel, Thomas, 2244
Werner, Emmy E., 378
Wernimont, Kenneth, 746
Weschler, Louis F., 1228
Wesser, Robert F., 1953, 2075–2076
West, E. G., 1042
West Virginia University, Bureau for Government Research, 2474
Wheare, K. C., 101
Wheeler, Gerald R., 1043
Wheeler, John P., 256
Whelchel, C., 1405
White, H., 896
White, Jean B., 2386
White, John P., 257, 1779
White, Leonard D., 1044
White, Lonnie J., 1111
White, Samuel L., 1880
Whitfield, J. B., 1395
Wickens, James F., 1302
Wiggin, J. Walker, 1975
Wiggins, Charles W., 382, 412, 560, 589, 740, 1515, 1584–1586
Wigmore, John H., 966
Wilber, L., 1881
Wilbern, York Y., 1556
Wilcox, Allen, 636
Wildgen, J. K., 1694
Wilkenfield, H. C., 435
Wilkes, James C., 500
Williams, Banjamin B., 1063
Williams, Henry N., 2313–2315
Williams, J. O., 566, 1031
Williams, James R., 651
Williams, John A., 2475
Williams, Max R., 2108–2109
Williams, Meg, 2402
Williams, Murat W., 2428
Williams, W., 501
Williamson, C. G., 1663
Williamson, Homer E., 1852
Williamson, Hugh P., 1902
Willis, Simeon S., 102
Willoughby, William F., 179
Wills, George S., 1728
Wilson, Darrell C., 2216
Wilson, Don W., 1629

Wilson, Marjorie H., 1098
Wilson, Paul E., 1045
Wilson, S. L., 765
Wiltz, John E., 286
Wimberly, W. C., 1516
Winkler, James H., 1045
Winslow, Clinton I., 436–439
Winston, Sheldon, 2476
Winter, William, 1882
Wissel, Peter, 967
Witt, Stuart K., 897, 2077
Witte, Edwin E., 968, 2522
Wohlenberg, E. H., 664
Wolf, T. Philip, 413
Wolfinger, Henry J., 2387
Wolfinger, Raymond, 103
Wood, John W., 781
Wood, Thomas J., 1751
Wood-Simons, May, 1517
Woodward, Earl F., 2366
Woodward, Walter, 2367
Woody, Carroll H., 2523
Woolfolk, Sarah V., 1079–1080
Wooster, Ralph A., 1695, 2368–2372
Worman, Michael A., 1396
Worthley, John A., 502, 766, 969, 1397
Wright, Deil S., 705
Wright, James R., 2184
Wright, John P., 1081
Wright, N. Dale, 730
Wyman, Roger E., 2524
Wyner, Alan J., 767, 1275
Wynes, Charles E., 2429

Yarwood, Dean L., 328
Yin, Robert K., 1046
Young, C. C., 1276
Young, Chester R., 2245
Young, George D., 1903

Zahorsky, Jeri, 958
Zeigler, Harmon, 40, 811–813
Zeller, Belle, 104, 329, 814, 2078
Zemsky, Robert M., 561, 1752
Zenor, Dean, 131
Ziegler, Martha J., 330, 1518
Zimmerman, Joseph F., 2079
Zisk, Betty H., 539

Subject Index

Abortion, 1847
Accountability, 326
Administrative rules, 2091, 2482
Adoption, 986A
Agenda setting, 576
Aging, 292
Agriculture, 786, 1817
Aid to Families with Dependent Children, 982
Aiken, George D., 2393
Alabama
  constitution of, 1072
  governors of, 1048, 1054, 1068, 1071, 1073
  history of, 1047, 1063, 1080
  legislative behavior in, 1070, 1081
  legislative structure in, 1057, 1066, 1075–1076
  legislators of, 1052
  political parties in, 1061, 1079
  politics of, 1059, 1064
  reapportionment of, 1062
  urban policy in, 1060
Alaska
  legislative structure in, 1083, 2189
  legislators of, 1082
Alcohol, 1038
Altgeld, John Peter, 1499
Anderson, William J., 2398
Anti-Catholicism, 1378
Anti-Communist legislation, 1251
Apportionment. See Reapportionment
Appropriations, 673, 1368, 1794
Arizona
  constitution of, 1097
  governors of, 1087, 1089, 1098
  legislative behavior in, 1092
  legislative committees in, 1091
  legislative structure in, 1088, 1094, 1096
  politics of, 1090
  redistricting of, 1086
Arkansas
  governors of, 1111
  legislative behavior in, 1683
  legislative structure in, 1101, 1106
  legislators of, 1104
  political parties in, 1103
  politics of, 1105
Auditing, 718

Bailey, Josiah W., 2089
Banking, 1128, 2071
Bargaining, 400
Barton, David, 1899
Bates, Edward, 1899
Bell, Peter Hansborough, 2366
Bicameralism, 161, 860, 1167, 1357, 1517, 2007, 2033, 2128–2129, 2136. See also Unicameralism
Bifactionalism, 1675, 1680
Black code, 1384, 1857
Blacks, 246–247, 320, 806, 1049, 1399. See also Legislators
Blair, Austin, 1767–1769
Blue laws, 2323
Bradley, Aaron Alporia, 1399
Broadcasting, 918
Brough, Charles H., 1102
Brown, Joseph E., 1415
Browning, Gordon, 2288
Budgeting, 666, 682–689, 1302, 1431, 1613, 2405
Burnett, Peter H., 1162

California
- campaigning in, 1227, 1229
- constitution of, 1194
- courts of, 1168
- elections in, 1134, 1161, 1178
- and executive branch, 1217, 1219, 1236, 1267
- governors of, 1113, 1162, 1177, 1232
- history of, 1124, 1166, 1180, 1189, 1218, 1224
- interest groups in, 1130
- legislative behavior in, 1122, 1126, 1133, 1154, 1235, 1259
- legislative committees in, 1136, 1144, 1163, 1186, 1188, 1199, 1240, 1258
- legislative structure in, 1120, 1146, 1160, 1201, 1215, 1225, 1250
- legislators of, 1123, 1132, 1202, 1205, 1276
- lobbying in, 1143
- political parties in, 1127, 1147, 1187, 1195, 1241
- politics of, 1121, 1138, 1151, 1172, 1174, 1176, 1185
- reapportionment of, 1112, 1116, 1139, 1164, 1173, 1204
- redistricting of, 1165
- referendum in, 1125, 1150
- urban policy in, 1216, 1242

Campaign
- costs, 261
- and elections, 274, 1742
- financing, 1380, 2185
- spending, 1227, 1229
- *See also* Elections

Campbell, Lewis D., 2138
Campbell, Thomas M., 2354
Campbell, Tunis G., 1400
Canada, 550
Canwell Committee, 2438
Capital buildings, 1557
Carey, Joseph M., 2526
Caucus rule, 1978
Census, 233
Chicanos, 1230
Child abuse, 1013
Citizens
- associations, 1731
- groups, 1825

City
- councils, 896
- relations with state, 1747, 2043, 2068

Civil rights legislation, 385, 1392–1393
Clergy, 1314
Coalitions, 387, 651, 2334
Coles, Edward, 1451
Collective bargaining, 986
Collins, LeRoy, 1392–1393
Colorado
- economics of, 1302
- and executive branch, 1292, 1296
- governors of, 1290
- history of, 1278, 1295
- legislative behavior in, 1288
- legislative committees in, 1285
- legislative structure in, 91, 1284, 1286
- legislators of, 1299
- politics of, 1297
- reapportionment of, 1277
- urban policy in, 1280, 1282

Commissions, 419, 1518, 1552
Committees
- advisory, 1641
- appointments to, 429, 439
- assignments, 1240, 1257, 1259, 1260
- budget, 1157, 1302, 1431, 1437, 1613, 2207
- conference, 1915–1916
- interim, 414, 416–417, 1518, 1552
- investigating, 1144, 1163, 2145
- joint, 1327, 2047
- membership of, 428
- power of, 435, 1345
- recess, 1076
- standing, 437, 439, 1077, 1136, 1561, 1890, 2122
- system of, 421, 423, 430, 433, 1188

Communism, 78, 2030
Comparative studies, 18, 39, 146, 153, 164, 231, 535, 550, 553, 593, 607, 984, 1036, 2041
Compensation, 2196, 2294, 2359
Computers
- data processing, 906, 909, 916,

Subject Index

920, 935, 959, 962, 965
simulations, 284, 952, 1527, 1529
Connecticut
  courts of, 1311
  and executive branch, 1316, 1334
  governors of, 1325
  history of, 1303, 1312
  interest groups in, 1331
  legislative behavior in, 1335
  legislative committees in, 1318, 1327
  legislative structure in, 1306, 1308, 1310, 1319, 1321, 1328
  political parties in, 1322
  politics of, 1304, 1317
  reapportionment of, 1313
  redistricting of, 1307
  representation of, 1330, 1337
Conner, Mike, 1882
Consent theory, 118
Conservative Party, 2049
Constituency
  representation of, 287, 293, 296, 301, 307, 310, 313
  views of, 219, 294, 300, 305, 309, 327
Constitutional conventions, 107, 123, 128, 131, 1666, 1672, 1693, 1858, 2070, 2082, 2153, 2412
Constitutions
  amendments, 115
  interpretation of, 1349, 1350, 1659, 1759, 1766, 1860, 1975, 2389
  legislative provisions, 2287, 2307, 2344
  limitations, 1587, 2144, 2223, 2352, 2464
  model of, 120, 122
  reform of, 126, 1886, 1985, 2053, 2098
  revision of, 121, 1072, 1352, 1361, 1369, 1459, 1666, 1814, 1977, 2329, 2363
Cook County, Illinois, 1455
Cornwell, John J., 2461
Corruption, 557, 559, 731-732
Costs, 919
Council of State Governments, 500
Councill, William H., 1053
County unit system, 1398

Courts, 792
  and reapportionment, 206, 226
Cox, Jonathan Elwood, 2097
Crime, 837
Cross, Wilbur L., 1325
Cuney, Norris Wright, 2319
Curtis, A. H., 1050

Davis, John J., 2409
Davis, Westmoreland, 2417
Delaware
  history of, 1341
  political parties in, 1340
  politics of, 1339
Delegation of power, 1135
Democratic Party, 1148, 1180, 1301, 1500, 1530, 2248, 2345
Detroit, 220
Devanter, Willis Van, 2529
Direct legislation, 1149, 1245, 2164, 2435
Districts
  multi-member, 193, 221, 295, 306, 1376
  sub-, 1567
  See also Redistricting
Dozier, John, 1051
Drew, George F., 1385
Dunklin, Daniel, 1898

Education
  desegregation of, 594-595
  higher, 609, 838, 1005, 1372, 2465
  policy, 972, 988, 1003, 1027, 2494
Elections
  cross-filing in, 1134
  gubernatorial, 269, 275, 278, 283
  outcome of, 259, 263, 277, 281
  presidential, 116
  and representation, 272, 282
  services, 2187
Energy, 1015
Environment, 129, 321, 478
Epperson, Ben H., 2369
Equal rights, 2139
Equal Rights Amendment, 664
Ethics, 861, 2058, 2457
Ethnicity, 325

Executive
  succession, 1395
  veto, 582, 583, 589
Expenditures, 674, 686, 700, 1440, 1702, 1844

Farmer-Labor Association, 1833
Farmer-Labor Party, 1846, 2439
Federal government
  aid, 1030, 1033, 1041, 2183
  funds, 665, 667, 735, 762
  grants, 744, 753–754
  relations with states, 742, 746, 759
  reorganization, 135
Federalism 258, 741, 745, 749
Ferguson, Thompson Benton, 2163
Financial powers, 1755
Fiscal
  policy, 208, 1153
Florida
  campaigning in, 1380
  constitution of, 1349–1350, 1361, 1369
  economics of, 1368
  education in, 1372
  governors of, 1359–1360, 1373, 1385, 1392
  history of, 1381, 1386
  legislative committees in, 1345
  legislative structure in, 1343, 1348, 1366, 1375, 1387
  legislators of, 1365, 1367
  political parties in, 389, 1356
  politics of, 1355, 1362
  reapportionment of, 1353–1354, 1388
  representation of, 1364
  urban policy in, 1363
Floyd, John, 2401
Fox, Dixon Ryan, 2035
Frantz, Frank, 2168

Game theory, 1503
Georgia
  constitution of, 1418
  governors of, 1401, 1415
  history of, 1399–1400, 1420, 1423
  legislative behavior in, 1409
  legislative structure in, 1411–1412, 1416, 1421–1422
  legislators of, 1407
  political parties in, 1408
  politics of, 1403, 1414, 1417
  reapportionment of, 1410, 1419
Gerrymandering, 251, 1230, 1820
Giannini, A. P., 1113
Gibbs, Jonathan C., 1379
Gilmer-Aikin bills, 2358
Goldwater, Barry, 262
Governors
  as executive, 563, 566, 581, 857
  as legislator, 564, 580, 584, 588, 613
  as party leader, 602, 608, 637, 1623
  powers of, 567, 579, 601
Governor's mansion, 61
Graham, William A., 2109
Grantsmanship, 1212
Greenback Party, 1763
Gresham, Walter Q., 1522
Gubernatorial elections. See Elections

Hamilton, Alexander, 2027
Hartness, James, 2395
Hawaii
  legislative structure in, 1424, 1427–1428
  reapportionment of, 1425
Hayes, Rutherford B., 2147
Health, 717
Highway safety, 1038
Hispanics, 2004
Historical studies
  Civil War, 79
  colonial period, 12, 150, 898, 1752
  18th century, 31
  19th century, 10, 380, 476, 511, 1729, 1748, 1763
  Revolution, 64–65, 124, 353
Historic preservation, 1045
Hooper, Ben, 2298

Idaho
  governors of, 1433, 1435
  history of, 1438

Subject Index

legislative behavior in, 1431
legislative structure in, 1430, 1436–1437
Illinois
  campaigning in, 1514
  constitution of, 1459, 1504
  and executive branch, 1456, 1462, 1471, 1483, 1512
  government spending in, 1440
  governors of, 1451, 1458, 1499
  history of, 1447, 1477, 1482, 1500
  interest groups in, 1439
  legislative behavior in, 1455, 1478, 1487
  legislative committees in, 1457, 1518
  legislative stucture in, 1452–1453, 1463, 1468, 1470, 1479, 1509
  lobbying in, 1475
  political parties in, 1450, 1476, 1484
  politics of, 1449, 1454, 1461, 1472
  reapportionment of, 1446, 1466, 1480, 1485, 1495
  redistricting of, 1464
India, 7
Indiana
  campaigning in, 1553
  elections in, 1540
  governors of, 1531
  history of, 1522, 1542, 1549
  legislative behavior in, 1521, 1526, 1532, 1546
  legislative committees in, 1552
  legislative structure in, 1520, 1534, 1543
  legislators of, 1533, 1536, 1550
  political parties in, 1519, 1523, 1530
  politics of, 1538, 1551
  reapportionment of, 1528, 1545, 1554
Indians, 2004
Informal groups, 1789
Information
  access to, 927
  processes, 835, 1592
  scientific, 921–922, 953
  technical, 1078, 1114, 1223
Initiative. See Referendum

Innovation, 983, 1017–1018, 1039, 1041
Institutional analysis, 66, 138, 140
Interest groups
  attitudes of, 788, 797, 808, 1130, 2078
  effectiveness of, 760, 784, 800, 1869, 2493
  politics of, 1553, 1584, 1760, 1774, 1828, 1894
Intergovernmental relations, 90A, 751
Internships, 1211
Interpersonal relations, 1790, 2507
Investigations
  authority, 1214
  committees for, 1144, 1163, 2145
Iowa
  constitution of, 1587
  interest groups in, 1584
  legislative behavior in, 1562, 1564
  legislative committees in, 1580
  legislative structure in, 1565–1566, 1585
  political parties in, 1586
  politics of, 1581–1582
  reapportionment of, 1569
  redistricting of, 1567
  urban policy in, 1560

Jefferson, Thomas, 31
Jim Crow Laws, 2267, 2429
Jones, Bob, 1089
Jones, John Rice, 1899
Jones, Norman L., 1514
Judiciary
  control, 772, 1168
  and legislatures, 769, 773, 775, 779
  policy of, 777
  powers of, 770, 774, 776, 778
  selection of, 781
Justice, Edward J., 2096

Kansas
  campaigning in, 1625
  governors of, 1611, 1615, 1623, 1629
  history of, 1619

legislative behavior in, 1604, 1608
legislative structure in, 1588, 1596, 1603, 1607, 1609, 1626
legislators of, 1624
lobbying in, 1593
political parties in, 1610
politics of, 1600
reapportionment of, 1591, 1601, 1618, 1621
Keating, Edward, 1291
Kentucky
 constitution of, 1653, 1659, 1662
 and executive branch, 1661
 governors of, 1654
 history of, 1638, 1651
 legislative behavior in, 1640
 legislative committees in, 1631, 1641, 1657
 legislative structure in, 1633, 1642, 1648
 legislators of, 1635
 politics of, 1636, 1639, 1656
 redistricting of, 1632, 1655, 1660, 1663
Key, V. O., 1036, 2300
Knott, William V., 1360
Know-Nothing Party, 1109, 1647, 1668, 2138, 2254–2255, 2368
Ku Klux Klan, 2179

Labor, 727, 995, 1001, 1010, 1221, 2318, 2454, 2478
Landon, Alfred M., 1611
Lawyers, 486, 545, 641, 856, 1688, 2018
Leadership
 legislative, 591, 600, 605, 614, 2040, 2327
 party, 590, 597, 1730, 2332
Legal
 codes, 2119–2120, 2213
 counsel, 1332
 services, 910, 941
Legislatures
 accountability, 722
 behavior, 503–561, 1538, 2175
 bill-drafting, 472, 933, 945, 960, 1558
 commissions, 863, 1199
 conferences, 1539, 1556
 councils, 928, 963, 1145, 1305, 1394, 1490, 1502, 1510, 1589, 1594–1595, 1605–1606, 1622, 1627, 1649, 1652, 1703–1704, 1715, 1764, 1803, 1972, 2160, 2173, 2333, 2360, 2453, 2501, 2512
 decision making, 617, 620, 627, 630, 1431, 1933, 2103, 2487
 districts, 298–299, 306, 1263, 1307, 1568, 1761
 effectiveness, 974
 elites, 2211
 expertise, 1797
 immunity, 540
 influence, 1193, 1525
 investigations, 712–713, 723, 1442, 1518
 journals, 898, 925, 1630, 2263–2265
 municipal, 598
 norms, 503, 517, 524, 528, 2176
 oversight, 714–715, 721, 725, 729, 730
 partisanship, 1133, 1203
 power, 562–589, 1416, 1683, 1708, 1750
 procedure, 133, 142, 151, 163, 178, 1745, 1837, 1848, 1850, 2204, 2219, 2351, 2367
 program review, 707, 711, 716, 724, 733
 publications, 2146
 recording, 900, 918
 reference services, 487, 908, 915, 928, 961, 963, 1326, 1394, 2151, 2305, 2499, 2503, 2505, 2517
 reform, 842, 864, 873, 883, 1275, 1315, 1463, 1543, 1677, 1728
 relations with executive, 680, 1071, 1365, 1409, 1702, 1723, 1830, 1852, 1998, 2051, 2094, 2271, 2304, 2315, 2406
 reorganization, 165, 865–866, 1160, 1465, 1467, 1728
 research, 52, 917, 924, 926, 932, 934, 943, 948, 1051, 1056, 1271, 1391, 1645–1646, 1900, 2114, 2249, 2481
 resolutions, 2341
 rules, 175, 2496

Subject Index

security, 929
services, 2015, 2149, 2262, 2309
sessions, 466–467, 479, 481, 498, 501, 1065, 1067, 1074, 1081, 1115, 1118, 1333, 1493, 1633, 1700, 1782, 2003, 2172, 2269, 2295–2296, 2343, 2359, 2459
socialization, 1122, 1235
stability, 505, 541
staffing, 424, 1155, 1253, 1389, 1432, 1489
structure, 139, 144, 149, 155, 177
studies groups, 46
tenure, 1288, 1532–1533, 1564, 2347
turnover, 373, 507, 521, 533, 543–544, 547, 560, 578, 1288, 1532–1533, 1564, 1604, 1868, 2113, 2276, 2281, 2339, 2347
vacancies, 280
withdrawal, 2470
workload, 2283
Legislators
background of, 508, 1131, 1289, 1478, 1536, 1732, 1785, 1808, 2017, 2065, 2199
behavior of, 1821, 1871, 1923
Black, 1104, 1496, 1692, 1706, 1897, 1979, 2081, 2125, 2258, 2291, 2398
careers of, 339, 341, 347, 361
compensation of, 333–336, 364, 371, 533
personality of, 1148, 2086, 2266
recruitment of, 606, 813, 1131, 1810, 2195
relations with constituents, 522, 525, 1203, 1217, 1729, 2242, 2498
retirement of, 336, 360, 376
role behavior of, 48, 337, 523
training of, 1099, 1358, 1590, 1736, 1862, 1872
Lewis, David P., 1069
Liberty Party, 1968
Lincoln, Abraham, 1447, 1506
Liquor control, 288, 1226
Lobbying, 1143, 1475, 1548, 1593, 1762, 1927, 1970, 2180, 2431
Long, Huey, 1679, 1682, 1685–1686

Louisiana
constitution of, 1666, 1672
governors of, 1671, 1678, 1682, 1686
history of, 1667
legislative behavior in, 1665, 1684
legislative structure in, 1689, 1695
legislators of, 1681
politics of, 1674
reapportionment of, 1664, 1694
redistricting of, 1673

Magoffin, Beriah, 1637
Maine
legislative structure in, 1698
political parties in, 1697
Malapportionment. *See* Reapportionment
Maryland
economics of, 1707
and executive branch, 1723
government spending in, 1702
governors of, 1713, 1717, 1719
history of, 1709, 1721, 1725, 1727
legislative behavior in, 1728
legislative structure in, 1701, 1708, 1710, 1714, 1726
legislators of, 1699, 1724
political parties in, 1705, 1712, 1722
politics of, 1720
representation of, 1716
Masons, 2226
Massachusetts
campaigning in, 1742
courts of, 1745, 1751
elections in, 1744
and executive branch, 1750
history of, 1748, 1752
legislative behavior in, 1739
legislative structure in, 1738
legislators of, 1732, 1740, 1746
political parties in, 1729
politics of, 1741
urban policy in, 1747
Mathews, Samuel, Jr., 2404
McNutt, Alexander G., 1873
Meagher, Thomas Francis, 1907
Media, 821–822, 1370, 1676

Medical legislation, 1107
Mental health, 979
Michigan
  constitution of, 1759, 1814
  courts of, 1885
  economics of, 1793
  and executive branch, 1770, 1781
  government spending in, 1755, 1760, 1792
  governors of, 1767, 1784, 1794, 1798
  history of, 1776, 1801
  interest groups in, 1774
  legislative behavior in, 1753, 1772, 1775
  legislative committees in, 1766, 1809
  legislative structure in, 1756, 1780, 1786, 1795, 1799, 1812
  legislators of, 1785, 1797, 1808, 1813
  lobbying in, 1762
  political parties in, 1754, 1763, 1771, 1778
  politics of, 1757, 1777, 1783
  reapportionment of, 1765, 1779, 1804, 1806
  redistricting of, 1805
  referendum in, 1796
  representation of, 1761, 1773
Midwest (region), 10, 67, 75, 417
Migration, 325
Miller, John, 2112
Minimum wage, 1028, 1042, 2450
Minnesota
  courts of, 1845
  and executive branch, 1834, 1839, 1852
  governors of, 1830
  history of, 1824, 1829, 1835
  interest groups in, 1828
  legislative behavior in, 1831, 1841, 1847
  legislative committees in, 1826
  legislative structure in, 1837, 1840, 1848
  legislators of, 1821, 1823, 1851
  lobbying in, 1825
  politics of, 1838
  reapportionment of, 1822, 1827, 1842
  redistricting of, 1820
Mississippi
  constitution of, 1859
  elections in, 1856
  and executive branch, 1855
  governors of, 1854, 1861, 1870, 1873
  history of, 1863, 1877
  interest groups in, 1869
  legislative behavior in, 1871
  legislative structure in, 1865, 1874, 1878
  legislators of, 1868
  political parties in, 1853, 1875
  politics of, 1866
  reapportionment of, 1858, 1867, 1879, 1881
  redistricting of, 1880
Missouri
  constitution of, 1886
  governors of, 1898
  interest groups in, 1894
  legislative behavior in, 1892
  legislative committees in, 1890
  legislative structure in, 1891, 1896
  legislators of, 1897
  political parties in, 1903
  politics of, 1889, 1893
  reapportionment of, 1883, 1888
  referendum, 1901
Mock legislature, 1323
Models, 514, 659, 1031, 2220, 2331
Montana
  governors of, 1907
  history of, 1908
  legislative structure in, 1904
  legislators of, 1909
  politics of, 1906
  reapportionment of, 1910
Morehead, John Motley, 2101–2102
Morgan County, Indiana, 1541
Mormons, 1961
Morrison, De Lesseps, 1678
Municipal leagues, 765
Murphy, Frank, 1784

Natural law, 114
Nebraska
  governors of, 1936, 1949
  history of, 1939, 1953
  legislative behavior in, 1925

Subject Index 225

legislative committees in,
    1915–1916
legislative structure in, 1913,
    1918, 1920, 1937, 1945, 1948
lobbying in, 1927
political parties in, 1951
redistricting of, 1917
representation of, 1923
urban policy in, 1932
Nevada
    constitution of, 1960
    economics of, 1954
    elections in, 1958, 2379
    governors of, 1956–1957
    history of, 1961
    political parties in, 1962
New England, 19, 57
New Hampshire
    constitution of, 1966, 1975
    courts of, 1965
    and executive branch, 1971
    governors of, 1964
    legislative structure in, 1967,
        1972
    lobbying in, 1970
    political parties in, 1963, 1968,
        1973
    politics of, 1969
    reapportionment of, 1974
New Jersey
    constitution of, 1977, 1985
    and executive branch, 1998
    government spending in, 1976
    history of, 1994
    interest groups in, 1988
    legislative behavior in, 1983
    legislative structure in, 1980,
        1984, 1997
    legislators of, 1979
    political parties in, 1986
    politics of, 1993
    reapportionment of, 1982, 1992,
        1995–1996
    urban policy in, 1981
New Mexico
    history of, 2012
    legislative behavior in, 2003
    legislative committees in, 2008
    legislative structure in, 2002,
        2007, 2011
    legislators of, 2016
    politics of, 2001, 2009
    public opinion in, 2010

    reapportionment of, 1999, 2013
New York
    constitution of, 2031, 2053, 2070
    courts of, 2063
    economics of, 2069
    education in, 2056
    governors of, 2050, 2075
    history of, 2035, 2038, 2049,
        2060
    interest groups in, 2052
    legislative behavior in, 2021,
        2066, 2071
    legislative committees in, 2047
    legislative structure in, 2020,
        2028, 2033, 2044, 2059
    legislators of, 2061, 2065
    lobbying in, 2078
    political parties in, 2037, 2048,
        2073
    politics of, 2023, 2029
    reapportionment of, 2019, 2034,
        2036, 2046, 2067
    representation of, 2074
    urban policy in, 2043
Nonpartisan League, 2110
Nonpartisanship, in legislatures,
    615, 662–663, 1818–1819,
    1843, 1845, 1853, 1925
Norris, George W., 1953
North Carolina
    campaigning in, 2101
    constitution of, 2082, 2098
    elections in, 2080, 2097, 2109
    and executive branch, 2092
    governors of, 2094, 2107
    history of, 2084
    legislative behavior in, 2086
    legislative committees in, 2088
    legislative structure in, 2087
    legislators of, 2081
    political parties in, 2085, 2093,
        2100, 2108
    politics of, 2083, 2106
    redistricting of, 240
North Dakota
    governors of, 2112
    legislative behavior in, 2113
    legislative committees in, 2114
    politics of, 2110
    referendum in, 2111

Ohio
  constitution of, 2144, 2153
  and executive branch, 2132, 2150
  governors of, 2147, 2155
  history of, 2118, 2140
  legislative behavior in, 2121
  legislative committees in, 2117, 2122, 2145
  legislative structure in, 2126, 2131, 2136, 2143
  legislators of, 2125
  political parties in, 2138
  politics of, 2115, 2127, 2130, 2135
  reapportionment of, 2124
Oklahoma
  constitution of, 2171
  government spending in, 2157
  governors of, 2163, 2167
  history of, 2161, 2168
  legislative behavior in, 2175
  legislative structure in, 2169, 2176
  lobbying in, 2180
  politics of, 2166, 2182
  reapportionment of, 2156, 2159, 2170, 2177
Ombudsman, 1269, 1397
One-party
  legislatures, 646, 657, 1071, 1377
  system, 404, 409, 647
Open meetings, 1233
Oregon
  campaigning in, 2185
  constitution of, 2203, 2208
  education in, 2212
  elections in, 2187
  government spending in, 2194
  governors of, 2188
  legislative behavior in, 2186, 2195, 2198, 2216
  legislative committees in, 2207
  legislative structure in, 2190, 2200, 2204
  legislators of, 2199
  political parties in, 2193
  reapportionment of, 2205, 2209
Osborn, Sidney P., 1087

Parliamentary procedure, 18, 469
Partisanship, 398, 1513, 2231
Party
  chairman, 412
  cohesion, 401, 1127
  competition, 387–388, 390, 406, 1036, 1319, 1356
  control, 382, 385, 405
  elites, 394
  formation, 1962
  identification, 383
  loyalty, 413, 1204, 1241, 2030
  platforms, 384
  politics of, 392, 395, 397, 403
  size, 1546
  voting, 411
  See also individual parties
Patronage, 1512, 2174
Patterson, John M., 1073
Peay, Austin, 2303
Pennsylvania
  constitution of, 2223, 2230
  history of, 2224, 2227, 2245
  legislative behavior in, 2220
  legislative committees in, 2221, 2234
  legislative structure in, 2219, 2235, 2237, 2239
  legislators of, 2222, 2240
  political parties in, 2228, 2231
  politics of, 2217, 2241
  reapportionment of, 2232
  referendum in, 2236
  representation of, 2238
People's Party, 1294
Performance auditing, 708–710
Philadelphia, 189
Pledger, William A., 1408
Poindexter, George, 1855
Policy
  development, 1389
  making, 402, 407, 1154, 1186
  outputs, 1388
  public, 1521, 1542
Political socialization, 512, 539, 549, 556, 1562, 1810
Polls, 830, 839
Pollution, 2139
Pope, John, 1111
Population trends, 1032, 1390
Populism, 2233, 2279, 2377, 2524, 2527

Subject Index

Populists, 1293–1294
PPBS (Planning Programming Budgeting System), 681
President, 54
Press, 815, 819, 821, 832, 836, 1505
Pressure groups. See Interest groups
Primaries, 266–267, 269, 271, 1320, 2348
  direct, 1231, 1516
Professionalism, 520, 2152
Program
  commission, 2133–2134
  evaluation, 1043
Progressive movement, 1161, 1237, 1244, 2442, 2519
Prohibition, 1448
Proposition 13, 1153
Public opinion
  formation of, 60, 308, 315, 1040, 2010
  and legislatures, 817, 827, 829, 1577–1578

Race relations, 1103, 1351, 1679
Railroads, 976, 998
Ralston, Samuel M., 1531
Ramsey, Alexander, 1832
Reapportionment
  effects of, 187, 192, 203, 210, 232, 1006
  and the law, 181, 195, 200, 226, 241
  and malapportionment, 324, 1036, 1529, 1694
  methods of, 180, 197, 214, 222, 237
  politics of, 185, 205, 211, 216
Record keeping, 902
Redistricting, 1086, 1307, 1464, 1632, 1655, 1660, 1673, 2321, 2443, 2510, 2520
Referendum
  legislation of, 1849, 2236
  politics of, 303, 1125, 1796, 1901, 2111, 2278, 2520
Regional development, 987, 1002
Religion, 106, 2479
Representation, 136, 257, 1434, 2074

Republican National Committee, 258
Republican Party, 262, 1187, 1408, 1610, 1824, 1963, 2076, 2290, 2419
Revenue sharing, 688, 695, 705
Rhode Island
  history of, 2251
  legislative structure in, 2246, 2253
  legislators of, 2258
  political parties in, 2248, 2250, 2254, 2257
  politics of, 2256
  reapportionment of, 2247
Richards, Deforest, 2531
Ritchie, Albert C., 1719
Robinson, Charles, 1629
Roll-call analysis, 636, 640, 645, 652, 654–655, 661, 1234
Roosevelt, Theodore, 2076
Ross, C. Ben, 1435

Safe seats, 260A
Salaries, 1138, 1141–1142, 1169
Samish, Art, 1249
Sharpe, Horatio, 1717
Shelby, Isaac, 1654
Short-form bill, 1426
Sifting Committee, 1563
Small, Len, 1514
Small business, 795
Smith, Al, 2054
Smith, Melancton, 2027
Socialism, 2072
Socialization. See Political socialization
Social programs, 1043
South (region), 6, 42, 50, 72, 583
South Carolina
  and executive branch, 2270
  governors of, 2271
  legislative structure in, 2268
  legislators of, 2259, 2266
  politics of, 2261
South Dakota
  constitution of, 2287
  courts of, 2280
  legislative behavior in, 2276, 2281
  legislative committees in, 2284

legislative structure in, 2274, 2277, 2284
legislators of, 2285
politics of, 2272, 2275, 2286
referendum, 2278
Southeast (region), 13, 89, 190, 248
Spending. See Expenditures
St. Louis, 1884
State
   capitals, 1084, 1110, 1931
   relations with local officials, 736, 738, 748, 755, 758, 765
   senates, 172
Statute law, 905, 966, 1198, 2142, 2191
Stearns, Marcellus L., 1359
Stevens, Isaac Ingalls, 2441
Subversive activities, 1119
Sulzer, William, 2075
Sunset laws, 706, 726, 1283

Tape recording, 2462
Taxes, 691, 694, 1749, 1976, 2157, 2378
Technology, 1018, 1046
Television, 822, 1370, 2165–2166
Tennessee
   campaigning in, 2311
   constitution of, 2295, 2307, 2313
   governors of, 2288, 2298, 2301, 2308
   history of, 2289
   legislative behavior in, 2304
   legislative structure in, 2296, 2315
   legislators of, 2291, 2310, 2312
   political parties in, 2290, 2303
   politics of, 2306
   reapportionment of, 2292, 2299, 2314
Tenney, Jack B., 1251
Tenney Committee, 1119
Testimonial privilege, 461
Texas
   constitution of, 2329, 2344, 2352, 2363
   courts of, 2350
   economics of, 2323
   elections in, 2348
   and executive branch, 2349
   governors of, 2325, 2338, 2354

history of, 2326, 2355, 2366
legislative behavior in, 2328, 2340, 2347
legislative structure in, 2342, 2351, 2353, 2361, 2364
legislators of, 2339, 2346, 2372
political parties in, 2319, 2324
politics of, 2316, 2335, 2337, 2357
reapportionment of, 2320, 2322, 2330
redistricting of, 2321
representation of, 2331
Time and motion studies, 1070
Transportation, 991
Turner, Joseph Addison, 1406

Un-American activities, 2438
Unemployment
   compensation, 2139
   insurance, 2090
Unicameralism, 73–74, 887, 894, 1137, 1156, 2243, 2293, 2365, 2392, 2447
Urban
   legislation, 242, 1033, 1466, 1560, 2182
   legislators, 265, 358
   reform, 1280–1281
   relations with rural, 1060, 1216, 1242, 1282, 1363, 1887, 1932
   representation, 182, 253, 257, 290, 317, 794, 1404
Utah
   constitution of, 2387
   and executive branch, 2374, 2383
   government spending in, 2378
   history of, 2375, 2380
   legislative behavior in, 2376
   legislative structure in, 2384
   politics of, 2382
   reapportionment of, 2385

Vermont
   campaigning in, 2393
   constitution of, 2389
   and executive branch, 2396
   governors of, 2395
   history of, 2388

Subject Index

legislative structure in, 2392
legislators of, 2398
politics of, 2391
reapportionment of, 2390
representation of, 2394
Veto, 123A, 2079
Virginia
   campaigning in, 2408
   constitution of, 2412, 2415
   and executive branch, 2423
   governors of, 2401, 2404
   history of, 2399, 2409, 2411, 2425
   legislative behavior in, 2405–2406
   legislative committees in, 2403
   legislative structure in, 2407, 2413
   legislators of, 2416
   political parties in, 2419, 2426
   politics of, 2402, 2410, 2414, 2420, 2422
   reapportionment of, 2421
   urban policy in, 2427
Volunteerism, 332
Voting
   behavior, 635, 643, 653, 656, 658
   cumulative, 1443, 1491, 1497, 1503, 1515
   party, 648–649, 650
   plurality, 1491
Voting Rights Act of 1965, 1673

Warren, Earl, 1177
Washington (state)
   courts of, 2443
   governors of, 2441
   history of, 2433, 2449
   interest groups in, 2444
   legislative structure in, 2447, 2452
   lobbying in, 2448
   political parties in, 2439
   politics of, 2430, 2440
   reapportionment of, 2432, 2434
   redistricting of, 2445
Washington, D.C., 2189
Water, 1171
Wathen, Richard B., 1555

Welfare, 381, 558–559, 977, 997
West (region), 14–15, 91, 191, 1014
West Virginia
   constitution of, 2464
   education in, 2465
   elections in, 2467
   governors of, 2455, 2461
   history of, 2472, 2475
   legislative behavior in, 2460, 2470
   legislative structure in, 2459, 2463, 2474
   lobbying in, 2469
   politics of, 2458, 2466
   reapportionment of, 2471
Whig Party, 2022, 2108
White, Albert B., 2455
White, William Allen, 1625
Wisconsin
   courts of, 2521
   and executive branch, 2490, 2513
   government spending in, 2494
   governors of, 2506
   history of, 2477, 2489
   legislative behavior in, 2483, 2488, 2493, 2514
   legislative committees in, 2495, 2501
   legislative structure in, 2480, 2485, 2508, 2512, 2523
   legislators of, 2498
   political parties in, 2484, 2486
   reapportionment of, 2502, 2504, 2509, 2511, 2516
   redistricting of, 2510, 2520
   social policies in, 2491
Women, 1012, 1284, 1347, 2103. *See also* Legislators
Woman suffrage, 2184, 2373
Workmen's compensation, 2478
Wyoming
   governors of, 2531
   history of, 2526, 2530
   legislative behavior in, 2529
   legislative structure in, 2525
   politics of, 2532
   reapportionment of, 2528

Zero-base budgeting, 720

Ref Z 7164 .R4 G574 1985
Goehlert, Robert, 1948-
State legislatures

NOV 1 8 1985